Money

Money

The Unauthorised Biography

FELIX MARTIN

ALFRED A. KNOPF   NEW YORK   2014

THIS IS A BORZOI BOOK
PUBLISHED BY ALFRED A. KNOPF

Copyright © 2013 by Failu Ltd.

All rights reserved.
Published in the United States by Alfred A. Knopf, a division of
Random House LLC, New York, and in Canada by Doubleday Canada,
a division of Random House of Canada Limited, Toronto, Penguin Random House
Companies. Originally published in Great Britain by The Bodley Head,
a division of the Random House Group Limited, London, in 2013.

www.aaknopf.com

Knopf, Borzoi Books, and the colophon are registered
trademarks of Random House LLC.

Library of Congress Cataloging in Publication Data is available.

ISBN 978-0-307-96243-0 (hardcover)   ISBN 978-0-307-96244-7 (eBook)

Jacket design by Evan Gaffney

Manufactured in the United States of America

First American Edition

To Kristina

Contents

Money

1 What Is Money?

Everyone, except an economist, knows what "money" means, and even an economist can describe it in the course of a chapter or so . . .
—A.H. Quiggin, *A Survey of Primitive Money: the Beginnings of Currency*, p. 1

THE ISLAND OF STONE MONEY

The Pacific island of Yap was, at the beginning of the twentieth century, one of the most remote and inaccessible inhabited places on earth. An idyllic, subtropical paradise, nestled in a tiny archipelago nine degrees north of the equator and more than 300 miles from Palau, its closest neighbour, Yap had remained almost innocent of the world beyond Micronesia right up until the final decades of the nineteenth century. There had, it is true, been a brief moment of Western contact in 1731 when a group of intrepid Catholic missionaries had established a small base on the island. When their supply ship returned the following year, however, it discovered that the balmy, palm-scattered islands of Yap had not proved fertile ground for the Christian gospel. The entire mission had been massacred several months previously by local witch doctors aggrieved at the competition presented by the Good News. Yap was left to its own devices for another one hundred and forty years.

It was not until 1869 that the first European trading post—run by the German merchant firm of Godeffroy and sons—was established in the Yap archipelago. Once a few years had passed, with

Godeffroy not only avoiding summary execution but prospering, Yap's presence came to the attention of the Spanish, who by virtue of their colonial possessions in the Philippines—a mere 800 miles to the west—considered themselves the natural overlords of this part of Micronesia. The Spanish laid claim to the islands, and believed that they had achieved a *fait accompli* when in the summer of 1885 they erected a house and installed a Governor in it. They had not counted, however, on the tenacity of Bismarck's Germany in matters of foreign policy. No island was so small, or so remote, as to be unworthy of the Imperial Foreign Ministry's attention if it meant a potential addition to German power. The ownership of Yap became the subject of an international dispute. Eventually, the matter was referred—somewhat ironically, given the island's track record—to arbitration by the Pope, who granted political control to Spain, but full commercial rights to Germany. But the Iron Chancellor had the last laugh. Within a decade and a half, Spain had lost a damaging war with America, and its ambitions in the Pacific had disintegrated. In 1899, Spain sold Yap to Germany for the sum of $3.3 million.

The absorption of Yap into the German Empire had one great benefit. It brought one of the more interesting and unusual monetary systems in history to the attention of the world. More specifically, it proved the catalyst for a visit by a brilliant and eccentric young American adventurer, William Henry Furness III. The scion of a prominent New England family, Furness had trained as a doctor before converting to anthropology and making his name with a popular account of his travels in Borneo. In 1903 he made a two-month visit to Yap, and published a broad survey of its physical and social make-up a few years later.[1] He was immediately impressed by how much more remote and untouched it was than Borneo. Yet despite being a tiny island with only a few thousand inhabitants—"whose whole length and breadth is but a day's walk," as Furness described it—Yap turned out to have a remarkably complex society. There was a caste system, with a tribe of slaves, and special clubhouses lived in by fishing and fighting fraternities. There was a rich tradition of dancing and songs, which Furness took particular delight in recording for posterity. There was a vibrant native religion—as the missionaries had previously discovered to their cost—complete with an elaborate genesis myth locating the origins of the Yapese in a giant barnacle attached to some floating driftwood. But undoubtedly the most striking thing that Furness discovered on Yap was its monetary system.

The economy of Yap, such as it was, could hardly be called developed. The market extended to a bare three products—fish, coconuts, and Yap's one and only luxury, sea cucumber. There was no other exchangeable commodity to speak of; no agriculture; few arts and crafts; the only domesticated animals were pigs and, since the Germans had arrived, a few cats; and there had been little contact or trade with outsiders. It was as simple and as isolated an economy as one could hope to find. Given these antediluvian conditions, Furness expected to find nothing more advanced than simple barter. Indeed, as he observed, "in a land where food and drink and ready-made clothes grow on trees and may be had for the gathering" it seemed possible that even barter itself would be an unnecessary sophistication.[2]

The very opposite turned out to be true. Yap had a highly developed system of money. It was impossible for Furness not to notice it the moment that he set foot on the island, because its coinage was extremely unusual. It consisted of *fei*—"large, solid, thick stone wheels ranging in diameter from a foot to twelve feet, having in the centre a hole varying in size with the diameter of the stone, wherein a pole may be inserted sufficiently large and strong to bear the weight and facilitate transportation."[3] This stone money was originally quarried on Babelthuap, an island some 300 miles away in Palau, and had mostly been brought to Yap, so it was said, long ago. The value of the coins depended principally on their size, but also on the fineness of the grain and the whiteness of the limestone.

At first, Furness believed that this bizarre form of currency might have been chosen because, rather than in spite, of its extraordinary unwieldiness: "when it takes four strong men to steal the price of a pig, burglary cannot but prove a somewhat disheartening occu-

The stone currency of Yap as photographed
by William Henry Furness III in 1903,
with people and palm trees for scale.

pation," he ventured. "As may be supposed, thefts of *fei* are almost
unknown."[4] But as time went on, he observed that physical transportation of *fei* from one house to another was in fact rare. Numerous transactions took place—but the debts incurred were typically
just offset against each other, with any outstanding balance carried
forward in expectation of some future exchange. Even when open
balances were felt to require settlement, it was not usual for *fei* to
be physically exchanged. "The noteworthy feature of this stone currency," wrote Furness, "is that it is not necessary for its owner to
reduce it to possession. After concluding a bargain which involves
the price of a *fei* too large to be conveniently moved, its new owner
is quite content to accept the bare acknowledgement of ownership
and without so much as a mark to indicate the exchange, the coin
remains undisturbed on the former owner's premises."[5]

When Furness expressed amazement at this aspect of the Yap monetary system, his guide told him an even more surprising story:

> [T]here was in the village near by a family whose wealth was unquestioned—acknowledged by everyone—and yet no one, not even the family itself, had ever laid eye or hand on this wealth; it consisted of an enormous *fei*, whereof the size is known only by tradition; for the past two or three generations it had been and was at that time lying at the bottom of the sea![6]

This *fei*, it transpired, had been shipwrecked during a storm while in transit from Babelthuap many years ago. Nevertheless:

> [I]t was universally conceded . . . that the mere accident of its loss overboard was too trifling to mention, and that a few hundred feet of water off shore ought not to affect its marketable value . . . The purchasing power of that stone remains, therefore, as valid as if it were leaning visibly against the side of the owner's house, and represents wealth as potentially as the hoarded inactive gold of a miser in the Middle Ages, or as our silver dollars stacked in the Treasury in Washington, which we never see or touch, but trade with on the strength of a printed certificate that they are there.[7]

When it was published in 1910, it seemed unlikely that Furness' eccentric travelogue would ever reach the notice of the economics profession. But eventually a copy happened to find its way to the editors of the Royal Economic Society's *Economic Journal*, who assigned the book to a young Cambridge economist, recently seconded to the British Treasury on war duty: a certain John Maynard Keynes. The man who over the next twenty years was to revolutionise the world's understanding of money and finance was astonished. Furness' book, he wrote, "has brought us into contact with a people whose ideas on currency are probably more truly philosophical than those of any other country. Modern practice in regard to gold reserves has a good deal to learn from the more logical practices of the island of Yap."[8] Why it was that the greatest economist of the twentieth century believed the monetary system of Yap to hold such important and universal lessons is the subject of this book.

GREAT MINDS THINK ALIKE

What is money, and where does it come from?

A few years ago, over a drink, I posed these two questions to an old friend—a successful entrepreneur with a prospering business in the financial services industry. He responded with a familiar story. In primitive times, there was no money—just barter. When people needed something that they didn't produce themselves, they had to find someone who had it and was willing to swap it for whatever they did produce. Of course, the problem with this system of barter exchange is that it was very inefficient. You had to find another person who had exactly what you wanted, and who in turn wanted exactly what you had got—and what is more, both at exactly the same time. So at a certain point, the idea emerged of choosing one thing to serve as a "medium of exchange." This thing could in principle be anything—so long as, by general agreement, it was universally acceptable as payment. In practice, however, gold and silver have always been the most common choices, because they are durable, malleable, portable, and rare. In any case, whatever it was, this thing was from then on desirable not only for its own sake, but because it could be used to buy other things and to store up wealth for the future. This thing, in short, was money—and this is where money came from.

It's a simple and powerful story. And as I explained to my friend, it is a theory of money's nature and origins with a very ancient and distinguished pedigree. A version of it can be found in Aristotle's *Politics*, the earliest treatment of the subject in the entire Western canon.[9] It is the theory developed by John Locke, the father of classical political Liberalism, in his *Second Treatise of Government*.[10] To cap it all, it is the very theory—almost to the letter—advocated by none other than Adam Smith in his chapter "Of the Origin and Use of Money" in the foundation text of modern economics, *An Inquiry into the Nature and Causes of the Wealth of Nations:*

> But when the division of labour first began to take place, this power of exchanging must frequently have been very much clogged and embarrassed in its operations . . . The butcher has more meat in his shop than he himself can consume, and the brewer and the baker would each of them be willing to purchase a part of it. But they have nothing to offer in exchange, except the productions of their respective trades, and the butcher is already provided with all the bread and beer which he has immediate occasion for . . . In order to avoid such situations, every prudent man in every period of society, after the first establishment of the division of labour, must naturally have endeavoured to manage his affairs in such a manner, as to have at all times by him, besides the peculiar produce of his own industry, a certain quantity of some one commodity or other, such as he imagined few other people would be likely to refuse in exchange for the produce of their industry.[11]

Smith even shared my friend's agnosticism as to which commodity would be chosen to serve as money:

> Many different commodities, it is probable, were successively both thought of and employed for this purpose. In the rude ages of society, cattle are said to have been the most common instrument of commerce . . . Salt is said to be the common instrument of commerce and exchange in Abyssinia; a species of shells in some parts of the coast of India; dried cod in Newfoundland; tobacco in Virginia; sugar in some of our West India colonies; hides or dressed leather in some other countries; and there is to this day a village in Scotland where it is not uncommon, I am told, for a workman to carry nails instead of money to the baker's shop or the alehouse.[12]

And like my friend, Smith also believed that in general, gold, silver, and other metals were the most logical choices:

> In all countries, however, men seem at last to have been determined by irresistible reasons to give the preference, for this employment, to metals above every other commodity. Metals can not only be kept with as little loss as any other commodity, scarce any thing being less perishable than they are, but they can likewise, without any loss, be divided into any number of parts, as by fusion of those parts can easily be re-united again; a quality which no other equally durable commodities possess, and which more than any other quality renders them fit to be the instruments of commerce and circulation.[13]

So I told my friend he could congratulate himself. Without having studied economics at all, he had arrived at the same theory as the great Adam Smith. But that's not all, I explained. This theory of money's origins and nature is not just a historical curiosity like Ptolemy's geocentric astronomy—a set of obsolete hypotheses long since superseded by more modern theories. On the contrary, it is found today in virtually all mainstream textbooks of economics.[14] What's more, its fundamental ideas have formed the bedrock of an immense body of detailed theoretical and empirical research on monetary questions over the last sixty years. Based on its assumptions, economists have designed sophisticated mathematical models to explore exactly why one commodity is chosen as money over all others and how much of it people will want to hold, and have constructed a vast analytical apparatus designed to explain every aspect of money's value and use. It has provided the basis for the branch of economics—"macroeconomics" as it is known—which seeks to explain economic booms and busts, and to recommend how we can moderate these so-called business cycles by managing interest rates and government spending. In short, my friend's ideas not only had history behind them. They remain today, amongst amateurs and experts alike, very much the conventional theory of money.

By now, my friend was positively brimming with self-congratulation. "I know that I'm brilliant," he said with his usual modesty, "but it does still amaze me that I—a rank amateur—can match the greatest minds in the economic canon without ever having given it a second thought before today. Doesn't it make you think you might have been wasting your time all those years you were studying for your degrees?" I agreed that there was certainly something a bit troubling about it all. But not because he had hit upon the theory without any training in economics. It was quite the opposite. It was that those of us who *have* had years of training regurgitate this theory. Because simple and intuitive though it may be, there is a drawback to the conventional theory of money. It is entirely false.

STONE AGE ECONOMICS?

John Maynard Keynes was right about Yap. William Henry Furness' description of its curious stone currency may at first appear to be nothing more than a picturesque footnote to the history of money. But it poses some awkward questions of the conventional theory of money. Take, for example, the idea that money emerged out of barter. When Aristotle, Locke, and Smith were making this claim, they were doing so purely on the basis of deductive logic. None of them had ever actually seen an economy that operated entirely via barter exchange. But it seemed plausible that such an arrangement might once have existed; and if it had existed, then it also seemed plausible that it would have been so unsatisfactory that someone would have tried to invent a way to improve on it. In this context, the monetary system of Yap came as something of a surprise. Here was an economy so simple that it should theoretically have been operating by barter. Yet it was not: it had a fully developed system of money and currency. Perhaps Yap was an exception to the rule. But if an economy this rudimentary already had money, then where and when would a barter economy be found?

This question continued to trouble researchers over the century after Furness' account of Yap was published. As historical and ethnographic evidence accumulated, Yap came to look less and less of an anomaly. Seek as they might, not a single researcher was able to find a society, historical or contemporary, that regularly conducted its trade by barter. By the 1980s, the leading anthropologists of money considered the verdict to be in. "Barter, in the strict sense of moneyless market exchange, has never been a quantitatively important or dominant mode of transaction in any past or present economic system about which we have hard information," wrote the American scholar George Dalton in 1982.[15] "No example of a barter economy, pure and simple, has ever been described, let alone the emergence from it of money; all available ethnography suggests that there has never been such a thing," concluded the Cambridge anthropologist Caroline Humphrey.[16] The news even began filtering through to the more intellectually adventurous fringes of the economics profession. The great American economic historian Charles Kindleberger, for example, wrote in the second edition of his *Financial History of Western Europe*, published in 1993, that "Economic historians have occasionally maintained that evolution in economic intercourse has proceeded from a natural or barter economy to a money economy and ultimately to a credit economy. This view was put forward, for example, in 1864 by Bruno Hildebrand of the German historical school of economics; it happens to be wrong."[17] By the beginning of the twenty-first century, a rare academic consensus had been reached amongst those with an interest in empirical evidence that the conventional idea that money emerged from barter was false. As the anthropologist David Graeber explained bluntly in 2011: "[T]here's no evidence that it ever happened, and an enormous amount of evidence suggesting that it did not."[18]

The story of Yap does not just present a challenge to the conventional theory's account of money's origins, however. It also raises serious doubts about its conception of what money actually is. The conventional theory holds that money is a "thing"—a commodity chosen from amongst the universe of commodities to serve as a medium of exchange—and that the essence of monetary exchange is the swapping of goods and services for this commodity medium of exchange. But the stone money of Yap doesn't fit this scheme. In the first place, it is difficult to believe that anyone could have chosen "large, solid, thick stone wheels ranging in diameter from a foot to twelve feet" as a medium of exchange—since in most cases, they would be a good deal harder to move than the things being traded. But more worryingly, it was clear that the *fei* were not a medium of exchange in the sense of a commodity that could be exchanged for any other—since most of the time, they were not exchanged at all. Indeed, in the case of the infamous shipwrecked *fei*, no one had ever even seen the coin in question, let alone passed it around as a medium of exchange. No, there could be no doubt: the inhabitants of Yap were curiously indifferent to the fate of the *fei* themselves. The essence of their monetary system was not stone coins used as a medium of exchange, but something else.

Closer consideration of Adam Smith's story of commodities chosen to serve as media of exchange suggests that the inhabitants of Yap were on to something. Smith claimed that at different times and in different places, numerous commodities had been chosen to serve as the money: dried cod in Newfoundland; tobacco in Virginia; sugar in the West Indies; and even nails in Scotland. Yet suspicions about the validity of some of these examples were already being raised within a generation or two of the publication of Smith's *Wealth of Nations*. The American financier Thomas Smith, for example, argued in his *Essay on Currency and Banking* in 1832 that whilst Smith thought that these stories were evidence of commodity media of exchange, they were in fact nothing of the sort.[19] In every case, these were examples of trade that was accounted for in pounds, shillings, and pence, just as it was in modern England. Sellers would accumulate credit on their books, and buyers debts, all denominated in monetary units. The fact that any net balances that remained between them might then be discharged by payment of some commodity or other to the value of the debt did not mean that that commodity was "money." To focus on the commodity payment rather than the system of credit and clearing behind it was to get things completely the wrong way round. And to take the view that it was the commodity itself that was money, as Smith did, might therefore start out seeming logical, but would end in nonsense. Alfred Mitchell Innes, the author of two neglected masterworks on the nature of money, summed up the problem with Smith's report of cod-money in Newfoundland bluntly but accurately:

> A moment's reflection shows that a staple commodity could not be used as money, because *ex hypothesi* the medium of exchange is equally receivable by all members of the community. Thus if the fishers paid for their supplies in cod, the traders would equally have to pay for their cod in cod, an obvious absurdity.[20]

If the *fei* of Yap were not a medium of exchange, then what were they? And more to the point, what, in fact, was Yap's money if it wasn't the *fei*? The answer to both questions is remarkably simple. Yap's money was not the *fei*, but the underlying system of credit accounts and clearing of which they helped to keep track. The *fei* were just tokens by which these accounts were kept. As in Newfoundland, the inhabitants of Yap would accumulate credits and debts in the course of their trading in fish, coconut, pigs, and sea cucumber. These would be offset against one another to settle payments. Any outstanding balances carried forward at the end of a single exchange, or a day, or a week, might, if the counterparties so wished, be settled by the exchange of currency—a *fei*—to the appropriate value; this being a tangible and visible record of the outstanding credit that the seller enjoyed with the rest of Yap. Coins and currency, in other words, are useful tokens to record the underlying system of credit accounts and to implement the underlying process of clearing. They may even be necessary in an economy larger than that of Yap, where coins could drop to the bottom of the sea and yet no one would think to question the wealth of their owner. But currency is not itself money. Money is the system of credit accounts and their clearing that currency represents.

If all this sounds familiar to the modern reader—even obvious—it should. After all, thinking of money as a commodity and monetary exchange as the swapping of goods for a tangible medium of exchange may have been intuitive in the days when coins were minted from precious metals. It may even have made sense when the law entitled the holder of a Federal Reserve or Bank of England note to present it on Constitution Avenue or Threadneedle Street and expect its redemption for a specified quantity of gold. But those days are long gone. In today's modern monetary regimes, there is no gold that backs our dollars, pounds, or euros—nor any legal right to redeem our banknotes for it. Modern banknotes are quite transparently nothing but tokens. What is more, most of the currency in our contemporary economies does not enjoy even the precarious physical existence of a banknote. The vast majority of our national money—around 90 per cent in the U.S., for example, and 97 per cent in the U.K.—has no physical existence at all.[21] It consists merely of our account balances at our banks. The only tangible apparatus employed in most monetary payments today is a plastic card and a keypad. It would be a brave theorist indeed who maintained that a pair of microchips and a Wi-Fi connection are a commodity medium of exchange.

By a strange coincidence, John Maynard Keynes is not the only giant of twentieth-century economics to have saluted the inhabitants of Yap for their clear understanding of the nature of money. In 1991, the seventy-nine-year-old Milton Friedman—hardly Keynes' ideological bedfellow—also came across Furness' obscure book. He too extolled the fact that Yap had escaped from the conventional but unhealthy obsession with commodity coinage, and that by its indifference to its physical currency it acknowledged so transparently that money is not a commodity, but a system of credit and clearing. "For a century or more, the 'civilized' world regarded as a manifestation of its wealth metal dug from deep in the ground, refined at great labor, and transported great distances to be buried again in elaborate vaults deep under the ground," he wrote. "Is the one practice really more rational than the other?"[22]

To win the praise of one of the two greatest monetary economists of the twentieth century may be regarded as chance; to win the praise of both deserves attention.

MONETARY VANDALISM: THE FATE OF THE EXCHEQUER TALLIES

The economic worldview of Yap which both Keynes and Friedman applauded—of money as a special type of credit, of monetary exchange as the clearing of credit accounts, and of currency as merely tokens of an underlying credit relationship—has not been without its own forceful historical proponents. Amongst those who have had to deal with the practical business of managing money—especially *in extremis*—the view of money as credit, rather than a commodity, has always had a strong following. One famous example is provided by the siege of Valletta by the Turks in 1565. As the Ottoman embargo dragged on, the supply of gold and silver began to run short, and the Knights of Malta were forced to mint coins using copper. The motto that they stamped on them in order to remind the population of the source of their value would have seemed perfectly sensible to the inhabitants of Yap: *Non Aes, sed Fides*—"Not the metal, but trust."[23]

Nevertheless, it is undoubtedly the conventional view of money as a commodity, of monetary exchange as swapping goods for a medium of exchange, and of credit as the lending out of the money commodity, that has enjoyed the lion's share of support from theorists and philosophers over the centuries, and thereby dominated economic thought—and, for much of the time, policy as well. But if it is so obvious that the conventional theory of money is wrong, why has such a distinguished canon of economists and philosophers believed it? And why does today's economics profession by and large persist in using the fundamental ideas of this tradition as the building blocks of modern economic thinking? Why, in short, is the conventional theory of money so resilient? There are two basic reasons, and they are worth dwelling on.

The first reason has to do with the historical evidence for money. The problem is not that so little of it survives from earlier ages, but that it is virtually all of a single type—coins. Museums around the world heave with coins, ancient and modern. Coins and their inscriptions are one of the main archaeological sources for the understanding of ancient culture, society, and history. Deciphered by ingenious scholars, their graven images and their abbreviated inscriptions give up vast libraries of knowledge about the chronologies of ancient kings, the hierarchy of classical deities, and the ideologies of ancient republics. An entire academic discipline—numismatics—is devoted to the study of coins; and far from being the scholarly equivalent of stamp collecting, as it might appear to the uninitiated, numismatics is amongst the most fruitful fields of historical research.

But of course the real reason why coins are so important in the study of ancient history, and why they have dominated in particular the study of the history of money, is that coins are what have survived.[24] Coins are made of durable metals—and very often of imperishable metals, such as gold or silver, which do not rust or corrode. As a result, they tend to survive the ravages of time better than most other things. What is more, coins are valuable. As a result, there has always been a tendency for them to be squirrelled away in buried or hidden hoards—the better to be discovered decades, centuries, or even millennia later by the enterprising historian or numismatist. The problem is that in no field so much as the history of money is an approach fixated upon what physically survives likely to lead us into error. The unfortunate story of the wholesale destruction of one of the most important collections of source material for the history of money ever to have existed shows why.

For more than six hundred years, from the twelfth to the late eighteenth century, the operation of the public finances of England rested on a simple but ingenious piece of accounting technology: the Exchequer tally. A tally was a wooden stick—usually harvested from the willows that grew along the Thames near the Palace of Westminster. On the stick were inscribed, always with notches in the wood and sometimes also in writing, details of payments made to or from the Exchequer. Some were receipts for tax payments made by landowners to the Crown. Others referred to transactions in the opposite direction, recording the sums due on loans by the sovereign to prominent subjects. "9£ 4s 4d from Fulk Basset for the farm of Wycombe" reads one that has survived, for example—relating a debt owed by Fulk Basset, a thirteenth-century Bishop of London, to Henry III. Even bribes seem to have been recorded on Exchequer tallies: one stick in a private collection bears the suspicious-sounding euphemism "13s 4d from William de Tullewyk for the king's good will."[25]

Once the details of the payment had been recorded on the tally stick, it was split down the middle from end to end so that each party to the transaction could keep a record. The creditor's half was called the "stock," and the debtor's the "foil": hence the English use of the term "stocks" for Treasury bonds, which survives to this day. The unique grain of the willow wood meant that a convincing forgery was virtually impossible; while the record of the account in a portable format—rather than just inscribed in the Treasury account books at Westminster, for example—meant that Exchequer credits could be passed from their original holder to a third party in payment of some unrelated debt. Tallies were what are called "bearer securities" in modern financial jargon: financial obligations such as bonds, share certificates, or banknotes, the beneficiary of which is whoever holds the physical record.

Historians agree that the vast majority of fiscal operations in medieval England must have been carried out using tally sticks; and they suppose that a great deal of monetary exchange was transacted using them as well.[26] A credit with the Exchequer, as recorded on a tally stick, would after all have been welcomed in payment by anyone who had taxes of his own coming due. It is, however, impossible to know for certain. For although millions of tallies must have been manufactured over the centuries, and though we know for sure that many thousands survived in the Exchequer archives up until the early nineteenth century, only a handful of specimens exist today. The ultimate culprit for this unfortunate situation is the famous zeal of England's nineteenth-century advocates of administrative reform.

Despite the fact that the tally-stick system had proved itself remarkably efficient over the preceding five hundred years, by the late eighteenth century it was felt that it was time to dispense with it. Keeping accounts with notched sticks—let alone using wooden splints as money alongside the elegant paper notes of the Bank of England—was by then considered little short of barbaric, and certainly out of keeping with the enormous progress being made in commerce and technology. An Act of Parliament of 1782 officially abolished tally sticks as the main means of account-keeping at the Exchequer—though because certain sinecures still operated on the

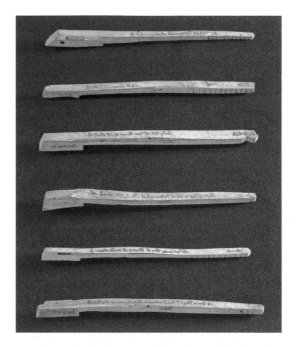

A collection of English Exchequer tallies: rare survivors of one of the
great episodes of historical vandalism of the nineteenth century.

old system, the Act had to wait almost another half-century, until
1826, to come into effect. But in 1834, the ancient institution of the
Receipt of the Exchequer was finally done away with, and the last
Exchequer tally replaced by a paper note.

With the tally-stick system finally abolished, the question arose
of what to do with the vast archive of tallies left in the Exchequer.
Amongst the partisans of reform the general feeling was that they
were nothing but embarrassing relics of the way in which the fiscal
accounts of the British Empire had been kept, "much as Robinson
Crusoe kept his calendar on the desert island," and it was decided
without hesitation to incinerate them.[27] Twenty years later, Charles
Dickens recounted the unfortunate consequences:

> It came to pass that they were burnt in a stove in the House of
> Lords. The stove, overgorged with these preposterous sticks, set

fire to the panelling; the panelling set fire to the House of Lords; the House of Lords set fire to the House of Commons; the two houses were reduced to ashes; architects were called in to build others; we are now in the second million of the cost thereof . . .[28]

The Houses of Parliament could be rebuilt, of course—and were, to leave the splendid Palace of Westminster that stands on the banks of the Thames today. What could not be resurrected from the inferno, however, was the priceless record of England's fiscal and monetary history constituted by the tallies.[29] Historians have had to rely on a handful of tallies that survived by chance in private collections, and we are fortunate that there are a few contemporary accounts of how they were used.[30] But as for the immense wealth of knowledge that the Westminster archive embodied about the state of England's money and finances throughout the Middle Ages, it is irretrievably lost.

If this is a problem for the history of money in medieval England, the situation is infinitely worse for the history of money more generally. All too often, the only physical trace of money that remains is coins: yet as the example of the English tally-stick system shows, coinage may have been only the very tip of the monetary iceberg. Vast hinterlands of monetary and financial history lie beyond our grasp— simply because no physical evidence of their existence and operation survives. To appreciate the seriousness of the problem we have only to consider what hope the historians of the future would have of reconstructing our own monetary history if a natural disaster were to destroy the digital records of our contemporary financial system. We can only trust that reason would prevail, and that they would not build their understanding of modern economic life on the assumption that the pound and euro coins and nickels and dimes that survived were the sum total of our money.

THE BENEFIT OF BEING A FISH OUT OF WATER

The second reason why the conventional theory of money remains so resilient is directly related to a still more intrinsic difficulty. There is an old Chinese proverb: "The fish is the last to know water." It is a concise explanation of why the "social" or "human" sciences—anthropology, sociology, economics and so on—are different from the natural sciences—physics, chemistry, and biology. In the natural sciences, we study the physical world; and it is—at least in principle—possible to get an objective view. Things are not so simple in the social sciences. In these fields, we are studying ourselves, as individuals and in groups. Society and our selves have no independent existence apart from us—and by contrast to the natural sciences, this makes it exceptionally difficult to get an objective view of things. The closer an institution is to the heart of our daily lives, the trickier it is to step outside of it in order to analyse it—and the more controversial will be attempts to do so. The second reason why the nature of money is so difficult to pin down, and why it has been and remains a subject of such controversy, is precisely *because* it is such an integral part of our economies. When we try to understand money, we are like the fish of the Chinese proverb, trying to know the very water in which it moves.

This doesn't mean that all social science is a waste of time, however. It may not be possible to get an absolutely objective view of our own habits, customs, and traditions; but by studying them under different historical conditions we can get a more objective view than otherwise. Just as we can use two different perspectives on a point in the distance to triangulate its position when out hiking, we can learn a lot about a familiar social phenomenon by observing it in other times, in other places, and in other cultures. The only problem in the case of money is that it is such a basic element of the economy that finding opportunities for such triangulation is tricky. Most of the time money is just part of the furniture. It is only when the normal monetary order is disrupted that the veil is snatched from our eyes. When the monetary order dissolves, the water is temporarily tipped out of the fishbowl and we become for a critical moment a fish out of water.

So it is precisely to occasions when disorder erupts in society and the economy that we must look in order to learn what money really is. And since, as the fate of the Exchequer tallies shows, we are at the mercy of scant evidence in investigating the distant past, we would be better off learning from recent history, where evidence is easiest to come by. If we want to understand the nature of money, in other words, our best bet is to study episodes of acute monetary disorder in modern times.

Fortunately, there is no shortage of those.

MONEY IN AN ECONOMY WITHOUT BANKS

On 4 May 1970, a prominent notice appeared in Ireland's leading daily newspaper, the *Irish Independent*, with a simple but alarming title: "CLOSURE OF BANKS." The announcement—placed by the Irish Banks" Standing Committee, a group representing all of Ireland's main banks—informed the public that as a result of the severe breakdown in industrial relations between the banks and their employees, "a position has now been reached where it is impossible for the undermentioned banks to provide even the recent restricted service in the Republic of Ireland." "In these circumstances it is with regret," the notice continued, "that these banks must announce the closure of all their offices in the Republic of Ireland on and from Friday, 1st May, until further notice."

It may come as a shock to learn that virtually the entire banking system in an advanced economy could have shut down overnight as recently as in 1970. At the time, however, this development was widely expected—not least because it had happened once before, in 1966. The matter of dispute between the banks and their employees was a familiar one in the Europe of the late 1960s: the extent to which pay was keeping up with prices. High inflation throughout 1969—by the autumn, the cost of living had risen by more than 10 per cent over the previous fifteen months—had prompted a demand by the employees' union for a new pay settlement. The banks had refused, and the Irish Bank Officials' Association had voted to strike.

From the beginning, it was expected that the banks' closure would not be short-lived, so preparations were made. The first reaction of businesses was to stockpile notes and coins. The *Irish Independent* reported that:

> ## IRISH BANKS' STANDING COMMITTEE
>
> # CLOSURE
> # OF
> # BANKS
>
> As a result of industrial action by the Irish Bank Officials' Association for the past eight weeks, a position has now been reached where it is impossible for the undermentioned banks to continue to provide even the recent restricted service in the Republic of Ireland.
>
> In the circumstances it is with regret that these banks must announce the closure of all their offices in the Republic of Ireland on and from Friday, 1st May, until further notice.
>
> Notwithstanding this closure and the suspension of normal banking services, the Special Import Deposit Scheme, whereby the Irish Banks provide the funds to meet the U.K. deposit requirements on manufactured goods, will continue to function.
>
> **Bank of Ireland**
> **Hibernian Bank Limited**
> **Munster and Leinster Bank Limited**
> **The National Bank of Ireland Limited**
> **Northern Bank Limited**
> **Provincial Bank of Ireland Limited**
> **Royal Bank of Ireland Limited**
> **Ulster Bank Limited**
> **Chase and Bank of Ireland (International) Limited.**
>
> **IRISH BANK'S STANDING COMMITTEE.**
> **R. F. BRENNAN, Secretary.**

There were massive withdrawals of cash throughout the country as firms built up their reserves in anticipation of a shutdown. Insurance companies, safe dealers, and security firms are expected to do brisk business while banks remain closed. Factories and other concerns with large payrolls have arranged to obtain ready cash from large retailers such as supermarkets and department stores to meet wage bills.[31]

But in the first month of the crisis, it became apparent that things might not turn out quite as badly as feared. The Central Bank of Ireland had deliberately accommodated the additional demand for cash in March and April, so there were about £10 million more notes and coins in circulation in May than usual. There was an inevitable tendency for the stream of payments to give rise to gluts of small change in some places—generally shops and other retail operations—and dearths in others—usually wholesalers and public institutions which had no reason to take in cash in the course of their daily business. The Central Bank even made a vain plea to the state-owned bus company to have it distribute cash to passengers. But these blockages in the circulation of coins and notes proved a relatively minor inconvenience.

The reason was that the vast majority of payments continued to be made by cheque—in other words, by transfer from one individual's or business' current account to another's—despite the fact that the banks at which these accounts were all held were shut. In its review of the whole affair, the Central Bank of Ireland noted that prior to the closure "some two-thirds of aggregate money holdings are in the form of credit balances on current accounts, the remainder consisting of notes and coin."[32] The critical question, therefore, was whether this "bank money" would continue to circulate. For individuals in particular, there was really no other option: for any expenses in excess of the cash they had in hand when the banks shut their doors on 1 May, their only hope was to write IOUs in the form of cheques and hope that they would be accepted.

Remarkably, as the summer wore on, transactions continued to take place and cheques to be exchanged almost exactly as usual. The one difference, of course, was that none of the cheques could be submitted to the banks. Normally, this facility is what relieves sellers of most of the risk of accepting credit payments: cheques can be cashed at the end of every business day. With the banking system shut, however, cheques were for the time being just personal or corporate IOUs. Sellers who accepted them were doing so on the basis of their own assessment of buyers' credit. The main risk, therefore, was of abuse of the improvised system. Since cheques were not being cleared, there was nothing in principle to prevent people writing cheques for amounts that they did not have. For the system to work, payees would have to take it on trust that payers' cheques were not going to bounce—and all this when they had no clear idea when the banks would reopen and allow them to find out. *The Times* of London was following events over the Irish Sea with interest—and in July it noted both the extraordinary fact that nothing much seemed to have changed, and the apparent fragility of the situation. "Figures and trends which are available indicate that the dispute has not had an adverse effect on the economy so far," wrote its correspondent. "This has been due to a number of factors, not least of which is the prudence which business has exercised against overspending." But could the balancing act continue? "There is now, however, a psychological risk that if the dispute drags on, caution will be cast aside, particularly by smaller businesses."[33]

Sure enough, cracks did begin to appear here and there. A month into the closure, there was a scare when some livestock markets announced that they would no longer accept private cheques.[34] In July, a farmer from Omagh who had been convicted of smuggling seven pigs into the Republic was unable to pay the £309 fine handed down to him, for want of ready cash.[35] And over the summer, the business lobby—encouraged by the banks and exasperated by the expenses they were incurring to find ways round the closure—began planting scare stories in the newspapers claiming, for example, that "a rapidly growing paralysis is spreading through the economy because of the banks dispute."[36] But the evidence collated by the Central Bank of Ireland once the crisis was finally resolved in November 1970 showed quite the opposite. Their review of the closure concluded not only that "the Irish economy continued to function for a reasonably long period of time with its main clearing banks closed for business," but that "the level of economic activity continued to increase" over the period.[37] Both before and after the event, it seemed unbelievable—but somehow, it had worked: for six and a half months, in one of the then thirty wealthiest economies in the world, "a highly personalized credit system without any definite time horizon for the eventual clearance of debits and credits substituted for the existing institutionalized banking system."[38]

In the end, the main impediment imposed by this highly successful system turned out to be logistical. By the time the banks and their employees finally reached a new pay settlement, and it was announced

that the banks would reopen on 17 November 1970, an enormous
volume of uncleared cheques had accumulated with individuals and
businesses. Advertisements were placed in the newspapers warning
customers not to submit all of them at once, and forewarning that it
was unlikely that account balances would be reconciled fully for several weeks. It was another three months—until mid-February, 1971—
before matters had returned completely to normal. By then, a total
of over £5 billion of uncleared cheques written during the period of
the closure had been submitted for clearing. This was the money that
the Irish public had made for itself while its banks were on strike.

How had this apparent miracle of spontaneous economic co-
operation come to pass? The general consensus after the event was
that several features of Irish social life were uniquely conducive
to its success: not least, that most famous feature of all, the Irish
public house. The basic challenge was that of screening the creditworthiness of those paying by unclearable cheque. Ireland had an
advantage in that communities, both in the countryside and in the
cities, were close-knit. Individuals had personal knowledge of most
of the people they transacted with, and so were comfortable form-
ing judgements as to their creditworthiness. But by 1970 Ireland was
nevertheless a diverse and developed economy, so this could not
always be the case. It was here that the Republic's pubs and small
shops came into their own, by serving as nodes in the system, collecting, endorsing, and clearing cheques like an ersatz banking system. "It appears," concluded the Irish economist Antoin Murphy,
with admirable circumspection, "that the managers of these retail
outlets and public houses had a high degree of information about
their customers—one does not after all serve drink to someone for
years without discovering something of his liquid resources."[39]

THE HEART OF THE MATTER

The case of the Irish bank closure provides an unusually useful
opportunity to understand more clearly the nature of money. Like
Furness' report from Yap, it forces us to reconsider what is essential to the functioning of a monetary system. But because the Irish

case is so much closer in time and technology to our own, it is much more suitable for economic triangulation. The story of Yap showed that the conventional theory of the origins and nature of money is confused. The story of the Irish bank closure helps point the way to a more realistic alternative.

The story of Yap stripped away a central, misleading preconception about the nature of money that had bedevilled economists for centuries: that what was essential was the currency, the commodity coinage, which functioned as a "medium of exchange." It showed that in a primitive economy like Yap, just as in today's system, currency is ephemeral and cosmetic: it is the underlying mechanism of credit accounts and clearing that is the essence of money. We were left with a very different picture of the nature and origins of money from the one painted by the conventional theory. At the centre of this alternative view of money—its primitive concept, if you like—is credit. Money is not a commodity medium of exchange, but a social technology composed of three fundamental elements.[40] The first is an abstract unit of value in which money is denominated. The second is a system of accounts, which keeps track of the individuals' or the institutions' credit or debt balances as they engage in trade with one another. The third is the possibility that the original creditor in a relationship can transfer their debtor's obligation to a third party in settlement of some unrelated debt.[41]

This third element is vital. Whilst all money is credit, not all credit is money: and it is the possibility of transfer that makes the difference. An IOU which remains for ever a contract between just two parties is nothing more than a loan. It is credit, but it is not money. It is when that IOU can be passed on to a third party—when it is able to be "negotiated" or "endorsed," in the financial jargon—that credit comes to life and starts to serve as money. Money, in other words, is not just credit—but *transferable* credit. As the nineteenth-century economist and lawyer Henry Dunning Macleod put it:

> These simple considerations at once shew the fundamental nature
> of a Currency. It is quite clear that its primary use is to measure
> and record debts, and to facilitate their transfer from one person

to another; and whatever means be adopted for this purpose, whether it be gold, silver, paper, or anything else, is a currency. We may therefore lay down our fundamental Conception that Currency and Transferable Debt are convertible terms; whatever represents transferable debt of any sort is Currency; and whatever material the Currency may consist of, it represents Transferable Debt, and nothing else.[42]

As we shall see, this innovation of the transferability of debts was a critical development in the history of money. It is this, rather than the graduation from a mythical barter economy, which has historically revolutionised societies and economies. In fact, it is barely an exaggeration—if we make allowance for the unmistakable overtone of Victorian melodrama—to say, as Macleod did:

> If we were asked—Who made the discovery which has most deeply affected the fortunes of the human race? We think, after full consideration, we might safely answer—The man who first discovered that a Debt is a Saleable Commodity.[43]

The recognition of this third fundamental element of money is important. It explains what determines money's value—and why money, even though it is nothing but credit, cannot just be created at will by anyone. For sellers to accept buyers' IOUs in payment, they must be convinced of two things. They must have reason to believe that the debtor whose obligation they are about to accept will, if it comes to it, be able to satisfy their claim: they must believe, in other words, that the money's issuer is creditworthy. This much would be enough to sustain the existence of bilateral credit. The test for money is more stringent. For credit to become money, sellers must also trust that third parties will be willing to accept the debtor's IOU in payment as well. They must believe that it is, and will remain indefinitely, transferable—that the market for this money is liquid. Depending on how powerful are the reasons to believe these two things, it will be easier or harder for an issuer's IOUs to circulate as money.

It is because of this third critical element of transferability that money issued by governments, or by the banks which governments endorse and backstop, is thought to be special. Indeed, there is an influential school of thought—known as chartalism—which argues that governments and their agents are the only viable issuers of money.[44] But the story of the Irish bank closure exposes this as another misleading preconception. The closure of the Irish banks showed that the system of credit creation and clearing need not be the officially sanctioned one. The official system—the banks—was suspended for the best part of seven months. But money did not disappear. Like the infamous *fei* that sank to the bottom of the sea, the associated banks suddenly vanished—and with them the official apparatus of credit accounts and clearing—and yet money continued to exist.

The Irish bank closure demonstrates that the official paraphernalia of banks and credit cards and solemnly printed notes with unforgeable insignia is not what is essential to money. All of this can disappear and yet money still remains: a system of credit and debt, ceaselessly expanding and contracting like a beating heart, sustaining the circulation of trade. What matters is only that there are issuers whom the public considers creditworthy, and a wide enough belief that their obligations will be accepted by third parties. For governments and banks to fulfil those two criteria is generally easy; whereas for companies, let alone individuals, it is generally hard. But as the Irish example goes to show, these rules of thumb do not apply universally. When the official monetary arrangements disintegrate, it is surprising how effective society is at improvising an alternative.

SO WHAT?

My friend the entrepreneur was looking distinctly unimpressed.

"Fine," he said, "you may be right. Maybe on closer inspection my—I mean, Adam Smith's—theory has a few holes in it. But I've got a question for you, then. So what? What difference does it make, in the real world, if I think of money as social technology rather than a thing? And why does it matter if it's a social technology that doesn't necessarily depend upon the state?"

These were fair questions, I answered. All I had been arguing for ultimately, was a simple change of perspective. But simple changes of perspective can have dramatic consequences. My own powers of persuasion were wilting. So I turned to a favourite story of the great physicist Richard Feynman for help.

In one of his famous television lectures on physics, Feynman wanted to convey how, in science, a small change of perspective can sometimes produce a radically different view of the world—and how our preconceptions might make that change of perspective seem counter-intuitive.[45] He gave the example of how the static electricity generated by using a plastic comb can be used to levitate a piece of paper. We never cease, he explained, to be entertained and amazed by this feat. The reason is that we are used to forces that we can see—for example our hand touching the comb itself, experiencing resistance, and therefore being able to grasp it and lift it up—and so we think only these forces are real. By contrast, forces that we can't see—for example the action at a distance caused by the electromagnetic field attracting the paper to the comb—seem like magic. But in fact we have it exactly the wrong way round. It is the force that we cannot see—the electromagnetic field—which is the fundamental force. The invisible electromagnetic field lies behind both the apparently magical action at a distance of the static electricity and the familiar solidity of everything we can see.

It is just the same with money. As we have seen, the great temptation has always been to think that coins and other currency, being tangible and durable, are money—on top of which the magical, incorporeal apparatus of credit and debt is constructed. The reality is exactly the opposite. It is the social technology of transferable credit that is the fundamental force—the primitive monetary reality. The stone *fei* of Yap, the willow tally sticks of medieval England, the banknotes, cheques, scrip money, and private IOUs of countless episodes of monetary disorder throughout history, and the billions of bits of electronic data that the banking systems of today's advanced economies use: they are all simply tokens to keep track of the underlying and ever-fluctuating balances of millions upon millions of credit and debt relationships.

The consequences of this change of perspective on money for our understanding of our economic reality are every bit as dramatic, in their sphere, as the consequences of the shift from the Newtonian to the quantum theoretic perspective have been for our understanding of our physical reality. The next chapter will begin to explain what they are.

2 Getting Money's Measure

THE BIOGRAPHY OF MONEY: A STORY OF IDEAS

In June 2012 a splendid new gallery devoted to the history of money was opened at the British Museum in London. The museum's management had concluded that the previous Money Gallery had lost the public's interest. Visitors just weren't that engaged by row upon row of old coins and scholarly explanations of where they came from: a new approach was needed. The result is a triumph of design. Alongside a more limited but more fascinating collection of coins are all kinds of exotic objects that have been used as currency: cowrie shells from Arabia and Africa, seeds from the Solomon Islands, a fourteenth-century Chinese banknote—even a *fei* from Yap. But there are now also a host of other intriguing objects that bring money's central role in human history to life, from a sixteenth-century maiolica donation box with which the pious citizens of Siena used to expiate God with Mammon, to a 1982 silkscreen homage to the U.S. dollar by Andy Warhol. There is, however, something strange about this magnificent new gallery. Its creation was generously sponsored by a bank; in fact, by what was then the largest bank in the world, the U.S. conglomerate Citibank. Banks are a pretty important part of the story of money, one would have thought. Yet there is no bank exhibited in the Money Gallery.

This is not because of some nefarious conspiracy to conceal the real workings of the financial system. It is because the gallery's designers were well aware that nothing very informative would result from putting a bank inside a museum. A bank is just an office building, pretty much indistinguishable from any other office building—and it would tell you little about money to look at that. The problem is that money is not really a thing at all but a social technology: a set of ideas and practices which organise what we produce and consume, and the way we live together. When it comes to money itself—rather than the tokens that represent it, the account books where people record it, or the buildings such as banks in which people administer it—there is nothing physical to look at.

This has an important implication for us if we want to investigate money's origins, nature, and influence on history and our own lives. The archaeological approach taken by the new Money Gallery at the British Museum is an important and interesting one in its own right. But if we really want to understand money, we need to embark on a different kind of archaeological expedition. Ours will be a mission to recover and analyse not bullion, coins, or the charred remains of tally sticks—or indeed any *thing* at all—but ideas, practices, and institutions; and, above all, the idea of abstract economic value, the practice of accounting, and the institution of decentralised transferability.

As with any excavation, the first question is where to dig. We have seen that if money is indeed the operating system on which we run our societies and economies, the challenge of getting an objective view is an imposing one. Locating a case in which the official monetary system took a holiday, as it did during the Irish bank strike, might have been easy enough; and through it we learned something about the extent to which money really depends upon the state. If we wish to delve more deeply, however, we need to achieve an altogether more radical triangulation: we need to explore a time and a place where money never existed. That may sound like a tall order—but as it happens, we are in luck. Not only do we possess a vivid and detailed description of the age immediately before the invention of money, but that description happens to be contained in two of the greatest poems ever composed.

THE WRATH OF ACHILLES:
THE WORLD BEFORE MONEY

The *Iliad* and the *Odyssey*—the two epic poems that represent the earliest surviving products of Greek culture—are celebrated as the fountainheads of all subsequent European literature. But it is not for their literary merits alone that the Homeric epics are valued. The *Iliad* and the *Odyssey* also comprise a unique historical record of Greek society and culture during a period of which we otherwise know remarkably little. The great palace civilisations of Knossos and Mycenae that flourished in the second millennium BC left a wealth of archaeological evidence. To understand the city states of classical Greece that emerged from the mid-eighth century BC onwards, we can turn not only to their art and architecture but to their literature and philosophy. But in between these two periods is an era for which almost no evidence of any sort exists: the so-called Greek Dark Ages. When Mycenaean society suddenly collapsed in around 1200 BC—probably as a result of assaults by invading enemies—virtually every vestige of the great civilisation disappeared within a single generation. The monumental palaces with their large populations, wealthy hinterlands, and cosmopolitan connections vanished. The Greek world reverted to a dispersed collection of isolated tribal communities: small, rustic, and illiterate. For the next four centuries almost our sole source for understanding the culture and society of the Greek Aegean is the tradition of oral poetry that culminated in the Homeric epics.

Fortunately, the canvas of these poems is vast. The *Iliad* is most famous for its evocative accounts of the carnage of war and the manly excesses of its heroes. A single account of an attack by a lone chieftain can run to over a thousand verses, most of them dedicated to vivid description of the gruesome ways in which he dispatches his enemies.[1] But the variety of life depicted in the poems is much broader than the heroic existence alone. In a famous passage of the *Iliad* describing the shield that the blacksmith-god Hephaestus fashions for Achilles, for example, we learn of Dark Age practice in fields ranging from agriculture to animal husbandry, and from marriage ritual to criminal litigation.[2] The subject matter of the *Odyssey* is more wide-ranging still. The hero Odysseus, returning from Troy, criss-crosses the known world. He is seduced by witches and imprisoned by one-eyed giants. He consorts with shepherds whilst disguised as a vagrant and dines with kings at the grandest palaces of the age. After exhausting all possibilities on earth, he even descends to the Underworld where he encounters his erstwhile brothers-in-arms and commiserates with them on their dreary fate. Yet in all this astonishingly rich panorama of Dark Age society there is something that is conspicuously missing. There is no money.

To those of us who live in a world where markets and money are the dominant tools for the organisation of social life, this begs an obvious question. If the tribal societies of Dark Age Greece had none of these things, how did they organise themselves? The shock at encountering a society that functions according to completely different rules from one's own is well captured by the question which the British economist Paul Seabright was asked by the director of bread production in the Russian city of St. Petersburg shortly after the collapse of the Soviet Union. "Please understand that we are keen to move towards a market system," the former Red Director explained, "but we need to understand how such a system works. Tell me, for example, who is in charge of the supply of bread to the population of London?"[3] The answer, of course, is that nobody is in charge—the decentralised system of money and markets is what keeps Londoners supplied with everything from Warburtons sandwich to artisan spelt. But just as the Soviet mind was astonished by the notion that the economy could operate without a plan and a planner to co-ordinate it, our minds are apt to be amazed by the opposite: the idea that society could function without any markets or money at all. What did the job before money and markets existed? The *Iliad* and *Odyssey* provide a rich and detailed answer.

The political apparatus is simple but rigid. It is an aristocratic world of chieftains, clerics, and common soldiers. But the hierarchy is flat: a chieftain amongst his followers seems more like a first among equals than a modern monarch, and Agamemnon, the Greek commander-in-chief at Troy, appears to stand in the same relation to the other chieftains. The relatively modest social distinctions are, however, rigidly observed. When a rancorous foot soldier accuses Agamemnon of arrogance in front of the assembled troops, the chieftain Odysseus responds to the breach of protocol in swift and brutal fashion, beating him with his staff and threatening to strip him and thrash him around the camp. This exercise of naked power, unmediated by any more civilised social institutions, might appal the modern reader. To the Dark Age Greek, nothing could have been more natural and appropriate. "Odysseus has done many thousands of great things for the Greeks before now both in government and in battle," the poet reports the troops as saying to one another approvingly, "but making this scurrilous chatterbox shut up is really the best of all of them: never again, I'll wager, will [he] dare to rebuke chieftains in this shameless manner."[4]

So much for the art of politics. How else did Dark Age Greek society organise itself in the absence of money? For the provision of the most basic needs—food, water, and clothing—the answer was simple, since it was essentially an economy of self-sufficient households in which the individual tribesman subsisted on the produce of his own estate. But the poems also emphasise three social institutions that played important roles in organising the community. The *Iliad* is concerned with the state of war. Here, it is the sharing out of booty following the sacking of a city or the defeat of enemies that is the most important mechanism. As a system for the distribution of income, it was evidently far from perfect. The rules appear to be subject to frequent dispute. Indeed, the plot of the poem turns on the dispute between the Greeks' best warrior, Achilles, and their commander-in-chief, Agamemnon, over their respective rights to captured booty.

By the time of the *Odyssey*, the world is at peace again. The poem

follows Odysseus as he wends his way home from Troy, and his son
Telemachus as he travels the Aegean in search of his father. A different institution now dominates the scene: the practice of exchanging
gifts between chieftains. It was the custom, on receiving or parting
from fellow aristocrats, to present gifts—gifts that would be recipro-
cated on one's own next visit. The purpose of this primitive form of
economic exchange was to express in visible and tangible form the
bond between social equals and to retouch the cement of the social
infrastructure for the future. Like booty distribution, its rules were
sometimes contested: the Trojan War itself was the result of a breach
of protocol by Paris, who stole Menelaus' bride, the beautiful Helen.
But outside times of war, it was the most important system of economic interaction in the Dark Age Greek world; one, indeed, so central to its worldview that when another poet writing two centuries
or so after Homer's time wished to capture the essence of the good
life in a single verse, he wrote: "Happy the man who has his sons, his
hounds, his horses—and a friend from foreign parts."[5]

The raw principle of "might is right" alone, albeit moderated by
booty distribution and reciprocal gift-exchange, seems a somewhat
threadbare fabric out of which to fashion even a simple society. And
indeed the poems describe a third crucial institution that was altogether more profound: the sacrifice of oxen to the gods and the distribution of the roast meat in equal parts to the congregation of the
tribe. Through this solemn ritual perhaps the most basic of all principles of Greek political organisation was expressed in visible—indeed,
in edible—form: the fact that every male member of the tribe was of
equal social worth, and, by the same token, owed an equal obligation
to the community as a whole.[6]

These three simple mechanisms for organising society in the
absence of money—the interlocking institutions of booty distribution, reciprocal gift-exchange, and the distribution of the sacrifice—are
far from unique to Dark Age Greece. Rather, modern research in
anthropology and comparative history has shown them to be typical of the practices of small-scale, tribal societies.[7] Of course, such
pre-monetary social institutions have assumed many forms, reflect-

ing the peculiar circumstances and beliefs of the peoples in question. But the anthropologists Maurice Bloch and Jonathan Parry have identified a widespread twofold classification. Comparative studies of societies from Madagascar to the Andes reveal "a similar pattern of two related but separate transactional orders: on the one hand transactions concerned with the reproduction of the long-term social or cosmic order; on the other, a 'sphere' of short-term transactions concerned with the arena of individual competition."[8] The pre-monetary institutions of the Homeric world conform to the scheme. On the one hand, there was the primeval institution of the sacrifice and the egalitarian distribution and communal consumption of its roast meat—a ritual expression of tribal solidarity before deity probably inherited from the most distant Indo-European past.[9] This was the institution that governed the "long-term transactional order." On the other, there were the conventions of reciprocal gift-exchange and of booty distribution. These were the rules that governed the "short-term transactional order," concerned not with cosmic order and harmony between the classes but with the more mundane matter of ensuring that the everyday business of primitive society—drinking and hunting when at peace; rape and pillage when at war—did not dissolve into chaos.

ANCIENT MESOPOTAMIA: THE UR-BUREAUCRACY

Yet the primordial social practices described in the Homeric epics and attested in the Aegean archaeological evidence were far from the only known means of organising society in the era of the Greek Dark Ages. A mere thousand miles to the east were civilisations much older, much larger, and much more sophisticated. These were the ancient riparian societies of Mesopotamia. In stark contrast to the rocky, mountainous, seaboard geography of most of the Greek world, Mesopotamia was a landscape of tremendous fertility, encompassing the rolling hills of the Fertile Crescent in the north and the rich alluvial plain of the Tigris and Euphrates rivers in the south. No doubt it is on account of these basic environmental conditions that

Mesopotamia can claim to be the birthplace of so many of the basic aspects of human civilisation. It is close to the northern reaches of the Euphrates, in modern-day Turkey, that agriculture seems to have been invented and the very earliest evidence of sedentary human settlement has been found.[10] It was in the delta of the two great Mesopotamian rivers, in modern-day Iraq, that the technique of irrigation appears to have been first developed.

These fundamental scientific discoveries permitted what were, by the standards of the era, vast concentrations of people—and as a result, the development of Mesopotamia's greatest and most influential social innovation: the city. By the early third millennium BC, the city of Uruk was thriving on the banks of the Euphrates in the far south, covering five and a half square kilometres and housing thousands of inhabitants.[11] But Uruk was only the pioneer of a number of great city states that flourished throughout Mesopotamia, and which a thousand years later would be unified by the world's first regional state, headquartered in the great metropolis of Ur.[12] By the beginning of the second millennium BC, more than sixty thousand people lived within the city itself. In its hinterland, meanwhile, thousands of hectares of land were under cultivation for dates, sesame, and cereals, and hundreds more were devoted to dairy farming and sheep herding. There were fish farms and reed factories in the marshes of the south, and numerous artisans' operations in the city itself making pottery, reedwork, and prestige goods for use in religious ritual. The scale and diversity of these activities, and their concentration in a single centre of population, were unimaginable in Dark Age Greece.

Unsurprisingly, the social system that developed was also radically different from the primitive tribalism of the Dark Age Greek world. Ultimate power in Ur was shared between the palace—the seat of a semi-divine king who combined the roles of military leader and chief justice—and the temples—home both to the deities who were believed to regulate the universe, and to an extensive clerical bureaucracy whose job it was to do the same for the economy of the city on earth. Monumental temple architecture dominated the centre of the city—the great ziggurat dedicated to the god Nanna which still stands today; the temple of his heavenly spouse Ningal; and the Ganunmah, a vast storehouse which also served as the headquarters of the clerical administration.[13] These officials choreographed virtually every aspect of Ur's economy: "[t]he fields, the herds, and the marshes were owned mainly by the temples, who used citizens to take care of the daily work. The temple administrators were always, however, the ultimate authority."[14] The contrast with Greece could not be more stark. In Mesopotamia, geography and climate led to scale and complexity, which in turn led to the world's first bureaucratic society—and its first command economy.[15]

A state with such a complex, hierarchical, and bureaucratic form of organisation demanded altogether different technologies of social co-operation and control from the primitive institutions that governed the small, tribal societies of Dark Age Greece. It is therefore not surprising that Mesopotamia witnessed the invention of three of the most important social technologies in the history of human civilisation: literacy, numeracy, and accounting.

THE SILICON VALLEY OF THE ANCIENT WORLD

The ancient world was mystified by the origins of literacy. It seemed inconceivable that a technology so self-evidently fundamental to civilised life could have been dreamt up by feeble-minded mortals. The only possible explanation, therefore, was that it had come from the gods—either as a generous gift, or as stolen goods. The Egyptians, for example, believed that Thoth, the baboon-faced god of knowledge, presented writing to mortals, and the Greeks that Prometheus did the same. In ancient Mesopotamia, on the other hand, it was held that the secret of literacy had been acquired by stealth. The great goddess Inanna had stolen writing for her city of Uruk by taking advantage of Enki, the god of wisdom, while he was drunk.

When modern scholars began to show an interest in the same question in the eighteenth century, they demonstrated more confidence in the powers of human invention. Archaeological evidence was marshalled, and by the early twentieth century a reasonable theory, consisting of two hypotheses, had been constructed. First, writing had not evolved gradually, but had been invented—exactly by whom was unclear, but it was generally presumed to be by wise sages who "agreed upon a conventional method of recording [language] in written signs . . . intelligible to all their colleagues and successors."[16] Second, the earliest writing must have been "pictographic"—that is, it consisted of stylised pictures of what it was intended to represent— since it would otherwise have been difficult for the sages to agree on the symbols and disseminate them easily amongst the population.[17]

Until the early twentieth century, all available evidence seemed to corroborate this pictographic theory of the origins of literacy. The earliest writing indeed appeared suddenly in the archaeological record, and did so in the form of Egyptian hieroglyphs, ancient Chinese characters, and the colourful pictograms of the pre-Columbian Aztec codices. In 1929, however, a new discovery turned the theory on its head. Excavations at Mesopotamian Uruk uncovered a vast archive of clay tablets inscribed with detailed accounts of palace and temple transactions. Dating from the late fourth millennium BC, the writing on these tablets represented by far the oldest specimens ever discovered. But unlike the pictographic scripts of Egypt, China, and Central America, this script consisted of abstract signs composed of combinations of inscribed flicks of a reed pen—a so-called "cuneiform" script. As the excavations continued throughout the mid-twentieth century, more and more evidence accumulated. The earliest known writing was represented not by pictograms but by a script not qualitatively different from a modern alphabet. If the conventional theory's second hypothesis was incorrect, perhaps its first hypothesis of spontaneous invention was also flawed. All of a sudden, the origins of writing were plunged back into obscurity; four decades would pass before a new light was to illuminate the ancient question from a quite unexpected angle.

The interwar excavations at Uruk that discovered the earliest known writing were part of a golden age of archaeological exploration in Mesopotamia from the late nineteenth to the mid-twentieth century. American, German, and British campaigns throughout this period unearthed the sites of countless archaic settlements and yielded vast and impressive archives of the craftsmanship of the Mesopotamian civilisations, from monumental statuary to delicate jewellery. In amongst these highly prized finds, however, were also scattered many thousands of small clay artefacts—most of them no larger than children's marbles. They came in many shapes and sizes— cones, cylinders, balls—but were otherwise utterly nondescript. For decades, these uninspiring-looking bits of debris were therefore largely ignored by archaeologists. Until the 1970s there was not even general agreement on what they were. Typical speculations were that they were "children's playthings," "amulets," or "game pieces."[18] Often they were identified simply as "objects of uncertain purpose." One distinguished American archaeologist wrote in his site report that "[f]rom levels 11 and 12 come five mysterious . . . clay objects, looking like nothing in the world but suppositories."[19]

The truth was both more mundane and more momentous. In 1969, a young French archaeologist, Denise Schmandt-Besserat, decided to make a comprehensive catalogue of these mysterious bits of clay. Once analysed together, it became clear that they came in various generic shapes and sizes common to sites from all over Western Asia, from south-eastern Turkey to present-day Pakistan. Schmandt-Besserat realised that these long-overlooked artefacts were not primordial chess pieces or primitive laxatives but tokens used for what is called "correspondence-counting"—keeping track of one quantity by maintaining a matching quantity of something else. Correspondence-counting requires no numerical sophistication whatsoever, merely the ability to check whether two quantities are the same.[20] It is the earliest known technique for reckoning num- ber: notched animal bones thought to use correspondence-counting to record the passage of days or the number of animals killed have been discovered dating from the early Stone Age.[21] In Mesopotamia, Schmandt-Besserat realised, a complex system of clay tokens had enabled this ancient method to attain a previously unknown level of sophistication. Each different shape and size of token represented a different type and quantity of a particular staple commodity: incised cones for bread, ovoids for oil, rhomboids for beer, and so on.[22] Reckoning number using this elaborate system of tokens was put to use in the agricultural economy to keep account of numbers of animals or quantities of crops.

For thousands of years, this system remained unchanged in its essentials.[23] With the rise of urban civilisation and the temple economies, the demands on record-keeping increased dramatically. Around 3100 BC, in Mesopotamian Uruk, a critical innovation was made. Records began to be kept not using collections of the tokens themselves, but by making impressions of the tokens on moist clay tablets. Henceforth, a sheep would not be represented by a conical token kept in an account box, but by the triangular impression of such a token on a clay tablet. Once this system had been introduced, and the impressions corresponding to each token had been learned, it was a small step to dispense with the tokens themselves. An impression of the correct shape and size could be made in the wet clay of a tablet much more simply using a reed pen. The ancient system of three-dimensional objects had been translated into a new system of two-dimensional symbols. It was an epochal development: nothing less than the birth of literacy.

Stimulating the invention of writing was no mean achievement on its own; but the increasing complexity of the Mesopotamian economies meant that the pressure to devise ever more efficient and flexible techniques was unrelenting. Reckoning number using the new, written symbols was certainly more efficient than shaping, firing, and then storing thousand upon thousand of little clay tokens. But both techniques still relied upon correspondence-counting—one token or symbol corresponding to each thing being counted. Soon after the invention of writing, however, another momentous improvement was made. Instead of writing five sheep symbols to signify five sheep, separate symbols for the number five and the category sheep were introduced. Now, only two symbols were required, instead of five. When one considers that on a single surviving tablet the receipt of 140,000 litres of grain is recorded it is obvious that the practical advantages were considerable.[24] The longer-term implications were even greater, however. Correspondence-counting requires no notion of abstract number; no concept, that is, of number separate from the things being counted. The new system did. Not only had Ur invented writing, it had almost simultaneously invented the concept of number—and thereby opened the way to the development of mathematics.

The invention of writing and abstract number set the stage for the development of the third technology at the heart of Mesopotamian society: accounting. The hierarchical control of economic activity by clerical bureaucracies required a management information system: a technique for quantifying stocks and flows of raw materials and finished goods, for using these quantities in forward planning, and for checking that the plan was being correctly carried out on the ground. Accounting was a social technology that combined the ability to keep records efficiently using writing and number with standardised measures of time so that quantities could be tracked as stocks on balance sheets and flows on income statements.[25] For the economies of ancient Mesopotamia, as for large corporations today, it was a system of consistent book-keeping that allowed directives from on high to be translated into practical instructions—and for the fulfilment of those instructions then to be verified by that most familiar, most forbidding, and, as it transpires, most ancient of professional figures: the accountant.

Thus in almost every respect, the societies of ancient Mesopotamia represent a radical counterpoint to those of Dark Age Greece. In place of the primitive and egalitarian tribal society of Homer there was the city, with tens of thousands of inhabitants ruled by a semi-divine king and organised into a multi-layered hierarchy. Instead of the exercise of raw power by chieftains over commoners, there were the sophisticated rules of the accounting system administered by the temple bureaucracy. In place of a simple economy governed by principles of reciprocity and ritual sacrifice that would have been familiar to countless primitive tribes over the past several millennia, there was a complex economy governed according to an elaborate system of economic planning that would be familiar to a manager in a modern multinational corporation. Yet despite these yawning differences, there was one vital respect in which the economies of ancient Mesopotamia were identical to those of Dark Age Greece. For neither the bureaucratic plan of the temple, nor the primitive tribal institutions of Dark Age Greece, had any use for money.[26]

Why was it that this extraordinary commercial civilisation, the most advanced economy that the world had ever seen, the society that invented literacy, numeracy, and accounting, did not invent money? The answer is that it did not develop one critical ingredient—the single most important precondition for money and its central component. To understand what that ingredient was, we must take a detour to a bureaucratic environment of a much more recent vintage: the 11th meeting of the General Conference on Weights and Measures, on 14 October 1960, in Paris.

GETTING THE MEASURE OF THINGS

Faceless international bureaucracies have not typically been responsible for revolutionary advances in human civilisation. More often, they have been bastions of dogma and recidivism against which lonely pioneers have had to struggle in the daring quest for knowledge and truth. The field of metrology—the science of measurement—provides a notable exception to this general rule, however. On 14 October 1960, the quadrennial General Conference on Weights and Measures was convened to consider a set of proposals made by the International Committee for Weights and Measures, received by them from the International Bureau of Weights and Measures. It was as impressive an accumulation of faceless international bureaucracies as one could wish for—a certain recipe, one might have thought, for a turgid agenda of incidental points of order to be pored over in tedious detail by the delegates before adjournment for a long lunch on expenses. Nothing could have been further from the truth. For at this meeting was agreed, for the first time in history, a simple and universal system of units of measurement based on internationally agreed standards—the *Système International d'Unités*, or SI for short.

This was no small feat. Until the nineteenth century, consistent standardisation of units of measurement across any wide geographical area was virtually unheard of. In 1790, for example, a survey was commissioned to ascertain the standard length of the *arpent*, a common French unit of length. To the surveyors' dismay, they found nine different standards in use in the *département* of Basses-Pyrénées alone. In Calvados, there were no fewer than sixteen.[27] Nor were examples such as these by any means the most extreme: France was at the more enlightened end of the European spectrum when it came to consistency. "Altogether, a state of shocking confusion reigned," wrote the great metrological scholar Witold Kula of his native Poland: "in the single village of Jastrzebie, Upper Jastrzebie used the Pszczyna measure while Lower Jastrzebie used the measure of Wodzislaw, and the vicar kept both measures available until the 1830s."[28]

Then there was the proliferation of units themselves. Under the SI, length—any length, of anything—is measured by the metre, or its subdivisions or multiples. Metrological concepts applicable in such universal contexts were unknown in medieval and early modern Europe. Even today in the U.K., whisky is measured in gills, beer in pints, and petrol in gallons. But in the system of old Slavonic measures, for example, the foot was the length unit employed to measure out potato patches, while the pace was used to describe distances to be travelled. The fathom was used to record the depth of the sea, while the ell was used in the measuring out of cloth. Of course, what was actually being measured in all these cases was length. But a different unit was used for each specific context. This hodgepodge of vernacular units resulted in terminology which sounds almost nonsensical to modern ears: "[t]he peasant fisherman would refer to his net as being 30 fathoms long and ten ells wide."[29]

This was the lamentable state of affairs which the General Conference on Weights and Measures had been established to remedy, and the creation of the SI was the culmination of nearly a century's worth of international efforts to simplify and standardise the world's weights and measures. It was a revolutionary advance in both respects. With regard to simplification, it introduced a set of just six basic units, sufficient for the measurement of any aspect of the physical world: the metre for linear extension, the kilogram for mass, the second for time, the degree Kelvin for temperature, the candela for luminosity, and the ampere for electric current.[30] Its achievements in standardisation were even more dramatic. Not only did it establish internationally agreed standards for these basic units, but for the first time it defined them in terms of universal constants found in nature, rather than by reference to particular agreed examples. Henceforth, the SI metre, for example, was no longer defined in terms of a canonical metre rule kept in Paris, but in terms of the wavelength of radiation emitted by a particular chemical element.[31]

At first glance, this long march towards simplification and standardisation might seem to have been purely cosmetic. After all, regardless of their specific origins, even archaic units of measurement are all related to one another, and to modern units, in fixed proportions. What could be more harmless than the indulgence of local custom— or more typical of a faceless international bureaucracy than the urge to eradicate it? But this would be to misunderstand the nature and origins of systems of measurement. After all, the question can be reversed. Why did anyone ever settle for these limited-purpose units of measurement, when they could have had universally applicable ones? Why, in other words, did these absurd proliferations of local and limited-purpose units spring up in the first place?

The truth is that there was method in the apparent madness. The common feature of traditional metrological concepts was that they had been developed from the bottom up for use in specific contexts— and that they captured exactly the most relevant aspect of the activity at hand. Today, for example, we define the area of any piece of land by measuring its perimeter. To the medieval peasant farmer, however, the square dimensions of a piece of arable land were the least useful things to know about it. Instead, as Witold Kula explained, "[t]wo qualitative aspects of any cultivable field are of crucial importance: the time it takes to cultivate it, and the harvest it is capable of yielding."[32] As a result, traditional units for the measurement of agrarian land were typically defined in terms of the area that one

An early attempt at simplification and standardisation: a French cartoon
of 1795 explaining the merits of the new "metric" system.

man could plough in one day, or that would yield a given volume
of grain. The square dimensions of units so defined may of course
vary significantly with the quality of the land; but what seems to the
modern mind an unfortunate loss of generality was at the time a
gain in terms of precise usefulness for the task in hand. The example
illustrates a general point: the appropriate extent and standardisation
of any metrological concept depends upon its use.

Of course, metrology is not static: as the uses to which they are
put evolve, so do units of measurement and their standards. What is
more, there is feedback in both directions: if practices and techniques
give rise to units of measurement, the invention of broader metro-

logical concepts and the implementation of more consistent standards allow new forms of technological and economic co-operation to flourish. Myriad inconsistent systems of measurement and standards that varied village by village might have been sufficient for an economy of isolated agricultural smallholdings; but the industrial age—the age of machines and of mass production—demanded standardisation, and the burgeoning of international trade and industry demanded common units in the name of efficiency. Today, the need for universal units calibrated to common standards is more acute than ever. In August 2011 *The Economist* magazine analysed the origin of the 178 components that make up the Apple iPhone 4: a quarter were from South Korea, a fifth from Taiwan, a tenth from the United States, and other fractions from Japan, China, and a host of European countries.[33] Global industrial supply chains—to say nothing of international collaboration in medicine, science, and commerce—would be inconceivable without globally understood units of measurement. None of it could exist if the process crowned by the creation of the SI had not taken place.

So the gradual invention of general-purpose units of measurement was not a mere cosmetic development at all. At any given time, the units of measurement in existence reflect the concepts then available. When fathoms, furlongs, leagues, and hands were originally devised, for example, there simply was no universal concept of linear extension. The fact that dropping a weight to sound the depth of the sea measured fundamentally the same thing as pacing out the distance to the next village did not cross anyone's mind. In the absence of a universal concept of linear extension, there could hardly be a unit of its measurement. The creation of the SI was therefore the visible and material manifestation of a profound but invisible change in the evolution of human ideas. The process took centuries—probably even millennia. The century of work by the International Bureau of Weights and Measures only put the finishing touches to it. But the 14 October 1960 decision of the General Conference to codify the six basic units of the SI was more than just a practical watershed for any activity that requires co-operation across national borders and the quantification of the physical world. It reflected the success of an incremental abstraction over the course of history not only from the separate notions of the height of horses and the height of their riders, for example, to the idea of height in general, but from the general ideas of height and length and depth to the universal concept of linear extension. It marked nothing less than a fundamental transition in the concepts that the majority of humanity uses to quantify the physical world. All in all, not a bad day's work for a faceless international bureaucracy.

The invention of a universally applicable unit of measurement; its central role in knitting together the modern, globalised economy; and its dramatic impact on the development of human thought. Where else is this revolutionary triumvirate to be found? Where else, but in the case of money?

3   The Aegean Invention of Economic Value

THE INVISIBLE DOLLAR

What actually is a dollar? What is a pound or a euro or a yen? Not a dollar or yen bill, that is, or a pound or euro coin—but a dollar, pound, euro or yen, itself? It is tempting to think that these names refer to something physical. It may even be natural to think this when they are inscribed on something physical like a coin—particularly one made of precious metal. The urge may be almost irresistible if there is legislation in place—as there was throughout much of the world in the nineteenth and early twentieth centuries—requiring banks to redeem on demand their dollar, pound, or other notes for specified quantities of gold of a given fineness. Appearances then seemed powerfully to suggest that it was this—a certain weight of precious metal—that "was" a dollar. These appearances were misleading, however. A dollar, whether under a Gold Standard or not, is something that would be intimately familiar to the faceless bureaucrats of the International Bureau of Weights and Measures: it is a unit of measurement—an arbitrary increment on an abstract scale. So like a metre or a kilogram, a dollar itself doesn't refer to any physical thing at all—even if the length or mass or value of some particular physical thing has been agreed on as its standard. As the great monetary scholar Alfred Mitchell Innes lyrically put it, "[t]he eye has never seen, nor the hand touched a dollar."[1] Just as the eye has never seen, nor the hand touched, a metre or a kilogram either; even if they have gazed on or gripped a wooden metre ruler or a cast-iron kilo weight.

If the dollar is a unit of measurement, what does it measure? The answer, on the face of it, is simple: value—or, more precisely, economic value. But if that is so, then the story of the evolution of physical units of measurement and the concepts they reflected begs a couple of further questions. If the SI metre is now the single, universal unit of measurement of linear extension, how universal is this concept of economic value—and what is its standard? If, in other words, the mandate of the General Conference on Weights and Measures were to be extended to the social world as well, what would the bureaucrats in Paris find?

They would no doubt expect to discover it in the same state of dreadful backwardness that for centuries obtained in physical metrology. And initially, they would not be disappointed. They would find a great variety of notions of value contending for our attention in our decision-making. We preserve monuments because of their historic value; we admire paintings for their aesthetic value; we don't cheat or steal because of our moral values; we spurn alcohol and pray five times a day because of our religious values; we treasure our grandmother's costume jewellery because of its sentimental value. All these are limited-purpose concepts of value—each lord of its own sphere, none sovereign outside it. Like the old physical concepts of the height of a horse, the depth of the sea, and the width of a net, sentimental, aesthetic, and religious value are specific concepts invented in the context of specific activities. And as for the question of standardisation—that would seem to be even less advanced than it was for those antique physical units of measurement. Who, after all, ever heard of an international standard of sentimental value? When it comes to the social reality, it is more or less everyone, let alone every village, for himself. As the saying goes, *de gustibus non est disputandum*—there is no accounting for taste.

Yet just as they were admiring this vast new territory for their endeavours, the bureaucrats would get a nasty shock. For in the midst of this unruly rabble of limited-purpose concepts they would suddenly confront the concept of economic value; and when it comes to generality, the concept of economic value would inspire not only admiration but jealousy amongst the officials. For economic value can be applied not just to things that have a particular physical property—temperature, length, or mass, for example—but, at least in principle, to absolutely anything at all. Goods have economic value; but so do services. The three physical dimensions are no constraint: time is money, after all. Abstract notions are no strangers to monetary evaluation: what price success? Even a solely spiritual existence was no obstacle in the days when people cared about such things: the wages of sin could be readily offset by clerical indulgences whose value was measured, and paid for, in pounds, shillings, and pence. In fact, there seems to be no intrinsic limit to the parts that the concept of economic value can reach. Even human life itself is regularly assigned an economic value by government economists in the cost–benefit analyses that they use to weigh up new laws. In 2010, the U.S. Transportation Department raised its estimate of the value of a human life from $3.5 million to $6.1 million, for example, and thereby tipped the scales in favour of requiring truckers to double the roof strength of their cabins in order to prevent 135 deaths a year.[2] The Owner-Operator Independent Drivers Association was outraged. But they were indignant because a lower valuation would have justified less onerous regulation: they were not complaining that you can't put a price on life. Economic value has attained the last word in universality—without any input from the bureaucrats whatsoever.

Still, even if the bureaucrats found themselves redundant when it came to simplification, surely standardisation would still represent a respectable agenda? After all, the concept of economic value might be uniquely universal, but its standards are still clearly national: the pound in the U.K., the yen in Japan, the euro in the Eurozone. Only the U.S. dollar has serious aspirations to the international applicability beloved of the General Conference, and even then somewhat patchily. Here, therefore, would be something for the officials to get their teeth into: building agreement on a single, international standard—ideally defined in terms of universal constants found in nature. But here too the bureaucrats would quickly encounter an obstacle. The problem is that there is a fundamental difference between the concept of economic value and the concepts measured by the SI. Economic value is a property of the social world; whereas linear extension, mass, temperature, and so on are properties of physical world. The choice of standard for the measurement of physical concepts is a question of technical efficiency. But the uses to which measurement of the social property of economic value are put are qualitatively quite different; and so the choice of its standard is quite different as well. The choice of standard for the measurement of economic value—the choice of the standard for the monetary unit, in other words—affects not how easy it is to build bridges, but how wealth and income are distributed and who bears economic risks. It is, therefore, not just a technical, but also an ethical question; and the criterion for choosing it is not only which standard unit is efficient, but which is fair. Of course, the determination of what is fair is nothing but politics. And since politics is, in today's world, essentially a national competence, the standards used for the measurement of economic value—monetary units—are essentially national. If the bureaucrats wished to make an international standard, they would first need to forge an international polity—a task beyond even the International Bureau of Weights and Measures.

Deflated by the fact that economic value is already a universal concept and defeated by the fact that its standards are unresolvably political and national, there would, however, be one contribution that the International Bureau, with their experience of the assembly of the SI, could make: they could tell the history of its evolution. The mighty monetary unit—the degree of economic value—may already have in the social realm the universality that the six units of the SI enjoy in the physical world. But did it not, like they, undergo a transformation over time? If even the now familiar concept of linear extension once did not exist, can economic value really be any different? Was there a time and a place when there was no concept of universal economic value—when actions were motivated and society organised by traditional, incommensurable, and limited-purpose notions of worth alone?

There was. We have already been there. It was the world before money: Dark Age Greece and ancient Mesopotamia. It is the invention of the concept of universal economic value that was the missing link in the invention of money. It is time to return to the archaic Aegean to find out how that invention occurred.

MONEY'S MISSING LINK

Technological and cultural sophistication have never been any guarantee of progress. History is full of examples of ancient and advanced civilisations whose reluctance or inability to absorb new ideas has left the field open for more backward nations, less burdened by the weight of existing achievements, to outstrip them. The situation was no different in the ancient world. Mesopotamia had great cities and complex economies, administered by the most advanced and innovative social system of the day—bureaucracy—which optimised efficiency and performance using the cutting-edge social technologies of literacy, numeracy, and accounting. It was hardly likely that these pinnacles of human civilisation had anything to learn from tribes of uncultivated yahoos to the west who clustered together in tiny groups and still organised society on the basis of uncouth tribal institutions dispensed with in Mesopotamia literally millennia previously.

The other way round was a different matter, of course. It was only too clear to the Greeks what enormous practical benefits the adoption of literacy and numeracy could bring. It is therefore no surprise how thoroughly these new technologies were adopted throughout the Greek world once contact with the East was properly re-established. The initial medium of transmission was almost certainly the Phoenicians of the Levant—prodigious sailors and traders with whom the Greeks had extensive contact from the late

Dark Ages. The earliest archaeological evidence for Greek writing is a famous drinking cup inscribed with three simple verses discovered at Ischia in 1954 and dated to between 750 and 700 BC.[3] Within a matter of decades, both literacy and numeracy had succeeded in pervading the Greek world, from its easternmost reaches on the Black Sea to the colonies of Sicily and southern Italy in the west.

The effects of these new technologies on Greek culture were momentous.[4] The century after 650 BC witnessed an unprecedented intellectual revolution—an emancipation of thought by the new ability to quantify, to record, to reflect, and to criticise what was written.[5] The revolution began in the East, in the city of Miletus, the commercial capital of the Ionian seaboard of Asia Minor. There, in 585 BC the philosopher Thales correctly predicted a solar eclipse—a feat which astonished the Greek world. What was truly remarkable about it, however, was not the prediction itself; the astronomy required for such analysis had been understood in Egypt and Mesopotamia for centuries. It was the new, scientific method by which Thales arrived at it—and the new worldview on which it rested. Thales rejected the idea of a subjective world ruled by the whims of anthropomorphic gods who needed to be personally appeased with ritual or magic. In its place he installed for the first time the idea of a universe governed by impersonal, natural laws, and its equally revolutionary corollary— the idea of the individual observer separate from the objective, physical phenomena under scrutiny.

The power of this new perspective resonated throughout the subsequent century. Under the old worldview, the universe consisted simply of what one could see: even gods and goddesses, it was believed, resided in the physical world. Under the new dispensation, there was a metaphysical realm too: the realm of the natural laws that govern the visible world—an ultimate reality, beyond appearance. It was a revolution in man's understanding of the physical universe: nothing less than "the emergence of abstract rational thought, of philosophy and scientific theory in a form still recognizable to modern practitioners."[6] Precisely because of its extreme backwardness relative to the ancient civilisations of Mesopotamia and Egypt, it was in the Greek

Aegean, and within only decades of the transition from an entirely illiterate culture, that the modern scientific worldview was invented.

But it was not only man's understanding of the physical universe that the fertile encounter between the sophisticated East and the primitive West revolutionised: it profoundly changed his understanding of the social world as well. The organisation of society on earth was traditionally conceived of as the mirror image of the divine household in the heavens above. But if the idea of a subjective universe ruled by capricious gods had been displaced by the scientific notion of an objective reality governed by impersonal laws, then must not the old understanding of society be superseded too? Must not the principle of analogy carry through: was there not such a thing as society, separate from the self—an objective social reality, the counterpart of the objective physical reality, and one also governed by impersonal laws?

The idea was irresistible—and remains so today. But it begged a question. The new perspective on the physical universe postulated some fundamental substance of which the physical universe was really made and in terms of which its laws were formulated. Whether it was Heraclitus' fire or Pythagoras' number, there had to be something of which the reality behind the appearance was constituted—the ancient equivalent of the concept of energy that is the basic building block of today's theoretical physics. The new vision of society required some analogous concept in terms of which the basic structure of the objective social reality could be described and understood by the scientific mind. But what could it be? And why, in posing this question, was the primitive culture of the Greeks breaking ground which the supremely advanced civilisations of Mesopotamia had not explored?

The answer is that in this new understanding of society and the economy, as in the new science of the natural world, the ironies of historical progress were again strongly in evidence. It was because, rather than in spite, of its relative backwardness that Greek civilisation stood on the brink of a fundamental intellectual revolution. For Greece had one idea that Mesopotamia lacked: a concept that could answer the requirement of the new understanding of society for a single, universal, abstract substance in terms of which the objective social reality could be understood. It had, hidden amidst its barbarous and primitive cultural forms, one glittering prize: a nascent idea of universally applicable value.

The sophisticated Mesopotamian apparatus of accounting and forward planning did not operate without notions of value, of course. Though in the early stages of their evolution it had operated with plans expressed only in physical units, the temple bureaucracies later developed units of abstract value with which to allocate resources between different classes of inputs and outputs. But these units were designed for deployment only in specific sectors and as part of the planning process: because of the sophistication of the system of bureaucratic control itself, there was no need for a universal unit of value which could be applied more generally and outside of the administrative hierarchy. As the medieval peasant had limited-purpose units of length, each ideally suited to its particular task—his ells, fathoms, and feet—so the temple bureaucrats had limited-purpose concepts of value and corresponding accounting units: "[d]epending on the economic sector, the means of comparison or the measure of standardized norms and duties could be silver, barley, or fish, or 'laborer-days,' that is, the product of the number of workers multiplied by the number of days that they worked."[7]

When the ancient Mesopotamian technologies of literacy, numeracy, and accounting came into contact with the primitive, tribal institutions of Greece, they were transplanted into a wholly different environment. And one of those institutions—the ritual of sacrificial distribution—contained the germ of a quite different concept of value. The ritual of the sacrificial feast consisted of the ceremonial killing of the victim, the burning of its entrails as an offering to the gods, and the roasting and distribution of its meat to the congregation. All male members of the tribe participated, and the shares distributed were equal—for this was an ancient ritual, the purpose of which was to express, to rehearse, and to ensure understanding of, the communality of the tribe. Like gift exchange, it was a ritual based on reciprocity—but the reciprocity here was between the individual and the tribe: the individual was reaffirmed as an equal member of the tribe and as having an equal obligation to ensure its survival. The most basic ideas at work are so fundamental, and so familiar to us today, that they are easy to miss. But they were ideas completely alien to the hierarchical cosmology and caste society of Mesopotamia. They were the concept of social value—the property that every male member of the tribe enjoyed by virtue of being part of the community—and the notion that on this measure, every member counted equally.

For as long as these ideas remained in their original context of the tribal ritual of sacrificial distribution, they remained nothing more than a relic of barbarism. But when mixed with the new technologies from the East and the new perspective on the world which they provoked, the catalysis was volcanic. For the notion of social value was an atomic concept in terms of which an objective social reality could be construed. And the idea of the equal worth of every member of the tribe was a social constant: a standard against which social value could be measured. At the heart of Greek society, in other words, was nothing other than a nascent concept of universal value and a standard against which to measure it, prêt-à-porter. Here was an answer to the question begged by the new perspective on society and the economy. Where the new understanding of physical reality had man, the observer of an objective universe, the new understanding of the social reality had the idea of the self, separate from society— an objective entity consisting of relationships measurable in a standard unit on the universal scale of economic value. It was a critical conceptual development—the missing link, on the intellectual level, in the invention of money.[8]

Mesopotamia had for millennia possessed one of the three components of money—a system of accounting, based upon its discoveries of writing and numeracy. But the immense sophistication of Mesopotamia's bureaucratic, command economy had no need of any universal concept of economic value. It required and had perfected a variety of limited-purpose concepts of value, each with its respective standard. It therefore did not develop the first component of money: a unit of abstract, universally applicable,

Athenian youths leading bulls to sacrifice, from the North frieze
of the Parthenon: the most famous of all representations of one of
Greek civilisation's central rituals.

economic value. Dark Age Greece, on the other hand, had a primitive concept of universal value and a standard by which to measure it. But the Greek Dark Ages knew neither literacy nor numeracy—let alone a system of accounting. They had, in nascent form, the first component of money, but lacked the second. Neither civilisation had all the ingredients for money on its own. But when the ultra-modern technologies of the East—literacy, numeracy, and accounting—were combined with the idea of a universal scale of value incubated in the barbaric West, the conceptual preconditions for money were at last in place.

A RULE FOR ANARCHY

It did not take long for these preconditions to produce practical results. The notion of a single, universally applicable concept of value evolved in the context of a political institution—the ritual of the sacrificial distribution—and it was in other social, religious, and legal contexts that it first began to be applied more widely. What had since time immemorial been ritual obligations, the relative worth of which it would not have crossed anyone's mind to compare, began to be assessed in terms of the new measure of value—the monetary unit. Already in the early sixth century BC, inscriptions recording religious dedications at the temple of Hera on the island of Samos—the greatest Greek religious foundation of its day—had begun to proclaim their monetary value.[9] At Athens at around the same time, the rewards granted by the state to victors at the pan-Hellenic athletic competitions began to be prescribed in monetary terms—100 drachmas for a champion at the Isthmian Games; 500 drachmas for a champion at the Olympics.[10] Nor was the ingenious new concept of universal economic value colonising only official estimations of worth—it was catching on with private individuals as well. A quaint inscription on a metal belt from around 500 BC boasts that the fee its owner was paid for a contract as a public scribe was the tidy sum of 20 drachmas.[11]

This spread of money's first two components—the idea of a universally applicable unit of value and the practice of keeping accounts in it—reinforced the development of the third: the principle of decentralised negotiability. The new idea of universal economic value made possible the offsetting of obligations without reference to a centralised authority. And the new idea of an objective economic space created the confidence that this possibility would exist indefinitely. Markets require people to be able to negotiate a sale or agree a wage on their own, instead of feeding their preferences into a central authority in order to receive back a directive on how to act. But successful negotiation requires a common language—a shared idea of what words mean. For markets to function there needs to be a shared concept of value and standardised units in which to measure it. Not a shared idea of what particular goods or services are worth—that is where the haggling comes in—but a shared unit of economic value so that the haggling can take place at all. Without general agreement on what a dollar is, we could no more haggle in

the marketplace over prices in dollars than we can talk to the birds
and the bees.

Now money was opening up a still more radical horizon: traditional social obligations could not only be valued on a universal
scale, but transferred from one person to another. The miracle of
money had an equally miraculous twin—the miracle of the market.[12]
And with the invention of coinage, a dream technology for recording
and transferring monetary obligations from one person to another
was born. The earliest known coins were minted in Lydia and Ionia,
in present-day Turkey, in the early sixth century BC. But it was the
city states of the Greek Aegean that seized upon coinage as the ideal
means of representing the new concept of economic value, starting
in the late sixth century BC. Its spread throughout the Greek world
thereafter was rapid and pervasive: by around 480 BC, there were
nearly a hundred mints operating in the Greek world.[13]

The result was a further acceleration in the pace of monetisation.
Everywhere, traditional social obligations were transformed into
financial relationships. In Athens, traditional agricultural sharecroppers were converted into contractual tenants paying money rents.
The so-called "liturgies"—the ancient, civic obligations of the thousand wealthiest inhabitants of the city to provide public services ranging from choruses for the theatre to ships for the navy—were now
assessed in financial terms. By the last quarter of the fifth century BC,
"not only military stipends, public and private wages, rents and commodity prices, but also social payments such as dowries . . . regularly
appear as sums of cash."[14] The city states of classical Greece had
become the first monetary societies.

It is difficult to overstate the social and cultural impact of this
first, revolutionary experience of monetisation.[15] The age of traditional society—of the unchallenged authority of the centralised
economy and the immutable social hierarchy—was ending. The age
of monetary society—of the market as the organising principle of
trade, of prices as the instructions guiding human activity, of ambition, entrepreneurship, and innovation—had arrived. The old cosmology was dying, and with it the old idea of the just social order as

its microcosm on earth. In its place was developing an objective idea of the economy in which social position was constrained only by the ability to accumulate money. Under the old regime, social position had been absolute: born a peasant, died a peasant; born a chieftain, died a chieftain. In the new world, everything was relative. The only real measure of a man's worth was money—and the accumulation of money has no intrinsic limits. "Money! Money is the man!" was the famous aphorism of the Argive aristocrat Aristodemus, exclaimed with undying disgust at the degenerate new order of things when "he lost his wealth—and with it his friends."[16] Now that money determined social standing, birth, honour, and tradition counted for nothing. Lose your wealth, and you were nobody.

Complaints from those with vested interests in traditional society were to be expected. Yet the genius of money was that it did not just appeal to an alternative set of vested interests— those of the lumpen peasantry who had drawn the short straw under the old regime. The great fear associated with the transgression of customary rules of conduct had always been that the result would be anarchy: the traditional social order claimed to represent the sole bulwark against civil breakdown and a war of all against all. The monetary enlightenment argued otherwise. On the political and economic level, money promised something unprecedented: that it would combine social mobility with political stability. With money, society could have its cake and eat it too. The sterile constraints of an immutable and absolute social system could be jettisoned in favour of ambition, entrepreneurship, and social mobility: money would be the universal solvent that could dissolve all traditional obligations. Crucially, though, the society that resulted would not collapse into chaos. Because money, the concept of universal value, and the idea of an objective economic space, were founded upon the ancient institution of communal sacrifice; and as such upon the invisible but irresistible communality of mankind. And money made its miraculous promise to combine apparent opposites on the personal level as well. It catered to two fundamental aspects of human psychology: the desire for freedom and the desire for stability. The ethics of the traditional society had sacrificed the former on the altar of the latter. The new world of monetary society promised both.

Money's claim that its new way of organising society would not end in disaster, but would combine the power of social mobility and personal freedom with that of social stability and economic security, was startling enough. But there was a final implication of the new worldview that was even more astonishing: that the rule of money was not just efficacious, but just. For money claimed to fuse together both the short-term and the long-term "transactional orders"—to govern both the minutiae of getting and spending in the everyday and the profundities of social harmony for the ages. This was a truly revolutionary idea, quite alien to traditional theology and ethics: the notion that all of human conduct, from haggling over chickens in the marketplace to matters of state and the government of empires, could be best regulated by a single logic and a single social technology.[17] As we shall see, the Greeks themselves were never reconciled to this counter-intuitive idea: it would take another two thousand years for the philosophers of the European Enlightenment to realise that feat. But monetary society staked the claim in practice anyway— and it was a claim no other social system had staked before.

"THE GREAT QUESTION WHICH IN ALL AGES HAS DISTURBED MANKIND"

The tensions created by the spread of monetary society and the imperialism of markets are deeply familiar to us today. The extent to which monetary thinking has become second nature, and the dominance of the concept of universal economic value, are remarkable— even frightening. It is no longer just the best seats in the theatre or on the aeroplane that have a price: in California it is now possible to pay to upgrade one's prison cell.[18] Illicit traffic in ivory and in carcasses of rhinos and elephants has been known for decades: today, one can buy a permit to shoot them legally—the right to kill an endangered black rhino goes for $250,000. A century ago, to enjoy citizenship of one of the world's rich nations was to have "won first prize in the lottery of life."[19] Today, anybody can immigrate to the U.K., the U.S., and several other countries—as long as they bring enough money. And if a person cannot afford these desirables, he can sell advertising space on his forehead, put his health at risk as a human guinea pig in a new drug trial, or—a much more traditional way out of economic straits, though one no less alarming to the modern sensibility—hire himself out as a mercenary to one of the private military contractors at the sharp end of modern Western warfare. As the American philosopher Michael Sandel, who assembled this ghoulish litany, concluded: "There are some things that money can't buy—but these days, not many."[20]

It is easy to believe that the invasion of this way of thinking and the uneasiness it causes in us are modern phenomena. It is just as tempting to believe that they are the result of the spread of the capitalist economic system. What our biography of money's early years has taught us, however, is that they are not. Capitalism is indeed a modern phenomenon—a system that emerged in Europe in the sixteenth and seventeenth centuries, and which has come to dominate the world today. But beneath the relentless spread of the market mentality and the overweening dominance of the idea of universal economic value lies something much older, and much more deeply ingrained in the way our societies work: the social technology of money. And the tensions and dissonances that we feel today are not new at all: they have flexed and echoed down the centuries ever since money's first invention, more than two and a half thousand years ago, on the shores of the Greek Aegean.

If money was such a powerful invention—such a revolutionary force for the transformation of society and the economy—the next question is obvious. It is one posed with brilliant clarity by the father of English political philosophy John Locke, in his *First Treatise of Government*:

> The great question which in all ages has disturbed mankind, and brought on them the greatest part of those mischiefs which have

ruined cities, depopulated countries, and disordered the peace of the world, has been, not whether there be power in the world, nor whence it came, but who should have it.[21]

It is to the perennial battle over who controls money that we therefore turn next.

4   The Monetary Maquis
_____

FINANCIAL SOVEREIGNTY AND MONETARY INSURRECTION
In December 2001, the economic crisis that had been brewing in
Argentina for over three years came to a head. The country had
pegged the value of its peso to the U.S. dollar for over a decade
under a so-called "currency board" arrangement that had delivered
unprecedented stability and prosperity for much of the 1990s. But
when Brazil devalued its currency in January 1999, Argentina was
suddenly priced out of its largest export market and its economy
tipped into recession. As the world's craving for the United States'
new economy drove the U.S. dollar higher and higher over the next
two years, it took the Argentine peso with it—heaping yet more
misery on an economy that with its reliance on the production of
agricultural commodities looked decidedly old. By the middle of
2001, the country had been in recession for almost three years and
its public finances were unravelling despite several attempted auster-
ity programmes. Argentina's much-vaunted fixed exchange rate had
become a severe obstacle to its international competitiveness, and
both the public and the financial markets began to suspect that it
could not hold. In April 2002 they were proved correct, when the
sixth Economy Minister in a year announced the end of the currency
board. Within weeks, the exchange rate had collapsed from 1 to 4
pesos to the U.S. dollar, and Argentina had defaulted on its external

debts, entering an exile from the international capital markets that
continues to this day.

The government's strenuous efforts to stave off this catastrophic
outcome had meant that Argentina's monetary and financial system
had been in dire straits for months leading up to the crisis. A year previously, Domingo Cavallo—the father of the currency board arrangement, the man who had single-handedly delivered Argentina from its
troubled history of inflation and instability—had been recalled to the
government to galvanise popular support and regain the confidence
of the markets. Over the summer, he had committed unwaveringly
to the maintenance of the dollar peg. The consequence had been
that as the economy had continued to shrink and the banks become
yet more distressed, private capital had continued to flee the country and pesos had become more and more scarce. On 2 December
2001, the beginnings of a full-scale run on the banking system had
forced Cavallo to make the most embarrassing of announcements.
To preserve the liquidity of the banks, a strict limit was imposed
on the amount of cash that depositors could withdraw from their
accounts. It was a desperate measure that provoked extraordinary
popular resentment. Cavallo's so-called *"corralito"* ("little enclo-
sure") succeeded in preventing the imminent collapse of the banking
system—but at the cost of causing an immediate and acute shortage
of peso liquidity.

The Argentinian public's response to the sudden drought of
money was no less entrepreneurial than that of the Irish had been
thirty years before. Where the state would not oblige, substitute
moneys sprang up spontaneously. Provinces, cities, and even supermarket chains started to issue their own IOUs, which rapidly began to
circulate as money—in open defiance of the government's attempts
to keep liquidity tight to support the peso. By March 2002, such privately issued notes made up nearly a third of all the money in the
country.[1] A report in the *Financial Times* painted an evocative picture
of the situation:

> As they finish their tea and croissants, two elegantly dressed ladies
> at a Buenos Aires cafe ask their waiter how they might pay. As if

reciting the day's menu from memory, the waiter gives them several options: *pesos*, *lecops*, *patacones* (but only Series I) and all classes of tickets luncheon vouchers that circulate widely at restaurants and supermarkets in the city.[2]

The monetary authorities were mortified. But embarrassing as it might be for the Governor of the Central Bank of Argentina to witness his friends paying for their breakfast with *patacones* signed by officials of the province of Buenos Aires, at least they were liabilities of some level of government. And at least they were still denominated in the national unit of account. There was, however, worse to come. By July, nearly one in ten of the adult population was discovered to be using the *Crédito*—a mutual credit money issued by local exchange clubs on its own, independent standard.[3] Even the peso's much-reduced role as the natural denomination for financial contracts was fading away. A significant part of the Argentine economy was now operating using a glorified swap shop.

There are obvious similarities between this eruption of subsovereign and private moneys in Argentina in 2002 and the IOU economy that sprang up in Ireland during its bank closure. But there was also a crucial difference. In Ireland, the government had been trying earnestly to prevent the shutdown of the monetary system, and it had actively encouraged the search for sources of private monetary credit that could substitute for bank deposits in preparation for the closure. In Argentina, it was the government itself that imposed the effective closure of the banks, as the central plank of a policy to forestall a run and to prevent the flight of capital into foreign currencies. By the same token, the creation of quasi-currencies was not done in patriotic alliance with the government against a common enemy. It was an act of open defiance of the government's draconian monetary policy. The government, it was widely held, had lost its bearings. It was working for the interests of blood-sucking usurers and foreign capitalists: its policies were harmful and illegitimate. The local politicians, businesses, and communities that fought them by issuing their private currencies saw themselves as a monetary version of France's famous Maquis—the "Army of Shadows" that organ-

The stuff of central bankers' nightmares: a token
good for five *Créditos*.

ised popular resistance to the puppet Vichy government during the
Second World War.[4] To the dismay of the monetary authorities and
their advisers, their efforts were effective. In April 2002, the International Monetary Fund (IMF) warned the Argentine government that
the efflorescence of substitute moneys had "complicated economic
management, raised the threat of inflation, and undermined confidence in the public finances."[5] Until the peso regained its monopoly
over the monetary franchise, the government would not be in control of the country.

Argentina's experience is not the only example of a guerrilla war
waged by a Monetary Maquis against government economic policy.
When the Soviet Union disintegrated in the early 1990s, a similar
thing happened. Financial shock therapy aimed to impose hard budget constraints on companies that had lived off continuous subsidies
for decades. The idea was to liquidate the unviable enterprises in an
avalanche of creative destruction, from which a brighter corporate
future would emerge. But the managers of the enterprises themselves were not persuaded. When their access to the official banking
sector dried up and they were invited quietly to exit the stage, they
had a better idea. They created their own monetary networks with
which to settle trade—circles of companies connected by supply
chains that could accumulate trade credit with one another and then
use it to offset debts without the use of the national money. By 1997,

the share of inter-company trade settled in this way in Russia was estimated at around 40 per cent.[6] Workers were paid with tokens or vouchers. A Ukrainian analyst summed up the scale of their issuance: "The known number of such private and self-accounting moneys in the Ukraine is in the hundreds, and in Russia must amount to tens of thousands."[7] A contemporary study of the phenomenon had a title that neatly summed up the problem facing the authorities. It was called *The Vanishing Rouble*.[8]

Contesting the jurisdiction of a government whose country is disintegrating is perhaps easy to do. But attempts to escape the sovereignty of the national money are not confined to periods of crisis. In the developed West there are today thousands of private moneys in circulation—albeit most on a limited scale. Under the generic descriptions of LETS—Local Exchange Trading Schemes—and mutual credit networks, community and business organisations all over Europe and America actively maintain private monetary networks. The idiosyncratic ideologies of the issuing organisations are often advertised in the names of their currencies. The London district of Brixton, for example, has its Brixton Pound—a name which combines the organisers' objective of keeping purchasing power in the local economy with the historic lustre of the official British denomination. The upstate New York college town of Ithaca, on the other hand, has its Ithaca Hours—the Marxist undertones of which are deliberate, since the unit of account is an abstract hour of labour. The largest of these schemes are very large. The WIR mutual credit network—a sophisticated club of small businesses in Switzerland— has over 60,000 member companies, and settled the equivalent of more than 1.5 billion Swiss francs' worth of trade in 2011.[9] The smallest are very small: even the humble babysitting circle, after all, is a simple private monetary network.[10]

Private moneys like these pose no existential threat to the official, national money, and the authorities generally treat them as harmless sideshows. Yet at the back of every central banker's mind is the cautionary tale of Argentina—an example of what can happen if the state loses its franchise over the institution of money. And it is a tale familiar from the histories of even the most advanced and powerful nations. One of the most provocative acts of the British Crown's jurisdiction over its American possessions was to outlaw the colonies' printing of their own monies—and one of the first acts of the First Continental Congress was to authorise the printing of a new currency with which to finance the War of Independence. Were LETS schemes and mutual credit networks ever to outgrow their modest communitarian objectives, one could be sure that governments would soon condemn the infringement on a basic element of their constitutional power.[11] Not for nothing does the very first article of the Constitution of the United States give Congress the exclusive power to mint money.[12] In the mind of the conservative politician, with good historical reason, it is but a short step from the *Crédito* to the Continental Dollar—from cocking a picturesque snook at globalisation to monetary insurrection; and from monetary insurrection to political revolt.[13]

It is hardly surprising, as a result, that—except when frustrated by the direst of crises, and with the exception of the odd unthreatening community project—the modern state has always made absolutely certain that it has exclusive control over the institution of money within its jurisdiction.

Or has it?

MONEY IN UTOPIA—AND IN THE REAL WORLD

With the Aegean invention of economic value and of the economy as an objective space, the conceptual preconditions for money were in place. But conceptual preconditions are one thing: the practical business of organising society using money is another. How was money to work in practice? In theory, it was simple. With a universally understood language of economic value, prices could be argued over and agreed, credit and debt accumulated by individuals, and those balances then used to offset other debts and credits against other counterparties. Anyone who bought anything would, in effect, issue their own money—a liability to the value of the price agreed, precisely matched by the credit that accrued to the seller. That seller would then be able to transfer this credit to a third party when he, in turn, agreed a price at which to buy something. Everyone would have just as much money as he needed, there would always be enough money to go around, and money's promise to deliver both freedom and security would be fulfilled.

This monetary Utopia is none other than the model on which mutual credit networks like the Soviet trade credit rings and, more sustainably, the Swiss WIR are built. When one member provides goods or services for another, it receives in the opposite direction acknowledgement of credit. This credit, meanwhile, is agreed to be good to settle debts due not only to the original purchaser, but to any member of the network. Like the money balances that the inhabitants of Yap kept track of with their limestone *fei*, it is a credit not against the original issuer, but against society as a whole—or against the body politic of a credit network's members. There are two basic preconditions for the successful functioning of such a system. First, every member must maintain his creditworthiness. Only then can society be confident in the value of his money. Second, all members must know one another, if not at first hand, then at second; or have some other grounds, by convention or compulsion, to accept society's word for an unknown member's credit. In LETS networks enthused by a spirit of localism and community, in associations of small business screened and organised with legendary Swiss efficiency, and on tiny Pacific islands, it is possible for these preconditions to be met. In any larger, less cohesive, society—let alone any society that already enjoys the institutions of a state—their attainment is, however, altogether more challenging.

The generic problem is well known to political theorists. As James Madison, the chief architect of the United States Constitution, wrote in the *Federalist Papers*, "[i]f men were angels, no government would be necessary."[14] And if men were angels—if there was never any question of their overspending, or defaulting, or simply skipping town, and if they trusted one another implicitly—no government money would be necessary either.[15] Everyone could issue their own IOUs, those IOUs would be readily accepted by all, and the entire economy would operate as a vast mutual credit network. But men are no more angels in economics than in politics. In a utopian community, money can consist of credit accumulated against the abstract notion of society—because every member has actively opted into that community. But in the real world, the hard-nosed creditor is bound to see herself facing not the noble ideal of the community but the altogether less fanciful prospect of the individual issuer. And the problem with the individual issuer is that he may default on his liabilities—and that other people might believe he will default. Money on any significant scale can therefore never consist of liquid credit accumulated against "society." The alternative is obvious—and was so at money's birth. Money will naturally consist of liquid credit accumulated against society's more concrete manifestation: the sovereign.

However one looks at it, the sovereign enjoys some distinct advantages as an issuer of money. In purely practical terms, sovereigns make a lot of payments. This was true even in the ancient world. Under the constitution of Athens and other city states like it there were numerous public offices to be filled—to say nothing of the need for soldiers. Before the advent of money, the fulfilment of these roles was treated as a public duty. By the fifth century BC, however, Athens was, in the words of the great politician Pericles, "a salary-drawing city."[16] Jury, magistracy, and military service were all paid in money. Citizens were paid to attend public festivals and even, by the fourth century BC, to turn up to the assembly to vote on legislation.[17] So the sovereign conducted by far the largest volume of economic transactions, with by far the largest number of people. And the economic dominance of ancient sovereigns was as nothing compared to today's overwhelming presence of the state. In 2011, government spending as a percentage of Gross Domestic Product (GDP—a reasonable proxy for the total volume of transactions in an economy) in the United States was 41 per cent. In France, it was more than 56 per cent.[18] The trade credit networks of Russia and Ukraine often clustered around public utilities. Because they were both large buyers and large billers, credit against them was easy to come by and easy to spend. But how much easier to earn and discharge credit against the state itself.

The sovereign has other unique advantages. Above all, it enjoys, by definition and unlike any private agent, political authority. The sovereign's creditworthiness therefore rests not on our assessment of its ability to earn credit in the marketplace, but on the strength of this authority and on the sovereign's willingness to deploy it to accumulate credit from its subjects via taxation. More than its dominant size in the market, it is the sovereign's dominant power outside the market that makes its IOUs so effective as money.[19] And what is more, it has been argued, the sovereign's political power confers on its liabilities a status that transcends both the state's vast market and its legal power. So long as the state is held to be legitimate, its money enjoys trust not only on commercial or legal, but on ideological and even spiritual grounds.[20] None of these advantages imply that sovereigns cannot default, of course: they most certainly can, and in spectacular fashion. Nor is it to say that the sovereign's is always the most creditworthy balance sheet in the land. But they do suggest why the sovereign is unique.

So the fact that it is the sovereign's money that typically circulates seems to be perfectly natural. It is the necessary condition of money in the real world. But using the official, national money to settle private transactions brings its own dilemmas. In fact, on closer consideration, it is not immediately clear that this conventional solution is any less utopian than the universal private monetary networks of the monetary cranks. The problem is that although the sovereign may indeed be the closest thing there is to a concrete manifestation of society, it is not society. What if the interests of the two diverge? What if the sovereign were to use its near-monopoly on money for its own gain—for example by overissuing money in order to fund spending simply to secure its popularity or re-election? What if it were to manipulate the system so that it produced not the marvellous combination of freedom and stability promised by money, but something else altogether? Hard-nosed realism may dictate that sovereigns issue money—but, as the First Continental Congress demonstrated, that only begs the question of who one would like to be sovereign. Or even—to side with the Monetary Maquis—whether one wouldn't be better off without any of the available sovereigns at all.

The monetary thought of the ancient Greeks was ambiguous on these practical, political questions. Its concerns, as we shall see, were in other, even more fundamental, areas. Plato's only practical recommendation for monetary policy was to operate two inconvertible currencies, one for domestic transactions, and the other with which to settle foreign trade and official payments—the better to prevent the import of foreign luxuries to his austere communal paradise.[21] But he did not address the question of who should issue and govern these moneys. Since his Republic was by definition a utopian community, the question hardly arose. Within the ideal state, control of money by the Philosopher-Kings just as of anything else, went without question. Even Aristotle devoted little time to the politics of money. Perhaps in Athens the body politic was so small and so cohesive—at the time of Aristotle it probably numbered no more than 35,000 male citizens—that the possibility of a significant divergence between the interests of public officials and the society from which they were drawn was simply not compelling.[22] Whatever the reason, Greek monetary thought did not broach the topic.

At the same time that Aristotle's famous Lyceum was flourishing in Athens, however, another great scholarly academy was being founded five thousand miles away in a country where the identity of ruler and ruled was anything but taken for granted. The doctrines developed there were to provide quite a different understanding of money, and an unequivocal answer to the question of who should control it.

"PEACE AND ORDER IN THE SUBCELESTIAL REALM"

The fourth century BC was the height of what is called the "Warring States" period in China. The central authority of the ancient Zhou dynasty had long since collapsed, and its former vassal states had been embroiled in seemingly endless war to reunify the Chinese lands since the eighth century BC. They had not made much progress. After nearly four and a half centuries of sedition and warfare, the memory of a peaceful and united China remained as distant as ever. Numerous smaller territories had been swallowed up by larger neighbours, but by the fourth century the lords of the four most powerful states—Qin, Jin, Chu, and Qi—remained locked in interminable combat, constantly scheming to protect their power and defeat their peers. None was any closer to victory, or therefore to peace. It was in an effort to break this stalemate that in the middle of the fourth century BC, Duke Huan of Qi conceived a remarkably modern idea.

Traditional Chinese thought—the philosophy of Confucius and Mozi—was concerned predominantly with ethics: its contributions to the science of government were essentially elaborations of its moral teachings. If the ruler acted justly, and his officials acted efficiently, then the state would be a just and efficient one. In the chaotic situation at the time, this minimalist political theory offered Duke Huan little practical help. He therefore invited the best thinkers of the age to join a new academy in his capital, Linzi. These scholars would be accorded a high rank and granted generous funding. Their only obligation would be to advise the ruler of Qi on how best to govern his country and defeat his enemies. It was a prototype of the modern policy think tank—and the idea proved a prodigious success. In its heyday in the late fourth and early third centuries BC, the Jixia academy had a faculty of seventy-six professors and several thousand students, and became the most famous centre of learning in China. Moreover, it was responsible for a significant reformation of Chinese thought. No longer was moral philosophy the sole focus. New schools were born with an explicitly more worldly aim: to explain in detail how a ruler might most effectively organise his state to ensure its survival and eventual domination. Amongst the tools that scholars of the Jixia academy considered most important to this task was the institution of money.

The monetary theories developed at the Jixia academy were collected in the work known as the *Guanzi*. They were to attain near-canonical status in Chinese economic thought for the next two thousand years. Though composed at almost exactly the same time as Aristotle's works on money, they take a starkly different approach.

Aristotle had founded the conventional Western theory of money when he had written in his *Politics* that "for the purposes of barter men made a mutual compact to give and accept some substance of such a sort as, being itself a useful commodity, was useful to handle in use for everyday life, iron for instance, silver and other metals . . ."[23] The scholars of the *Guanzi* took an entirely different view. Money, they wrote, is a tool of the sovereign—part of his machinery of government: "[t]he former kings used money to preserve wealth and goods and thereby regulate the productive activities of the people, whereupon they brought peace and order to the Subcelestial Realm."[24]

If money was a tool of the sovereign, other important questions followed: how exactly did it work, and to what objectives should the sovereign deploy it? To answer these questions, the Jixia scholars developed a simple but powerful theory of money. First of all, the value of money, they explained, was unrelated to the intrinsic value of the particular token used: "[t]he three forms of currency [pearls and jades; gold; and knife- and spade-shaped coins] offer no warmth to the naked, nor can they fill the bellies of the hungry," the *Guanzi* proclaimed. Instead, money's value was directly proportional to how much of it was in circulation compared to the quantity of goods available. The role of the sovereign, therefore, was to modulate the quantity of money available in order to vary the value of the monetary standard in terms of those goods. He could choose a deflationary policy—"[i]f nine-tenths of the kingdom's currency remains in the hands of the ruler and only one-tenth circulates among the people, the value of money will rise and prices of the myriad goods will fall"; or an inflationary one—"[h]e transfers money to the public domain, while accumulating goods in his own hands, thus causing the prices of the myriad goods to increase ten-fold"—depending on the needs of the economy.[25]

Varying the monetary standard in this way could serve two purposes. First, it would provide a powerful means of redistributing wealth and income amongst the sovereign's subjects, as inflation eroded the claims of creditors and eased the burden of debtors, shifting wealth from the former to the latter—or deflation did the oppo-site. Moreover, the most important redistribution, if new money were minted, would be to the sovereign from his subjects as he spent new money into circulation at essentially no cost—the miraculous power that economists in the Western tradition would later come to call "seigniorage." Second, it would regulate economic activity by making the primary instrument for the organisation and settle-ment of trade more or less readily available. The goal of government should be a harmonious society, and monetary policy was a power-ful tool with which to achieve it. Of course, there was a catch. For money's powers to be effective, the Jixia scholars pointed out, the sovereign must retain exclusive control over them. If anyone else in the kingdom was able to issue money then they would arrogate to themselves control over the value of the standard, and usurp part of the sovereign's power.

From their inception, the precepts of the Jixia academy were hailed for their clarity and logic. But it took bitter experience to establish them as the unchallenged axioms of Chinese monetary thought—and in the meantime, the matter of monetary control was sometimes fiercely contested. In the chaotic decades following the overthrow of the Qin dynasty in 202 BC, the emperors of the newly installed Han dynasty pursued a loose fiscal and monetary policy, spending beyond their means and financing their deficit by issuing new money. Eventually, a radically deflationary monetary policy aimed at restoring confidence in the imperial currency had to be imposed. The squeeze that followed proved as painful and unpopular as ever: but in this instance so painful and unpopular that in 175 BC Emperor Wen was persuaded to attempt an unprecedented experi-ment that contravened the most sacred teachings of the Jixia school. Henceforth, issuers other than the emperor would be allowed to mint money. The Han dynasty Grand Historian Sima Chen explained the consequences:

The people were allowed to mint [coins] at will. As a result the king of Wu, though only a feudal lord, was able, by extracting ore from his mountains and minting coins, to rival the wealth of the Son of Heaven. It was this wealth that he eventually used to start his revolt. Similarly Teng T'ung, who was only a high official, succeeded in becoming richer than a vassal king by minting coins. The coins of the king of Wu and Teng T'ung were soon circulating all over the empire, and as a result the private minting of coinage was finally prohibited.[26]

Monetary entrepreneurs had managed to convince the emperor that to alleviate the effects of his stabilisation policy he should permit them to issue money. The problem was that private issuers require political authority in order to make their liabilities liquid. A vicious circle therefore emerged. The private issuers sought to build their political authority in order to enable the supposed monetary palliative to take proper effect; the financial power this gave them increased that authority, and so on. Before long, it became clear that whatever their economic merits, the private moneys and their issuers posed a political challenge to the integrity of the empire. Palace counsellors warned that the growing political chaos was the direct result of ignoring the monetary axioms of the Jixia academy, and in 113 BC the Emperor Wu re-established the imperial monopoly over money. Sang Hongyang, his chief adviser on economic matters, explained the explicitly political reasoning that lay behind the crackdown: "If the currency system is unified under the emperor's control, the people will not serve two masters."[27]

The experiment with monetary heterodoxy had failed. The academy's conception of money and the policy recommendations that derived from it had been proved correct. Whoever wished to remain in power and see his domain well governed should jealously guard the management of the monetary standard and the monopoly of issuance. As the *Guanzi* put it, "[t]he prescient ruler grasps the reins of the common currency in order to bridle the Sovereigns of Destiny."[28]

The ingenious initiative of Duke Huan of Qi meant that the first great work of Chinese monetary thought was a creation of court employees, intended to bolster the monetary franchise of the sovereign. In Europe, the situation was to be quite the opposite. Not only was European monetary thought to take many centuries to develop beyond the maxims of Plato and Aristotle, but when it did, it was not the sovereign but his subjects who were responsible for the progress—and its aim was not to reinforce the sovereign's control over money, but to relax it. In the next chapter, we will discover why.

5 The Birth of the Money Interest

With every passing year, we realise that the technological achievements of the Roman world are greater than we thought. Fifty years ago, we tended to take the view that Virgil popularised in a famous passage of the *Aeneid*: that the Romans may not have been much good at science, technology, or the arts, but that they made up for this by excelling at their vocation to build empires and rule the world.[1] Now, we know that their generals owned computers and that their entrepreneurs built mechanised factories.[2] But if Rome's technological achievements were impressive, they were as nothing to its financial sophistication. Within a few centuries of its birth in the Aegean, money was everywhere in Rome. The financial infrastructure was vast and complex. There was of course a trusted coinage, but as in any sophisticated monetary economy, coins were principally for small transactions. Big tickets—and in Rome's heyday, there were some very big tickets—were settled using *littera* or *nomina*—promissory notes or bonds. The great politician and orator Cicero summarised the normal method of large payments in the late Republic as *"nomina facit, negotium conficit"* ("[one] provides the bonds, and completes the transaction").[3] Nor did the credit economy extend only to large payments. In the poet Ovid's satirical textbook for young lovers, *The Art of Love*, he warns the prospective Lothario that girlfriends need presents—and it is no good making the excuse that you have no cash on hand, because you can always write a cheque.[4]

Already by the beginning of the Imperial age, the days when the smart Roman's wealth was entirely in land were long gone. *"Dives agris, dives positis in faenore nummis"* ("Rich in fields, rich in money out at interest") was how the poet Horace described the worldly Roman of his day.[5] He would hardly have seemed out of place in Victorian England, with its rentiers begging to be excused from paying a bill because they are "all in the funds at the moment." Then, as now, there were even those who spurned real assets entirely, and preferred to be rich in monetary form alone.[6] Bankers could take deposits, make loans, and settle international payments.[7] Then as now, this financial elite specialised in dazzling the uninitiated with the sophistication of their technique: the jaded Cicero wrote of them with pointed irony that "concerning the acquisition and placing of money and its use, certain excellent fellows, whose place of business is near the Temple of Janus, converse more eloquently than philosophers of any school."[8]

In such an extensively monetised economy, it is hardly surprising that the Romans were also well acquainted with another familiar feature of modern finance: the credit crisis. Occasionally, the similarities with the modern age are nothing short of eerie. In AD 33, the Emperor Tiberius' financial officials were persuaded that the recent boom in private lending had become excessive. It was decided that regulation must be tightened in order to extinguish this irrational exuberance. After a brief review of the statutes, it was discovered that none other than the father of the dynasty, Julius Caesar, had in his wisdom instituted a law many decades before specifying strict limits on how much of their patrimony wealthy aristocrats could farm out in loans.[9] He had, in other words, introduced a rigorous capital adequacy requirement for lenders. The law was clear enough: but not for the first time in history, industrious lenders had proved remarkably skilled at circumventing it. Their ingenious evasions, the historian Tacitus reported, "though continually put down by new regulations, still, through strange artifices, reappeared."[10]

Now the emperor decreed the game was up: the letter of the old dictator's law would be enforced. The consequences were chaotic. As soon as the first ruling was made, it was realised with some embarrassment that most of the Senate was in breach of it. All the familiar features of a modern banking crisis followed. There was a mad scramble to call in loans in order to comply. Seeing the danger, the authorities attempted to soften the edict by relaxing its terms and announcing a generous transitional period. But the measure came too late. The property market collapsed as mortgaged land was fire-sold to fund repayments. Mass bankruptcy threatened to engulf the financial system. With Rome in the grip of a credit crunch, the emperor was forced to implement a massive bailout. The Imperial treasury refinanced the overextended lenders with a 100-million sesterces programme of three-year, interest-free loans against security of deliberately overvalued real estate. To the Senate's relief, it all ended happily: "Credit was thus restored, and gradually private lending resumed."[11]

This first flowering of monetary society in Europe was not to last, however. As the military and political might of Rome declined, so did its rich financial ecosystem. In the late third century AD, as Rome's prize possession of Egypt passed in and out of foreign hands, there was serious monetary disorder, including an inflation in AD 274–5 when prices rose by 1,000 per cent in a single year.[12] After AD 300, bankers disappear from the records—the social and political stability required to underpin professional finance had, it seems, disintegrated.[13] As the institutions of government retreated from the outer reaches of the empire, so, largely, did the institution of money. The effects were most severe in the most remote and marginal colonies. In Britain, for example, the Roman monetary system disappeared completely within a generation of the departure of the legions at the beginning of the fifth century AD. For a full two hundred years, coinage was forgotten as a means of representing money despite having

The lowest point of Europe's descent into monetary barbarism:
a Roman coin, having lost all monetary significance, reworked
as jewellery in a 7th-century British pendant.

been in constant use for nearly five centuries before then.[14] Eventually, all over Europe—even in Rome itself—the splendid sophistication of monetary society faded away. Like Greece after the fall of Mycenae, Europe entered its own Dark Age—an age that saw a near-total regression from monetary to traditional society.

EUROPE'S MONETARY RENAISSANCE

Near-total—but not complete. While the rich panorama of financial technologies, from the elaborate techniques of high finance to the simple convenience of humble coinage, were forgotten, one ghostly, but vitally important, vestige of Roman monetary society remained: the concept of universal economic value. The recalcification of the fluid social fabric into fixed tribal and feudal relations was virtually

complete. But the persistence in the collective memory of this hallmark of monetary society proved in time to be a stock of intellectual fixed capital which would greatly facilitate the remonetisation
of European society. An initial resurgence of monetary society came
with the consolidation of the Frankish Empire in the late eighth century. Under Charlemagne, the monetary units of pounds, shillings,
and pence were introduced and money was issued on a standard
consistent across most of Europe. But this first renaissance proved
short-lived, and it was only in the second half of the twelfth century
that remonetisation began in earnest, following the relentless logic
established nearly two millennia earlier in the Aegean.[15] Starting in
the Low Countries in the last quarter of the twelfth century, feudal obligations traditionally payable in kind began to be transformed
throughout Europe into *fiefs rentes*—rents payable in money.[16] The
institution of the *corvée*—under which a lord's vassals were required
to render him service for a certain number of days a year—was
replaced with paid labour. Civil officialdom began to function as a
professional, salaried cadre, rather than a poor man's simulacrum of
the hereditary nobility. This in turn meant that in jurisdictions where
the economy could support it, direct taxation in money was reintro-
duced for the first time since the Roman era.[17]

The familiar consequences of the monetisation of previously
static social relations appeared: the re-emergence of social mobility, the revival of ambition and avarice as prime factors motivat-
ing behaviour, and the realignment of aristocratic competitiveness
from the battlefield and the jousting lists towards the accumulation
and ostentation of wealth.[18] *"Nummus nobilitas"* ("Money is nobility!") declaimed the poet Hildebert of Lavardin sarcastically, in an
uncanny echo of Aristodemus' complaint that "Money is the man!"[19]
But medieval Europe was a larger, richer, and more powerful forum
for monetary society than ancient Greece had ever been. The results
of its growth could therefore be both more spectacular and more
ridiculous—and so more reminiscent of the excesses of monetary
society in the modern age. The aristocrats of the Italian city of Bolo-
gna, for example—one of the richest cities of the early medieval

era—devoted their newfound energies to a very modern passion: vying with one another to build the tallest tower. The result was the Manhattan of the Middle Ages: 180 towers, some nearly a hundred metres tall, in a city less than four kilometres square.

The persistence of Charlemagne's monetary units formed the basis for this extensive remonetisation, but it also gave rise to its chaotic practical organisation. Whereas the original introduction of money to Europe had taken place under the auspices of a unified Roman political authority, its reconstitution was the definition of piecemeal. Since the collapse of Charlemagne's empire, Europe had lacked a unified political space. With the exception of England, no unitary jurisdiction extended beyond one or two major cities and their hinterlands—and many were very much smaller. So whilst the pounds, shillings, and pence of Charlemagne's empire were deployed throughout Europe to organise the revived monetary practices of evaluation, negotiation, and contracting, all standardisation was lost. A cornucopia of moneys were issued, corresponding to the enormous variety of jurisdictions which enjoyed the privilege of minting and money issuance—from great kingdoms and principalities to tiny baronial and ecclesiastical fiefdoms. The result was a monetary landscape that appeared superficially simple—since the monetary units of pounds, shillings, and pence were used almost everywhere—but was in reality extraordinarily complex, since the actual value of these units depended on the particular standard maintained by the individual feudal issuer.

This revitalised monetary regime had one especially attractive feature for its feudal issuers. In an age when the imposition of direct taxes remained a logistical and economic challenge for many of them, the levying of seigniorage by the manipulation of the monetary standard represented an invaluable source of revenue. An important feature of the monetary technology of the day made this simple to do. The dominant technology for representing money was coinage, with silver the metal of choice for higher-value coins, and bronze or other less valuable metals and alloys for smaller denominations. But unlike today's coins, medieval types were typically struck without any written indication of their nominal value: there was no number stamped on either face—only the face or arms of the issuing sovereign or some other identifying design. The value of the coins was then fixed by edicts published by the sovereign on whose political authority they were minted. This system had a great advantage for the sovereign. Simply by reducing the tariffed, nominal value of a coin, the sovereign could effectively impose a one-off wealth tax on all holders of coined money. A certain coin, the sovereign would announce, is no longer good for one shilling, but only for sixpence. The coin had been "cried down"; or equivalently, one could say that the standard had been "cried up." An offer might then be made to recoin the cried-down issue, upon presentation at the Mint, into a new type. The sovereign could then in addition levy a charge on the re-minting operation.

Naturally, this process was unpopular with users of the sovereign's coinage. Fortunately for them, there was one partial, natural defence. High-value coins—minted from silver, for example—had an intrinsic value regardless of the tariff assigned to them: the price at which their metal content could be sold on the open market to smiths and jewellers, or indeed to competing mints. They included, as it were, portable collateral for the sovereign's promise to pay. This meant that there was a lower limit to the tariffed value which the issuing sovereign could assign his coinage. If a coin was cried down too far, the collateral would be worth more than the credit the coin represented, and holders could sell it to a smith for its bullion value. On the other hand, the alert sovereign could respond by reducing the silver content of the new type when the coinage was re-minted—a so-called "debasement." It was a recipe for a constant game of cat-and-mouse between the coin-issuer and the coin-user, with even a coin's precious-metal content, which effectively served as collateral for the creditworthiness of its issuer, always vulnerable to erosion by the predations of the sovereign.

This vulnerability was more than a theoretical risk. Medieval sovereigns had few ways of raising revenue apart from the proceeds of their personal domains: levying direct or indirect taxes was far beyond most feudal administrative capabilities. Seigniorage was therefore a uniquely attractive and uniquely feasible source of income—and medieval sovereigns happily indulged in it. Under normal circumstances, when seigniorage was levied only on the gradual increase in the coinage supply demanded by a growing monetary economy, the revenues were relatively modest. But when the need arose, a sovereign could raise enormous sums by crying down or even demonetising altogether the current issue of the coinage and calling it in for re-minting off a debased footing. In 1299, for example, the total revenues of the French crown amounted to just under £2 million: of this, fully one half had come from the seigniorage profits of the Mint following a debasement and general recoining.[20] Two generations later, the recoinage of 1349 generated nearly three-quarters of all revenues collected that year by the king.[21] When such large sums could be raised, it is hardly surprising that there were no fewer than 123 debasements in France alone between 1285 and 1490.[22]

The remonetisation of Europe over the so-called "long thirteenth century," from the late twelfth to the mid-fourteenth century, therefore generated two phenomena that would eventually come into conflict. The first was the emergence of a class of individuals and institutions whose wealth was held, and whose business transacted, in money—a politically powerful "money interest" beyond the sovereign's court. The second was the growing addiction of sovereigns to the fiscal miracle of the seigniorage—a miracle which grew in proportion with the increasing use of money. The more activities were monetised, and the more people were drawn into the money economy, the larger the tax base on which seigniorage was levied. As sovereigns were to discover, this apparently magical source of fiscal financing did in fact have limits. They were not technical, however, but political. At some point, the new money interest was bound to assert itself against the sovereign's perceived excesses. This point was reached in the mid-fourteenth century. It produced the first work in the Western canon on a topic that was thereafter to receive considerably more attention but become considerably more obscure: monetary policy.

THE BIRTH OF THE MONEY INTEREST

In the summer of 1363, the fortunes of the royal house of Valois—the rulers of the Kingdom of France—were at a low ebb. Seven years previously, the king, Jean II, had suffered a calamitous defeat at the hands of the Black Prince of England at Poitiers, and been led across the Channel as a prisoner. Fortunately for Jean, the medieval understanding of captivity—for kings at least—was indulgent. He whiled away his time in England hunting and feasting with his hosts, enjoying his large court, and lodging on the Thames at the Savoy Palace—then, as now, a byword for high living. In the meantime, his French lands, with his eldest son the Dauphin Charles in nominal command, descended into near anarchy. At last, in 1360, a treaty was struck, under which Jean would return to France to raise a ransom of three million crowns while his second son, Louis, was confined in Calais as surety for the English. Reluctantly, Jean bade farewell to the Savoy and returned to his ravaged kingdom. His hardship was not to last long. In 1363, news reached Paris that Louis had escaped his captors, breaching the terms of the treaty. Jean was overcome by a sudden bout of *noblesse oblige* and lost no time in volunteering to return to his imprisonment in England. He died a year later, and the dilapidated Kingdom of France passed into the hands of the Dauphin for good.

King Jean's return to England in 1363 had astonished the French establishment—but they had quickly realised that it also presented them with a golden opportunity to brainwash his heir. Here was their chance to end the French crown's fiscal folly, and especially its reliance on the evils of excessive seigniorage. In the course of his war with the English, Jean had tested new extremes in this respect. In 1355, the year before Poitiers, there had been no fewer than eight devaluations, and even then the year had ended with the king forced to declare a moratorium on his debt service.[23] What was needed was to convince the prince that in the emerging era the age-old practice of milking the seigniorage would do more harm than good. The Dauphin was young and hopefully impressionable, but he was no fool. What was required was an advocate—a brilliant logician, economist, and rhetorician—who could marshal the most cogent arguments available from the schools and apply them to the real world. This was a tall order: the academic orthodoxy of the day placed more value on infinitesimal disputes over the precise meanings of classical texts than on scientific enquiry, let alone its application to policy. Luckily, there was an exception to this general rule: the newly appointed Grand Master of one of the most prestigious schools in Paris, the College of Navarre. His name was Nicolas Oresme. He accepted the assignment at once.

Oresme was a Norman from Lisieux who had come to Paris in the 1340s to study under the great scholiast Jean Buridan. Since then, he had proved himself the outstanding scholar of his day, making major contributions in many disciplines, from mathematics and astronomy to philosophy and theology. It was for the tract that he addressed to the Dauphin Charles in around 1360, however—*Tractatus de origine, natura, iure, et mutacionibus monetarum* ("A Treatise on the Origin, Nature, Law, and Alterations of Money")—that he would be best remembered.[24] The *Treatise* was both a powerful work of analysis and a powerful work of persuasion. Oresme stated clearly the two disputes it sought to untangle at its outset: was it right that the sovereign should manipulate the monetary standard? And if it was, then in whose interests should he do so?

Oresme's answers were revolutionary. Traditional scholastic thought held that money was part of the feudal domain of its issuer and that the minting authority could therefore do with it whatever it liked. Since the sovereign owned the Mint, the only interests to be considered were those of the sovereign. Oresme introduced a radically different perspective. Money, he said, is not the property of the sovereign but of the entire community that uses it. In a world in which the use of money had spread far beyond the settlement of royal expenses—a world in which private transactions were extensively conducted, and private wealth widely held, in monetary form—the issuance of money constituted an essential public service and should therefore be operated in the interests of the public at large. Naturally, Oresme's idea of the public at large was somewhat selective.

He was, after all, a spokesman for the great feudal landowners of the church and the aristocracy, whose rents and savings had been newly transformed from obligations in kind into monetary wealth. It was these people, whom Oresme unblushingly dubbed "the best classes of the community," who suffered most from the scourge of redistributive seigniorage—and in whose interests the sovereign should manage his money. The sovereign, Oresme pronounced, "is not the lord or owner of the money current in his principality. For money is a balancing instrument for the exchange of natural wealth . . . [i]t is therefore the property of those who possess such wealth."[25]

This vantage point gave Oresme a new perspective on the merits of the sovereign's manipulation of the standard—the great bugbear of the new moneyed classes. On the one hand, Oresme was quick to point out, this was basically a problem. In the normal course of things, the sole reason for such manipulation was for the sovereign to levy seigniorage from his subjects. "Can any words be too strong," he asked, "to express how unjust, how detestable it is, especially in a prince, to reduce the weight without altering the mark?"[26] Both social justice and economic efficiency required a more reasonable and predictable monetary system. But as a wily and circumspect pamphleteer, Oresme realised that to campaign for the abolition of the seigniorage altogether—by bringing the tariffed, nominal value of the coinage exactly into line with the market value of the precious metal that it contained—would never fly. He therefore recommended a more moderate course. In exchange for the benefit of using the sovereign money, the community should bear both the costs of minting and a modest seigniorage, so that the sovereign could continue to enjoy "a noble and honourable estate, as becomes princely magnificence or royal majesty."[27]

Yet Oresme was aware that this proposed monetary reform begged a further question. Eliminating—or at least strictly regulating—seigniorage would certainly reduce the sovereign's room for discretion in the management of money. But if the sovereign's choice of the level of seigniorage was not to determine the quantity of money in circulation, what should? In theory, there was a simple answer to this question. If the standard were simply to be fixed and immutable, then private demand for coinage could set the quantity of money. If people wanted coins, they could bring silver to the Mint and have it coined, with only minting costs and a minimal seigniorage tax to pay. The problem was that this laissez-faire solution was unlikely to work in practice, because there was no reason to suppose that the arbitrary supply of precious metal would necessarily accord with the demand for money.

There was, Oresme concluded, a limited role for sovereign monetary policy after all. In extreme cases, debasement might be necessary—but only in order to ensure that the supply of coined money was sufficient to meet the needs of the community, and only on the instructions of the community: "if [the community] trusts the Prince with [the debasement of money], within a reasonable limit . . . the Prince would not undertake it as main author, but as the executor of a public ordinance."[28] At all other times, the sovereign's monetary policy should consist of trying to discover new sources of precious metal to augment the supply of coined money. "It was this consideration," Oresme wrote, "that led Theodoric, king of Italy, to order the gold and silver deposited according to pagan custom in the tombs, to be removed and used for coining for the public profit, saying: 'It was a crime to leave hidden among the dead and useless, what would keep the living alive.' "[29]

Oresme had uncovered a genuine and profound paradox that would, as we shall see, haunt monetary thought over subsequent centuries. There had to be a means of restraining the sovereign's inveterate impulse to fund his innate profligacy for free via seigniorage. There needed, that is, to be a rule governing the issuance of money: the standard should not be infinitely flexible. But if such a rule resulted in periodic dearths of money, it would impose an undesirable constraint on commerce. This would seem to call for someone to have the discretion to adjust the supply of money in response: the standard should not be immutably fixed either. Oresme did not resolve this paradox—recommending that the sovereign resort to grave robbery was hardly likely to catch on as a mainstay of policy.

He did, however, introduce the innovative idea that in considering monetary policy's ability to redistribute wealth and incomes and its ability to stimulate or stifle trade, it was not the sovereign's fiscal needs that should take priority, but the wider community's commercial well-being.

This new perspective on money led to a radical political conclusion. For if monetary policy was to be directed at the public interest, it implied that the community—rather than the sovereign alone—should control it. The *Treatise*'s conclusion could not have been more blunt: "the community alone has the right to decide if, when, how, and to what extent [money] is to be altered, and the prince may not in any way usurp it."[30] What is more, it clearly implied more general limits on the sovereign's power, and was not afraid to acknowledge these as well: "he is greater and more powerful than any of his subjects, but of less power or wealth than the whole community, and so stands in the middle."[31] And in case the message was not clear enough, Oresme rounded off with a chapter discussing the likely fate of a sovereign that chose to ignore it. The portent of its ominous title can hardly have been lost on the Dauphin: *Quod tyrannus non potest diu durare*—"That a tyrant cannot last long."[32]

Persuasive as Oresme's arguments may have been, they were not obviously effective. The problem was that there was no way of forcing sovereigns to listen while there was essentially no alternative to sovereign money. There was certainly extensive use of small-scale credit and even of local token currencies in the Middle Ages. But the perennial constraints on the monetisation of private credit and the fragmented political geography of the day meant that the only viable general-purpose money was that issued under the authority of the sovereign. Indeed, the creditworthiness and political authority of sovereigns themselves was typically so weak that coins minted from precious metals remained the dominant form of money. When even the sovereign's money required portable collateral in the form of its precious-metal content, what hope could there be for issuers of a lower political and economic standing? Sovereigns therefore retained a practical monopoly on money issuance—and they knew it. The emerging money interest could hire the best brains in Europe to make the case that the sovereign should restrain his seigniorage and manage his money instead with their interests in mind—and in Oresme they had done just that—but they had no means of forcing the sovereign's hand. As an issuer of money, he simply had no serious competition.

As so often in the history of monetary thought, however, Oresme's arguments were becoming obsolete almost as they had been expressed. Outside of the traditional sources of sub-sovereign wealth and power—the aristocracy and the church—the commercial revolution was beginning to build a new mercantile class. Its practices may not have enjoyed the nice theoretical apparatus of Oresme—but then the merchants did not need scholastic logic to justify their activities. They were busily rediscovering an invention that would turn monetary society on its head in a way in which Oresme's brilliantly argued tract never could. That invention was the bank.

6 The Natural History of the Vampire Squid

In around 1555 there arose a scandal in the city of Lyons.[1] An Italian merchant had settled there and proceeded to make himself prodigiously rich in a remarkably short space of time. By itself, there was nothing particularly surprising about that. Lyons was one of the great commercial cities of France, and of Europe. It was no stranger to the business of international trade, or to the wealth that it could bring the enterprising merchant. Indeed, the magnificent fair it hosted four times a year was said to have been founded in Roman times, and by the mid-sixteenth century it was the greatest mercantile gathering in all of Europe.[2] It was the manner of the Italian's success that had caused a stir. He had come to the fair bringing no merchandise whatsoever; nothing, in fact, but a single table and an inkstand. He looked more like an itinerant scholar than a merchant, and had spent his days doing nothing more strenuous than signing his name to pieces of paper brought to him by fellow merchants. And yet by the end of the fair, a few weeks of such decidedly undemanding activity had made this pallid and bookish fellow astonishingly rich. The explanation was obvious: the man was a fraud.

The uneasiness of contemporary observers at this strange spectacle must have been brewing for some time: it was not an isolated case. It was indeed true that fairs like that at Lyons had once been grand occasions for Europe's great merchants to convene gigantic versions of the markets held on a weekly basis in villages and towns across the Continent. They had been the principal places of trade for the high-value luxury goods whose exchange across national boundaries was the most dynamic aspect of the medieval economy—as well as for myriad local transactions in small-scale and usually perishable goods. But in the course of the long thirteenth century, the organisation of cross-border trade had changed: the business of exchange had been subjected to a division of labour. The heads of the merchant houses no longer travelled with their goods. They remained at home, and kept agents permanently resident in their main export markets, while professional hauliers would transport cargoes by land or sea as contracted. The merchant became concerned primarily with the legal and financial aspects of international trade—the change of title to the goods, and to the money received in return; and the financial calculus of balancing revenues received in one currency with expenses incurred in another. The tedious business of getting the goods from one place to another was farmed out to a lesser class of businessmen.[3]

One result of this changing organisation of commerce was a gradual evolution in the nature of the mercantile fairs. Once upon a time, a fair like Lyons had operated for its duration as a great pyramid, incorporating the mass of local retail trade at the base, the commerce of wholesalers and international traders in the middle, and the netting out of the accounts accumulated at these lower levels at its apex. But over time, these periodic gatherings of Europe's merchant class came, as the great French historian Fernand Braudel put it, "to concentrate on credit rather than commodities, on the tip of the pyramid rather than the base."[4] Less and less were they opportunities for the physical exchange of goods. More and more, they were occasions for the clearing and settlement of credit and debit balances accumulated in the course of international trade over the preceding months. Between fairs, payments for international imports were generally made not in coin, but on credit, using bills of exchange—credit notes sold by the pan-European merchant houses to their clients, who could then present them to their suppliers in foreign cities in payment for goods. By 1555, the primary role of the fair of Lyons was as a clearing house for the credit and debit balances accrued by the merchant houses of Europe against one another in issuing these bills of exchange to finance trade. It had become the most important market in Europe not for goods, but for money.

This was the system of which the paper-pushing Italian was a part—and it was every bit as mysterious and confusing to the uninitiated as the global financial markets of today. In place of the vigorous and venial atmosphere of the fairs of yesteryear—the ambience of a gigantically exaggerated local market day, complete with fireworks and bonfires, gambling and girls, tumblers, tightrope walkers, and tooth-pullers—there were merely the etiolated shades of the merchant bankers with their ink-stained fingers and incomprehensible account books. Nothing real changed hands except bundles of bills. Commerce had become a branch of mathematics. The standard textbook on the subject, published in Venice in 1494 by the Franciscan friar Luca Pacioli, was called *De Arithmetica*—"On Arithmetic." Most observers found the activities of its practitioners "a difficult cabbala to understand": the fact that it led so mysteriously but inexorably to enrichment without apparent exertion was baffling.[5] Five hundred years later, the reaction of one fictional everyman to the most recent financial revolution was uncannily similar:

> Her English husband Ossie, now he's rich-for-life but he works in money, in pure money. His job has nothing to do with anything except money, the stuff itself. No fucking around with stocks, shares, commodities, futures. Just money. Sitting in his spectral towers on Sixth Avenue and Cheapside, blond Ossie uses money to buy and sell money. Equipped with only a telephone, he buys money with money, sells money with money. He works in the cracks and vents of currencies, buying and selling on the margin,

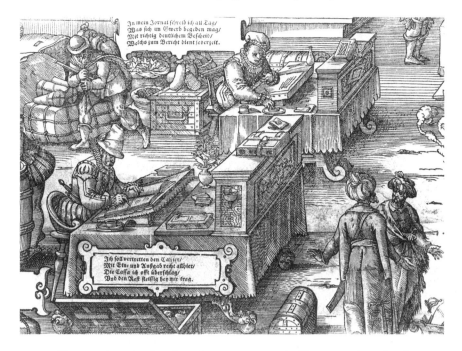

The merchant banker, for whom commerce had become a branch of mathematics, depicted in a sixteenth-century German print.

riding the daily tides of exchange. For these services he is rewarded with money. Lots of it.[6]

As the scandal of 1555 demonstrated, bafflement could easily turn to resentment. However difficult to understand in its details, the system of credit regulated by the fairs and their participants was commonly understood to be the pinnacle of the new system of monetised exchange that was increasingly governing even the humblest farmer's life. But such a general understanding only went so far. Numerous questions remained to nag the suspicious mind. What exactly did the merchants do with their bills of exchange, and why did it give them such enormous influence over the lives of people who never set eyes on their exclusive conclaves? How and why did it make them so rich? And how did the emergence of these powerful and unaccountable parliaments of merchants relate to the established political powers of the day—the sovereign, the nobility, and the church? It took better informed and more financially literate observers to solve such riddles.

These were few and far between; but they did exist. Claude de Rubys—a retired crown official who wrote a history of the Lyons fair in 1604—observed that the most remarkable feature of the great fair at Lyons was the way in which it enabled such a huge volume of trade to be settled without the use of cash. It was not unusual, he wrote, to see "a million pounds paid in a morning, without a single sou changing hands."[7] In other words, tens of millions of pounds' worth of business was being done, with the sovereign's money almost nowhere to be seen. The great merchant houses of Europe had rediscovered the art of banking—how to produce and manage private money on an industrial scale.

THE SECRETS OF THE PYRAMID

The new medieval mercantile classes faced in essence the very same problem that their modern counterparts faced in the disintegrating Soviet Union, in Argentina after its crisis, or in Greece today: how to operate a monetary economy when the sovereign's interests diverged from their own. They too yearned for a Utopia in which there would always be just enough money to satisfy the needs of trade, and in which the sovereign would not take advantage of his seigniorage prerogatives to extract unwarranted revenue. They had tried persuasion, in the guise of Oresme's ingenious arguments, but that had not worked.[8] The alternative, as in the latter-day cases of the Monetary Maquis, was rebellion.

The obvious means of escape was via the creation and clearing of private networks of mutual credit. Wherever merchants had dealings, it was natural for them to accumulate credit and debit balances against their clients and suppliers—and as far as possible to offset them and carry forward the residuals on an ongoing basis, rather than to settle every invoice back and forth using the sovereign's coin. As we saw, though, the problem with such mutual credit networks is that natural limits to commercial and personal familiarity and the fragility of confidence impose constraints on scale. They cannot function as mechanisms to organise a whole economy: in the real world, only the money of the sovereign enjoys sufficient currency for that. This was the unfortunate problem that had confronted the sponsors of Nicolas Oresme. They might not have liked the way the sovereign managed his money—but the only alternative was hardly up to supporting the growth of the new commercial economy.

As their operations increased in size and complexity, the great merchant houses of Europe realised that there was, however, an intermediate option. What they rediscovered was the possibility of a hierarchical organisation of credit. A local tradesman's promise to pay might not be worth much beyond his small circle of suppliers and clients. But the promise of one of the international merchant houses, with their much larger volume of trade, their great stocks of reserves, and their long histories of success, was a different matter. If a great merchant substituted his word for that of a local tradesman, an IOU that might previously have circulated at most within the local economy could be transformed into one that could circulate anywhere where the great merchant's prestige was acknowledged. A pyramid of credit could be constructed, with the obligations of local tradesmen as the base, larger wholesalers in the middle, and the most exclusive, well-known, and tight-knit circle of international merchants at the top. The international merchant house could interpose itself, in other words, between local merchants and their ultimate counterparties—and in doing so, transform inert, bilateral promises to pay into liquid liabilities that could easily be assigned from creditor to creditor and so circulate as money wherever the great house's credit was current. The private trade credit of even the humblest local merchant, in other words, could break its parochial bounds and, endorsed by a cosmopolitan mercantile name, become good to settle payments on the other side of Europe, where its original issuer and his business were entirely unknown.

It was here—in the creation of a private payments system—that the invention of modern banking originated. Such a humble birth may sound disappointing. Today, the banking sector's unglamorous routine of providing payment services takes a distant second place in the popular imagination to the exciting businesses of lending and trading. But their ability to finance and settle payments is the more fundamental activity. This is banks' specifically monetary role, and what makes them special. A bank is in essence an institution which writes IOUs on the one hand—these are its deposits, its bonds, its notes; generically, its liabilities—and accumulates IOUs on the other—its loans and its securities portfolio; generically, its assets. Every business has some promises to pay outstanding to suppliers, and owns some promises to pay from customers. But for most businesses, these financial assets and liabilities—the firm's accounts receivable and payable, as they are called in the book-keepers' jargon—are dwarfed by the value of the business' real assets: its plant, its premises, its inventory, and so on. In a bank, it is the other way round. The mysterious Italian at the fair of Lyons is entirely representative. A bank's real assets are always negligible. The balance sheets of modern banks are vast: in 2007 the balance sheet of a single British bank, the Royal Bank of Scotland, was larger than the GDP of the entire U.K. No manufacturing business could ever accumulate assets of this magnitude. The reason that a bank can do so is that almost all its assets are nothing but promises to pay, and almost all its liabilities likewise.

As we have seen, any IOU has two fundamental characteristics: its creditworthiness—how likely it is that it will be paid when it comes due—and its liquidity—how quickly it can be realised, either by sale to a third party or simply by coming due if no sale is sought. The risks associated with any promise to pay depend upon these two characteristics. Accepting a promise to pay in a year's time entails more risk than accepting a promise to pay tomorrow: a lot more can go wrong in year than in twenty-four hours. This is the dimension of liquidity risk—so called because unless it can be sold in the meantime, a private promise to pay only becomes liquid at the moment it is settled in sovereign money. Then there is the possibility that the IOU's issuer will not be able to pay at all, regardless of the time frame. Accepting a promise to pay from a NINJA—the banking industry acronym for someone with No Income and No Job or Assets—is more risky than accepting a promise to pay from Warren Buffett. This is the dimension of credit risk.

The whole business of banking resolves into the management of these two types of risk, as they apply both to a bank's assets and to its liabilities. Banks transform uncreditworthy and illiquid claims on the assets and income of borrowers into less risky and more liquid claims—claims which are so much less risky and so much more liquid that they are widely accepted in settlement of debts. They achieve this miraculous transformation through their management of the credit and liquidity risks of the loans they make to governments, companies, and individuals, on one side, and of the credit and liquidity risks of the obligations they owe to their depositors and bondholders on the other.[9]

The management of credit risk—working out which borrowers are NINJAs and which are Warren Buffetts, devising the best combination of borrowers in the overall portfolio, and monitoring borrowers over the lifetime of their loans—is the most obvious part of what banks do. But it is not the most important part.[10] Strip a bank's balance sheet back to its bare bones, and the simplest form of banking, the form practised by the most risk-averse of banks, is the short-term financing of trade. In this kind of banking, credit risk is minimal: loans are usually extended simply to cover the purchase and transport of goods for which a sale has already been agreed, and the goods themselves are often used as collateral. With sufficient insurance, the bank might even eliminate the credit risk altogether. The risk it can never get rid of, however, is liquidity risk. Even in the short-term financing of trade, when the loan is only for the days or weeks it takes to bring the goods from the producer to market, the banker is making a commitment for a definite length of time. And on the other side of its balance sheet it has its own liabilities—its deposits, bills, and bonds—which are coming due. When the higher complications of credit risk are absent, the essence of the banker's art comes into focus. It is nothing more than ensuring the synchronisation, in the aggregate, of incoming and outgoing payments due on his assets and liabilities—which are themselves, of course, the aggregated liabilities and assets of all his borrowers and creditors. This was the art that the great international merchants of the Middle Ages had rediscovered.[11]

Within domestic economies, the effects of this rediscovery began to be felt as early as the twelfth century. By the end of that century, in the Italian maritime city state of Genoa, merchants had founded local banks that both kept accounts for clients and maintained accounts with one another, so that payments could be made across the system, from the client of one bank to the client of another.[12] By the fourteenth century, payment via such bank transfers was the preferred method of making any sizeable payment in Florence; and there were as many as eighty banks offering the service.[13] To the extent that the account-holders were required to present themselves at their bank to approve payments—as was the case, for example, in Venice—the system remained limited by a degree of inconvenient centralisation. But by the mid-fourteenth century, payment by cheques and other written IOUs was becoming common in the city states of Tuscany, in Genoa, and in Barcelona. Such written instruments could circulate amongst the merchant community without notarisation at the bank, before being presented for redemption. Thus they facilitated fully decentralised clearing, just as the sovereign's coinage did. The first example that survives—a cheque drawn by the aristocratic Tornaquinci family of Florence on their bankers the Castellani—dates from 1368, less than a decade after Oresme addressed his *Treatise* to the Dauphin Charles.[14] Even as Oresme was pleading for more equitable management of the sovereign's money, the new mercantile class was devising ways to escape its tyranny altogether.

Operating as it did within the jurisdiction of a given sovereign, the business of domestic banking was subject to the close attention of the political authorities, however. The resuscitation of a profession which specialised exclusively in financial transactions revived ancient suspicions. The medieval schoolmen, starting with St. Thomas Aquinas, devoted the majority of their writings on money to parsing Aristotle's condemnation of lending at interest as unnatural. Even Oresme, the champion of the new monetary rentiers, was quick to criticise the "money-changers, bankers or dealers in bullion" who "augment their own wealth by unworthy business . . . a disgraceful trade."[15] Then there were the ominous lessons of the potential macroeconomic risks associated with large-scale banking contained in ancient texts like Tacitus' account of the Tiberian financial crisis. Above all, there was the sovereigns' interest in ensuring the continuing priority of their money, and hence their seigniorage. As a result, the new invention of banking was subjected to draconian regulation. When in 1321 the authorities in Venice discovered that merchants were practising fractional reserve banking—holding only a small proportion of their assets in coin of the state—they passed a law specifying that banks must be able to meet all requests for withdrawals in coin within three days.[16] In the same year the Catalonian authorities revised their 1300 order that failed bankers be forced to live on bread and water alone until all their clients were reimbursed. Henceforth, any banker who failed to meet his clients' demands was to be publicly denounced—and then summarily beheaded in front of his bank. It was no idle threat, as the hapless Barcelona banker Francesch Castello discovered in 1360.[17] Under such uncompromising regulatory regimes, domestic banking really was a risky business.

Conditions were altogether more propitious in the parallel world of international banking. To begin with, international trade was the most dynamic part of the medieval economy: the aristocracy benefited first from the monetisation of feudal relations, and it was their taste for foreign luxuries that drove high-value commerce. What's more, the great merchant house, with its resident agent in the foreign jurisdiction, its extensive operations in both countries, and its new expertise in banking, could supply the local merchant both with credit and with foreign exchange services. But most important of all, there was, by definition, no sovereign authority to regulate commerce between countries, and no sovereign money with which to transact. So it was here, in the international sphere, that banking's potential to accelerate the commercial revolution was first fully realised. The central innovation was the perfection, by the mid-sixteenth century, of the system of "exchange by bills": a procedure for financing international trade using monetary credit issued by the clique of pan-European merchant bankers, denominated in their own abstract unit of account, recorded in bills of exchange, and cleared at the quarterly fair of Lyons.

The system was simple.[18] An Italian merchant wishing to import goods from a supplier in the Low Countries could purchase a credit note known as a bill of exchange from one of the great Florentine merchant houses. He might pay for this note either in the local sovereign money or on credit. By buying such a bill of exchange, the Italian merchant achieved two things. First, he accessed the miracle of banking: he transformed an IOU backed by only his own puny word for one issued by a larger, more creditworthy house, which would be accepted across Europe. He transformed his private credit into money. His second achievement was to exchange a credit for a certain amount of Florentine money into one for a certain amount of the money of the Low Countries where he was making his purchase. The bill of exchange itself was denominated in a private monetary unit created specially for the purpose by the network of exchange-bankers: the *écu de marc*. There were no sovereign coins denominated in this *écu de marc*. It was a private monetary standard of the exchange-bankers alone, created so that they could haggle with one another over the value of the various sovereign moneys of the continent. Somewhat bizarrely to modern eyes, the foreign exchange transaction included in the bill of exchange therefore involved two exchange rates—one between Florentine money and the *écu de marc*, the other between the *écu de marc* and the money of the Low Countries.

The end result was to overcome a previously insurmountable series of obstacles. The exchange-banker would accept the importer's credit in payment, knowing him and his business well from the local market. Meanwhile, the supplier in the Low Countries would accept the exchange-banker's credit as payment, knowing that it would be good in its turn to settle either a bill for imports or for some local transaction—and satisfied that he was being paid in the local money. Of course, the banker ran the risk that the exchange rates of the two sovereign moneys against the imaginary *écu de marc* might change in between his issuing the bill of exchange and its being cashed in the Low Countries, but he made sure that his fees and commissions made this a risk worth taking.[19]

As they continually wrote and accepted bills of exchange to finance trade between the great European cities, the exchange-bankers would accumulate credit and debit balances. The circle of exchange-bankers was a close-knit one, and willingness to allow out-standing balances to build up was therefore high. Nevertheless, to ensure a clear picture of who owed what to whom, it was necessary to have periodic offsets. These could be done bilaterally on an ad hoc basis; but the regular fairs provided a natural opportunity for a more generalised clearing—and this is precisely what they gradually became. Every quarter, the clique of great merchant houses would meet at the central fair of Lyons in order to square their books. On the first two days of the fair there was a frenzy of buying and selling, of writing new bills or cancelling old ones, at the end of which all delegates' books were closed for the quarter and the resulting bal-ances between the houses were verified. The third day—the "Day of Exchange"—was the heart of proceedings. The exclusive cadre of exchange-bankers would convene alone to agree on the *conto*: the schedule of exchange rates between the *écu de marc* and the various sovereign moneys of Europe. This schedule was the pivot of the entire financial system, since it was at these exchange rates that any outstanding balances had to be settled on the final day of the fair—the "Day of Payments"—either by agreement to carry over balances to the next settlement date, or by payment in cash.[20]

The task of a judicious exchange-banker such as the mysterious Italian at Lyons was so to transact in the first days of the fair that by the time the Day of Payments came round, he could offset all his credit and debit balances perfectly, and turn a profit into the bargain. But the real source of the exchange-bankers' phenomenal enrichment and power was not simply their ability to speculate on the fluctuations of the fledgling foreign exchange market. The system of exchange by bills was not just a means of facilitating international trade or foreign exchange—remarkable as these achievements were. It was something much grander, and more politically significant. Bit by bit, the exchange-bankers had assembled all the moving parts of a great machine that enabled private credit to circulate as money throughout Europe. All three of money's fundamental components were there. Like the Argentine *Crédito*, the system had its own unit of abstract value, the *écu du marc*. It had its own system of accounting—the rules of book-keeping set out in Pacioli's *De Arithmetica*, and the standard protocols agreed between the great merchant houses for applying it. And it had its system for the transfer and clearing of credit balances using the bill of exchange and the great clearing house of the central fair. The system of exchange by bills had become nothing other than "a supranational private money interacting with domestic public monies."[21] By crowning a pan-European hierarchy of credit with the self-regulating network of their cosmopolitan but close-knit cabal, the exchange-bankers had succeeded, it seemed, in building Utopia. With their perfection of the system of exchange by bills, they had constructed a viable private money on a continent-wide scale.

The economic significance of this astonishing achievement was plain to see in both the commercial revolution that it facilitated and the fabulous wealth of the men who had built it. But there was more—much more—to the new system of bankers' money than that. It was the harbinger of an epochal political change as well—one that would change the face of finance for ever.

7   The Great Monetary
     Settlement

PRIVATE MONEY AND MARKET DISCIPLINE

Claude de Rubys, the historian of the Lyons fair, was one observer
who spotted the political significance of the international system of
exchange by bills: it enabled the mercantile class to escape from their
reliance on sovereign money. As an experienced statesman, de Rubys
was aware that control of a nation's money was one of the most basic
and lucrative sources of sovereign power. He also understood that the
creation and management of private money by bankers was an act
not only of economic innovation, but potentially of political revolution. The money interest was now equipped both with Oresme's
powerful arguments—the ideas of the public interest and the needs
of trade as guiding principles of monetary policy—and with a potential alternative, should the sovereign refuse to heed them. The great
merchant houses had discovered a means of producing an international
money beyond any one sovereign's jurisdiction. Moreover, so tightly
knit was this cosmopolitan elite, and so expertly constructed its hierarchy of credit networks, that it had no need of precious metal to
serve as collateral for its promises to pay. Its money was invisible,
intangible, consisting only of the confidence of the small group of
exchange-bankers at the tip of the pyramid in one another's abilities
to assess risks, to be able to meet payments as they came due, and to

limit the issuance of credit. This was an enemy impossible to grasp, let alone defeat—a Monetary Maquis with a real "Army of Shadows." Now it was the money interest that could back its arguments with threats—threats to abandon the sovereign's money if it was not managed in accordance with their interests. The boot was firmly on the other foot.

Unsurprisingly, sovereigns sought to wage a rearguard action against this new enemy. The most useful recruits were men who knew the secrets of the bankers from first-hand experience. Sir Thomas Gresham, England's royal agent at Antwerp from 1551, was one such poacher-turned-gamekeeper. Gresham came from a prominent mercantile family. His father had been one of the chief beneficiaries of Henry VIII's distribution of monastic assets, and had traded on these riches to become Lord Mayor of London. Gresham himself was in his own turn "a successful business man, a financial expert, and a confidential agent of the government."[1] His experience in the first two roles was to come to his aid in his capacity as the English crown's financier-in-chief in the Low Countries following the financial disasters of the last decade of Henry VIII's reign. From a high of 26 Flemish shillings in 1544, the English pound sterling had commenced a seemingly inexorable decline in value on the exchange at Antwerp, at one point in 1551 sinking to only 13 Flemish shillings—a 50 per cent depreciation in seven years.[2] Since the English crown was a major debtor in Antwerp, this precipitous decline was unwelcome: it increased the real burden of the king's debt in the same proportion. Moreover, whilst it was difficult to deny that the English crown's foreign borrowing might have been excessive, court opinion held—in the time-honoured tradition of government officials facing market pressures—that the real culprit was the exchange-bankers, whose low opinion of English creditworthiness was nothing but a scam to earn them unjustified profits. Most culpable of all, wrote the minister William Cecil, were none other than the mysterious Italians, who "go to and fro and serve all princes at once . . . work what they list and lick the fat from our beards."[3]

By 1551, the court was in despair. But Gresham had a plan. Following his appointment as agent, he pitched the idea of an exchange stabilisation fund to be deployed to combat unwarranted depreciation of the pound sterling. He requested a secret infusion of £1,200 or £1,300 a week for the purpose. With such ammunition, he said, he could neutralise the bankers' power to sell sterling whenever they disapproved of the English crown's policies. The young Edward VI's Regency Council was persuaded, and the plan was put into effect. Gresham's ploy was certainly prescient—government intervention in the foreign exchange markets using stabilisation funds was to become a standard tool of policy in the twentieth century. Unfortunately, it was also ahead of its time in discovering the limited abilities of such schemes to succeed in the face of market scepticism. After just two months, the English government balked at the cost of Gresham's apparently ineffectual interventions, and cancelled the programme. Undeterred, Gresham returned with a new plan; but this one was much more conventional. The foreign currency reserves of the English merchants at Antwerp were to be commandeered as a forced loan to the crown. The crown's foreign currency debts due to the slippery exchange-bankers would be refinanced into a sterling loan from its own subjects. It was ingenious and effective—but it was an admission of defeat. The exchange-bankers could not be beaten at their own game. The only remedy was for the sovereign to exert its power of coercion over its subjects. But that could only increase their incentive to join the resistance.

As so often in the history of monetary thought, theory lagged behind practice. Businessmen, policy-makers, and bankers themselves understood the developing system from the bottom up; Gresham even published a treatise on the topic. But a full appreciation of banking's general political significance had to wait nearly two more centuries for the furnace of the French Enlightenment to fuse together previously separate strands of economic and political thought. France in the mid-eighteenth century was ripe for such a catalytic role. Politically, it remained the bastion of the *Ancien Régime*—an unreconstructed feudal monarchy in a continent long since disturbed by the winds of constitutional change. Financially, France was one of the most backward states in Western Europe, but intellectually it was the centre of the world. The extraordinary contrast between its dazzling republic of letters and its moribund bodies politic and financial meant that it was the thinkers of the French Enlightenment who first fully articulated the link between money, banking, and politics.

The most brilliant analysis of all appeared in the masterwork of the greatest constitutional thinker of the age: Charles-Louis de Secondat, Baron de la Brède et de Montesquieu. Montesquieu's *The Spirit of the Laws* was a crowning achievement of the French Enlightenment— a masterful blend of history, anthropology, and political analysis that argued for the establishment of constitutional government on the English model. Montesquieu gave special attention—and special praise—to the role of commerce as a beneficial force in political development, and reserved his greatest admiration for international finance. "It is astonishing that the bill of exchange has been discovered only so late," he wrote, "for there is nothing so useful in all the world."[4] Even in France, though it remained a century behind England in political reform and monetary development, the discipline that the foreign exchanges imposed upon the king's policies meant that however absolute the sovereign's powers might appear, they were in practice severely circumscribed. Violent abuses of the sovereign money of the sort practised in the ancient world and the Middle Ages, he wrote, "could not take place in our time; a prince would confound himself, but would not fool anyone else. The foreign exchanges have enabled bankers to compare all the monies of the world and to evaluate what they are really worth . . . They have eliminated the great and sudden arbitrary actions of the sovereign—or at least the effectiveness of such actions."[5]

The irony that Gresham had confronted in practice was now fully understood and elegantly elaborated in theory. Feckless sovereigns' abuse of their monetary prerogatives had stimulated the rediscovery of banking and the invention of the great system of exchange by bills. As a result, it was sovereigns that now had to dance to the tune of the money interest rather than the other way round. All of a sudden, the eerie insubstantiality of the bankers' operations was not a source of suspicion, but a stealth weapon in the crusade for constitutional government. "In this manner we owe . . . to the avarice of rulers the establishment of a contrivance which somehow lifts commerce right out of their grip," wrote Montesquieu.[6] Or rather, they had inadvertently tied their own hands, finding themselves compelled to manage money ever more in the interests of the community for which Oresme had spoken. By forcing the money interest into a successful rebellion, "sovereigns have been compelled to govern with greater wisdom than they themselves might have intended . . . [Now] only good government brings prosperity [to the prince]."[7]

In 1993, James Carville, the chief strategist on U.S. president Bill Clinton's election campaign the year before, evoked the extraordinary power of money to constrain political action in the modern world, in an interview for the *Wall Street Journal*. "I used to think if there was reincarnation, I wanted to come back as the president or the pope or a .400 baseball hitter," he joked, "but now I want to come back as the bond market. You can intimidate everybody."[8] Carville's succinct formulation became justly famous; but the idea was far from original. He was evoking an Enlightenment vision of money as a force that can discipline even the mightiest sovereign. In fact, the most memorable sound bite on the topic in that earlier era was coined by another James—the Scotsman James Steuart, whose 1767 *Inquiry into the Principles of Political Economy* was one of the first works of economics in the English language.[9] Steuart's judgement neatly summarised the complete transformation in monetary thought that had taken place in the four centuries since Nicolas Oresme's *Treatise*, let alone since the days of the Jixia academy. These earlier authorities had held that money was ultimately an instrument of the sovereign—and that the best one could do was to plead with him to use it wisely. Steuart's vision was quite the opposite. Monetary society, he wrote, was nothing other than "the most effective bridle ever was invented against the folly of despotism."[10]

Two Jameses—Steuart (left) and Carville (right)—with one important idea:
that money can be a powerful tool to control the sovereign.

BANKING ON THE STATE: THE PHILOSOPHER'S STONE OF FINANCE

But things were not quite so simple. There are good reasons, we
recall, why sovereign money is generally the default. No private issuer
enjoys the same extent for its markets, the same capacity to coerce
demand for its liabilities, or the same psychological association with
confidence in society. The bankers might have built themselves a new
Jerusalem—but it was a monetary Utopia just as prone to invasion
by stark realities as any in history. Private issuers could default—and
their creditors be left with worthless bills drawn on insolvent counterparties. Liquidity could evaporate as confidence flagged, throwing
the most carefully laid plans for the synchronisation of payments into
disarray. Even the pyramid of credit erected by the bankers stopped
somewhere—at the exclusive circle of international financiers—and
even their money market could suffer from crises of confidence, or
simply from the impact of unexpected events.

Indeed, the fate of the new private money was no less ironic than that of the old sovereign money. On the one hand, it was essential that banking remain the exclusive preserve of a narrow elite. Only a self-regulating clique could incubate the interpersonal trust necessary to operate a private monetary network, and the barriers to new entrants were negligible once its principles were understood. Unlike the sovereign, the bankers had no power of coercion to enforce their franchise. As a result, bankers guarded their secrets jealously and started a proud tradition of "shroud[ing] their practices in a finicky formalism which lent itself perfectly to preserving their monopoly."[11] But these very same conditions also imposed obvious limits to its expansion. The credit notes of the international bankers could circulate amongst themselves, but outside that magic circle, they were bound to be a conundrum. The very features that made the bankers' private money work were the ones which meant it could not actually displace sovereign money.

The result was a chronically unstable monetary disequilibrium—a long-running guerrilla war between sovereigns and the private money interest which neither side could win. All this was to change with a final historic invention at the end of the seventeenth century. As had been the case with money itself, this was an innovation that was the result of transplanting advanced ideas from the most sophisticated commercial culture of the age into a financial backwater—but one which enjoyed a unique political inheritance. In this reprise of the old drama the part of the sophisticate was to be played by the Low Countries, and that of the bumpkin by England.[12] Holland's cutting-edge technology was "Dutch finance": the most advanced system for managing the national debt that then existed. England's contribution was its recent, painful adoption of constitutional monarchy. The resulting invention was the Bank of England—and with it, the basis of all modern banking systems, and all modern money.

At the close of the seventeenth century, England remained racked by the constitutional crisis that had erupted into civil war in the 1640s. The experiment with Republican government under the Cromwells had failed and the deposed King Charles I's son had been restored to power in 1660. But though the old divisions between

Royalists and Parliamentarians were fading, a new opposition driven by the divergent interests of land-owning Tories and commercially minded Whigs was emerging. The reason was nothing new. If anything, the fiscal incontinence of the sovereign that had been the immediate cause of the civil war had deteriorated further. So decrepit were the restored King Charles II's finances by 1672 that he was forced to default on his debts, announcing a "Stop of the Exchequer." The predictable result was a collapse in the crown's credit. By the end of the decade the terms on which the English sovereign could borrow were significantly worse than those available to private merchants.[13]

Nor was the fiscal situation improved by the ingenious solution to the constitutional crisis that eventually followed Charles II's death and his brother James' accession—the "Glorious Revolution" of 1688, which saw William of Orange invited to assume the throne of England. It rapidly transpired that William's leading motive in accepting the English Parliament's offer was not a selfless desire to save England from popery, but his appetite for more generous resources with which to defend Holland against the predatory ambitions of Louis XIV's France. No sooner had William taken the throne than he had joined England to a continental coalition that proceeded to launch a war against the French. Taxes were raised to yield £4 million a year—a sum unheard of in Charles II's day—but expenditure rose by even more, to £6 million a year. The difference had to be raised from creditors, using ever more desperate means. By the spring of 1694, England had endured five years of heavy war taxation—more than a third of it levied on land and therefore felt disproportionately by the Tory gentry. What was worse, there was no end in sight. The war dragged on, the king's credit was shot, and another year's vast deficit was yawning. A second default of the fraying Exchequer loomed.

Fortunately, the late seventeenth century in England was not only the era of constitutional chaos. It was also an age of vigorous innovation in the fields of money and public finance. The king's ministers and advisers were deluged by proposals from so-called "Projectors" for new ways to fund the deficit.[14] Some were ingenious, many crackpot. Almost all boiled down to the same basic idea of finding a mechanism for borrowing against future tax revenue. The trick was to discover a formula which satisfied creditors' desire for better security and more control, and yet preserved the dignity of the sovereign. But with the war deficit always threatening, the king's ministers were not in a position to be overly choosy. One novel plan was for a state lottery involving the sale of 100,000 lottery tickets at £10 each and marketed uncomplicatedly as "The Million Adventure."[15] The money raised was lent on to the Treasury in the usual way, but investors bored by the monotony of coupon payments enjoyed the chance to win an elaborately graded menu of cash prizes.[16] Fads of this sort proved successful at enticing jaded creditors to part with their money, but when all the prizes were paid out, they proved to be just as expensive as ever. No amount of actuarial ingenuity could disguise the fact that the standing of the king's credit with potential lenders remained abysmal.

There was one proposal, however, which was to prove altogether more effective. It was a plan for a bank which would fundamentally reorganise the funding of the king's debts. Investors would subscribe capital to the bank, and the bank would lend money to the government. The establishment of a bank to raise money for the sovereign was certainly not an innovation in itself. There had been public banks in the city states of the Mediterranean on and off since the Middle Ages. Holland had had a public bank at Amsterdam since 1609; Sweden, one in Stockholm since 1656. What was new about the Projector William Paterson's proposal was that this Bank of England would in effect be a public–private partnership. The Bank's primary role would undoubtedly be to put the sovereign's credit and finances on a surer footing. Indeed, its design, governance, and management were to be delegated to the mercantile classes precisely in order to ensure confidence in its operations and credit control. But in return the sovereign was to grant important privileges. Above all, the Bank was to enjoy the right to issue banknotes—a licence to put into circulation paper currency representing its own liabilities, which could circulate as money.[17] There was to be, quite literally, a quid pro quo.

Paterson's scheme might easily have been lost in the crowd. But the idea of the hybrid Bank of England found a powerful group of supporters in the circle of ambitious Whig grandees who were soon to dominate the first party-political administration of the country. They realised that Paterson's Project could deliver a Great Monetary Settlement. If they and the private money interest they represented would agree to fund the king on terms over which they, as the Directors of the new Bank, would have a statutory say, then the king would in turn allow them a statutory share in his most ancient and jealously guarded prerogative: the creation of money and the management of its standard. To be granted the privilege of note issue by the crown, which would anoint the liabilities of a private bank with the authority of the sovereign—this, they realised, was the Philosopher's Stone of money. It was the endorsement that could liberate private bank money from its parochial bounds. They would lend their credit to the sovereign—he would lend his authority to their bank. What they would sow by agreeing to lend, they would reap a hundredfold in being allowed to create private money with the sovereign's endorsement. Henceforth, the seigniorage would be shared.[18]

The worldlier men of the age were well aware that the outwardly technical business of reforming public financial management was in reality intensely political. Conservative types deemed any concessions to the Whig money interest to be unwise, if not seditious. It was not the first time that the mysterious magic of banking had been put forward as a solution to the problem of the crown's fiscal incontinence. In 1665, Sir Charles Downing had proposed that the Treasury become a virtual state bank. The Earl of Clarendon, the king's chief adviser, had dismissed the plan on explicitly political grounds as "introductive to a commonwealth, and not fit for a monarchy."[19] Such suspicions did not dissipate with the founding of the Bank of England in 1694. Ruling in a test case in 1702, the Chief Justice John Holt attempted a counter-reformation, calling the newfangled technology of bankers' promissory notes—of which the Bank of England's notes were by now establishing themselves as the pre-eminent representatives—"a new sort of specialty unknown to the Common Law, and invented in Lombard Street to give laws to Westminster Hall."[20]

Other observers saw that there were benefits to both parties, however—and this was to be the secret of the settlement's success. The quid pro quo nourished a virtuous circle. The state's blessing afforded general circulation to the Bank's notes. The commercial ownership and management of the Bank improved the state's credit-worthiness. Unreconstructed partisans of the money interest against the monarchy tended to stress this latter advantage to the exclusion of the former. Sir James Steuart, for example, was quick to remind doubters that "[t]he ruling principle of [the Bank], and the ground of their confidence, is mercantile credit."[21] That was true, as far as it went. But Steuart's compatriot and contemporary Adam Smith saw the bigger picture, and summarised it succinctly: "The stability of the Bank of England is equal to that of the British government."[22] Smith's epigram captured the nature of the virtuous circle exactly. Without the state, the Bank would have lacked authority; without the Bank, the state would have lacked credit.

Smith delivered his verdict in 1776. It had taken the best part of a century from the Bank of England's first charter in 1694 for the great monetary compromise that it represented to become so ingrained in the political economy of the United Kingdom. Over that period, the Bank's role as a source of emergency fiscal financing declined as the government bond markets expanded. Meanwhile, its role as the monetary agent of the state—the keeper of its accounts, the agent of its payments, the manager of its bond issues—grew inexorably, and its position at the apex of the monetary pyramid was continually rein-forced. In 1709 the Bank was given an effective monopoly on banknote issue within England.[23] In 1710 it was appointed receiver of public money for the state lottery, and five years after that of all payments for government annuities.[24] By the 1760s the Bank was administering more than two-thirds of the national debt.[25] By 1781, any doubts about the constitutionality of the Bank were long forgotten. In June of that year, the Prime Minister Lord North spoke to a febrile Parliament in the midst of Britain's traumatic war with its own colonists in America. Revolution was in the air—but there were still some constants from which to take comfort. When other gods were failing, the Prime Minister consoled the House, there was always the Bank, "from long habit and the use of many years . . . a part of the constitution," or "if not part of the constitution, at least . . . to all important purposes the public exchequer."[26]

With the foundation of the Bank of England, the money interest and the sovereign had found an historic accommodation. The Monetary Maquis at last had its share of power; and in return, the "Army of Shadows" worked—at least in part—for the government. This compromise is the direct ancestor of the monetary systems that dominate the world today: systems in which the creation and management of money are almost entirely delegated to private banks, but in which sovereign money remains the "final settlement asset," the only credit balance with which the banks on the penultimate tier of the pyramid can be certain of settling payments to one another or to the state. Likewise, cash remains strictly a token of a credit held against the sovereign, but the overwhelming majority of the money in circulation consists of credit balances on accounts at private banks. The fusion of sovereign and private money born of the political compromise struck in 1694 remains the bedrock of the modern monetary world.

If the practical consequences of the Great Monetary Settlement are obvious, its implications for monetary thought were just as revolutionary; and perhaps, in the long run, even more momentous. Western thought on the central question of who should control money was poised to undergo a second major transition. Before Oresme, money had been understood implicitly as a tool of government: part of the sovereign's feudal domain, and an instrument of his policy. Oresme had challenged this, and proposed an alternative objective of monetary policy—to supply the needs of the community. But he had done so from a position of weakness: there was no alternative to the sovereign money. The result had been stalemate. The rediscovery of banking, however, had turned the tables on the sovereign. Now there was genuine competition in the creation and management of monetary networks. Monetary thought abandoned its plaintive tone, and addressed itself to this new reality. Money was no longer a tool of the sovereign, but a tool against the sovereign—no longer an instrument with which the king could "bridle the Sovereigns of Destiny," as the Chinese *Guanzi* had put it, but James Steuart's "most effective bridle ever was invented against the folly of despotism."[27]

These successive answers to the question of who should control money seemed diametrically opposed—but the next revolution in monetary thought was to reveal how much they had in common. The Great Monetary Settlement was about to provoke a new theory of monetary society: the social science of economics. And in this theory, money would undergo a radical transformation. It would no longer be understood either as a tool of the sovereign, or a tool against the sovereign: it would cease to be understood as something political at all. Until now, money had been understood as a powerful social technology; its central idea of economic value as an ingenious shared concept for the co-ordination of social activity; and the monetary standard as a potent tool for the redistribution of wealth and the stimulation of commerce, whose manipulation was therefore the deserving object of heated contention. But money was about to become an inert lump of metal, value an innocuous property of the natural world, and monetary policy, let alone any debate over it, a contradiction in terms.

In short, the conventional view of money was about to make its entrance.

The Economic Consequences of Mr. Locke

THE GREAT RECOINAGE DEBATE

To its enthusiastic promoters in the City and in Parliament, the Great Monetary Settlement represented a magnificent advance in the progress of England's new constitutional monarchy. But there were others who were not so sure. For all the ingenuity of the new arrangements, one critically important question remained open: what was to be the standard on which the Bank of England was to issue its new public–private money?

It was the immemorial dilemma of monetary policy—the very question over which sovereigns and their subjects had argued interminably for hundreds of years. It was all very well to have cooked up a Project which claimed to be capable of mediating the interests of the sovereign and the commercial classes. But could it really engineer a monetary policy that would strike a compromise between their competing priorities? And if so, what would it look like? It was all wholly uncertain—and it was taking place at the very moment that the broader political settlement between King and Parliament was itself only just bedding down. It was a leap of faith to make the advocates of constitutional monarchy very nervous: the future of the system they had striven so long to see, and over which England had fought a civil war, was being risked on a financial scheme dreamt up by a cabal of City bankers. If the Great Monetary Settlement represented by the Bank of England turned out to be nothing more than a means for the money interest to get its way, it would surely collapse; and, more disastrously, bring the political settlement represented by the Glorious Revolution crashing down with it. There were no two ways about it: the supporters of the new system of government had to nip this baleful possibility in the bud. Fortunately, a golden opportunity to do so appeared almost immediately—and it was afforded by one of the oldest monetary problems in the book.

In 1696, less than two years after embarking on its historic experiment with a new form of currency issued by the Bank of England, Parliament resolved that the time had come to confront the problems of the old form—the coinage—as well. There was nothing particularly new about these problems: but they had become impossible to ignore. As we have seen, the use of precious-metal coinage involves an automatic technical challenge. If the market price of the bullion contained in the coins was allowed to exceed the legal value of the coin itself, disaster would quickly follow. Coins would be melted down and sold to silversmiths or exported from the country as bullion. Alternative means of representing money—wooden tallies, copper tokens, written notes—could in principle supply the deficiency. But in practice, the country's silver coinage was still the central support of the monetary architecture, and a shortage of coins was therefore a serious obstacle to trade. England had been suffering from a chronic case for decades: since the early years of the seventeenth century, the market price of silver bullion had consistently hovered around the critical value, and had frequently risen above it.[1] The result had been the gradual emaciation of the coin supply.

Parliament had taken remedial action in 1666 by passing an "Act for the Encouraging of Coinage" which took the unprecedented step of abolishing the seigniorage levy and raising the price paid by the Mint for silver bullion by the same amount in an attempt to bring it back into line with the market price—but the ground made up had not been enough.[2] The market price for silver continued to be a penny or two an ounce higher than the tariff, with a full-weight silver coin therefore worth 2–3 per cent more as bullion than as coin. As a result, although some £3 million worth of silver was minted into coins after 1663, almost all was found to have disappeared from circulation again by the early 1690s.[3] To make matters worse, the coins that did remain in circulation were subject to a merciless assault of clipping, filing, and shearing, as unscrupulous users scavenged as much bullion as they could without actually rendering the coins unrecognisable. Since the increasing general shortage meant that only the most monstrous mutilation could prevent coins from passing at their legal value, this was a racket that could be seriously profitable. By 1695, the authorities' samplings suggested that the vast majority of coins in circulation contained only around one half of the silver they had originally been minted with, and that full-weight silver coins were now worth nearly 25 per cent more as bullion than as coin.[4] It was clear that on the current trajectory, the little coin left in England would be shorn into oblivion. The question was what on earth could be done about it.

For an answer, Parliament turned to William Lowndes, a lifelong veteran of the Treasury and newly appointed its Secretary. Lowndes combined vast practical experience and an unrivalled network of financial and commercial contacts with a clear intellect and a comprehensive knowledge of English monetary history, and his report was a model of diligence, logic, worldliness, and common sense. He discovered that precisely the same difficulties had occurred on several occasions in the later Middle Ages. The underlying problem was that the value of sterling had, for one reason or another, fallen. There had been inflation, in other words—and the price of silver in pounds, shillings, and pence had risen. In response to such developments it had, he found, been "a Policy constantly Practised in the mints of *England* . . . to Raise the Value of the Coin in its Extrinsick Denomination from time to time, as Exigence or Occasion required."[5] The coinage had been periodically "cried up," in other words, with the tarriffed, nominal value of coins of a given silver content raised to reflect the depreciation of sterling. On both historical and logical grounds, Lowndes concluded, this was indeed the only reasonable policy response. The fall in value of money must be acknowledged by raising the price paid for silver by the Mint—or by reducing the quantity of silver in an official, full-weight coin. The monetary standard had shifted—a pound was worth less than before. The Mint policy had to accommodate itself to this fact: there was no point in fighting the market.

Lowndes estimated that a one-off, 20 per cent reduction in the silver content of the coinage would do the job.[6] The Mint price of silver was 62d. per ounce, but by the time of Lowndes' report, the market price was 77d.[7] As a result, the silver crown piece, containing just under an ounce of silver at its full, official weight, had a tariffed, nominal value of 60d. but a market value as bullion of 77d. It was hardly surprising that the coin was disappearing from circulation. Following the proposed recoinage, a full-weight English crown would contain only about four-fifths of an ounce of silver—worth around 60d. as bullion, in line with the crown's tariffed, nominal value and hence presenting no incentive for clipping or export. Barring any unexpected further increase in the market price of silver, the reset Mint price would remain attractive enough that silver bullion would start to be brought in for coining again, and the coin supply would recover. All in all, it was an eminently sensible and realistic solution, based on sound historical precedent. Unfortunately, it encountered an implacable opponent in the person of the most highly respected public intellectual of the age: the philosopher John Locke.

As the leading theorist of the new system of constitutional government, and the chief intellectual guardian of its principles, Locke was invited by Parliament to comment on Lowndes' report. He responded, in December 1695, with a scathing polemic against the proposal and the ideas underpinning it. In Locke's view, Lowndes' argument depended upon a fundamentally incorrect understanding of money and the monetary standard. Lowndes talked about money as if it were different from the coinage itself. This was, Locke warned, at best a confusion, and at worst a typical City smokescreen designed to conceal some no-good trickery. The reality was that money was nothing more nor less than silver itself. "Silver," Locke

John Locke: physician, philosopher, and, fatefully, monetary theorist.

began his response unequivocally, "is the Instrument and Measure of Commerce in all the Civilised and Trading Parts of the World" and "the Measure of Commerce by its quantity, which is the Measure also of its intrinsick value."[8] As for the monetary standard, that was therefore much less mysterious than Lowndes was making out. A "pound" was simply an objective reference to a definite weight of silver. The fact of the matter was that "[m]en in their Bargains contract not for denominations or sounds, but for the intrinsick value: which is the quantity of Silver by publick Authority warranted to be in pieces of such denominations."[9] Lowndes' fanciful justification that there was some metaphysical plane on which a coin would retain its "value" despite losing 20 per cent of its silver was therefore as bare-faced and ridiculous a deceit as claiming "to lengthen a foot by dividing it into Fifteen parts, instead of Twelve" while still "calling them Inches."[10]

Lowndes' conceptual errors meant that his policy recommendation was dangerously deluded, if not positively treasonous. His account had everything exactly the wrong way round. The idea that the pound could somehow simply lose or gain value, independently of the silver content of the coinage, was sheer nonsense. The monetary standard did not float around like an insubstantial ghost; it was a natural fact. A pound sterling was no more nor less than 3 ounces, 17 pennyweight, and 10 grains of sterling silver, and never could be.[11] It was categorically not the case that the pound had mysteriously lost 20 per cent of its so-called "value," and that the solution was to reduce the silver content of the coinage. What had really happened was that there had been an outbreak of mass criminal deviance unparalleled in English history. The coinage had been clipped, sheared, and melted down on a previously undreamt-of scale. Since money was just worth the silver it was made of, this amounted to nothing other than the robbing of unfortunate coin-users in broad daylight. The pound had lost its value because it had lost its silver content—not the other way round—and Lowndes' proposal actually to sanction this disaster by reducing the official silver content of the pound sterling was therefore nothing short of conniving with the coin-clippers. The only thing that Lowndes had got right, Locke concluded, was that a recoinage was in order. But it should not be one that meekly acquiesced in a criminal debasement of the national currency. It should be one that restored to the current, mutilated coin issues their full, official weight of silver.

To the horror of Lowndes and most of the financial establishment, Locke's prestige and political influence won the day. In January 1696 Parliament ordered that, from June, clipped and worn coins would no longer be legal tender. Holders were invited to use them before that date to pay their taxes or purchase government bonds. Clipped coin collected in this way would be re-minted at the official weight, with the Exchequer liable for any silver top-up that was required. Light coin not collected by June would be demonetised and accepted from July onwards only at the market value of its actual silver content. If one had taxes to pay, or could otherwise get one's light coins to the Mint in time, in other words, one's wealth would be safe. If one did not or could not, one would take a loss equal to the shortfall between the coins' bullion value and their now obsolete nominal value.[12]

The whole exercise was a debacle from start to finish. Before the deadline, shrewd profiteers toured the country buying up clipped coins from befuddled shopkeepers terrified that they would be marooned with devalued coins because they had no taxes due, and then bribed corrupt Revenue officials to pass the light coins through their accounts and pay out full-weight ones in return. When the deadline passed, those left holding light coin suffered a swingeing loss. £4.7 million worth of coin, for example, was collected by the Exchequer. This was found to contain sufficient silver for only £2.5 million when re-minted at the full, official weight. Galling as this was for Lowndes at the Treasury, at least he had understood these mechanics—and Parliament had assented to them, albeit against his advice. That could hardly be said of the thousands amongst the poorer and worse-informed classes who had failed to exchange their coins in time. There were riots in Yorkshire, Staffordshire, and Derbyshire, and in July the government was even forced into a partial concession, offering to exchange the silver in light coins for a special government bond issue at sixpence per ounce more than the Mint would pay.[13]

These abrupt redistributions of wealth between the well-informed and those left carrying the can were only the start of the mess. The operation took much of the existing coinage out of circulation. Fewer coins were then returned to circulation upon re-minting. And since the new, full-weight coins were still worth more as bullion abroad than as coins in England, many were immediately exported. There was an immediate and asphyxiating coin shortage. Deflation set in: prices fell, business confidence collapsed, and trade contracted. The growth and stability of the English economy was added to the litany of under-appreciated benefits sacrificed on the altar of Locke's monetary philosophy. The Tory pamphleteer Edmund Bohun hinted at the human cost of this self-inflicted economic trauma when he reported from Norwich in July 1696 that:

No trade is managed but by trust. Out tenants can pay no rent. Our corn factors can pay nothing for what they have had and will trade no more, so all is at a stand. And the people are discontented to the utmost; many self-murders happen in small families for want, and all things look very black . . .[14]

FROM THE PALM OF OLYMPIA
TO THE GOLD STANDARD

John Maynard Keynes once remarked of a book by his intellectual nemesis Friedrich von Hayek that it was "an extraordinary example of how, starting with a mistake, a remorseless logician can end in Bedlam."[15] Lowndes and other practical men of business had similar feelings about Locke's disastrous recoinage policy. They were baffled by the great philosopher's argument, which seemed to them to fly in the face of acknowledged facts—starting with the self-evident truth that there was no intrinsic link between the silver content of coins and their nominal value, nor had there ever been. The monetary standard had always been flexible: indeed, that was precisely what the perennial struggle between the sovereign and his mercantile subjects had always been about. The value of money depended not on the stuff that the coinage was made of but on the creditworthiness and authority of the sovereign who stood behind the tariff that specified the nominal value of the coin. "[M]oney has its *Value* from the authority of the government, which makes it currant, and fixes the price of each piece of Metal," explained the contemporary financier Nicholas Barbon; as a result "money will be of as good *Value*, to all intents and purposes, when it is coined lighter . . . [f]or the authority being the same, the value will be the same."[16] This understanding of the nature of money was derived not from any complicated philosophy or abstract economic theory, but from the plain fact that even much worn and clipped coins still circulated at their tariffed, nominal value. To Lowndes and his City colleagues such an understanding of money was as uncontroversial as it seemed innocuous.

Locke's ideas did, after all, depart substantially from the mainstream of ancient and medieval monetary thought. Amongst the ancients, the general understanding was that economic value was quite obviously a property of the social world, and that money was an archetypal social phenomenon. The very term that the Greeks used for money was *nomisma*, "something sanctioned by current or established usage or custom."[17] In the *Republic*, Plato called it "a symbol that exists for the sake of exchange."[18] His pupil Aristotle held the same view, arguing that "it exists not by nature but by convention, and it is in our power to change it and make it useless."[19] This understanding of money as a social institution, and of coins as symbols of social relations, had its roots in a Greek culture renowned in the ancient world for its "distinctive inclination . . . to symbolic substitution."[20] Herodotus reports that the Persians could scarcely believe their ears when they discovered that the prize for which the athletes at the Olympic Games competed was nothing but a crown of palm leaves.[21] Money was a technology built on the basis of the revolutionary notion of economic value—an invisible substance that was both everywhere and nowhere, and which had a presence in the physical world only via the symbolism of coinage. As such, the "nominalist" view that money has value only by convention came naturally to the Greeks.

In the hands of the medieval schoolmen, there even developed a more extreme position—the idea that the convention in question is a deliberate artefact of the sovereign. Monetary exchange, Aquinas said, "was invented by reason, not by nature."[22] It was the "one thing by which everything should be measured . . . not by its nature, but because it has been made a measure by men."[23] As such, it served at the pleasure of the relevant authorities, and "if the king or the community so decides, it loses its value."[24] This was an idea one step further on from the broad understanding of the ancients that value was a property of the social, rather than the physical, reality. It argued in addition that this social property was a creature of the sovereign political authority. It represented the origins of "chartalist" thought.[25]

Locke's conception of money was therefore unorthodox—all the more so, given that he was living in the middle of the financial revolution. Coinage, despite its continuing importance, was fast losing its franchise on the representation of monetary credit. The new financial technologies of banks and banking were taking over. The past two years had even witnessed the foundation of the Bank of England itself and the first emission of its paper currency. And this of course was what made Lowndes and the City men—the doyens of this new world—so incredulous of Locke's argument, and of its success.

But these worldly men were missing the point. The truth was that Locke was only too well aware of the political importance of the monetary standard. Indeed, the origins of Locke's monetary theory resided precisely in his political thought. For three decades, through all the turmoil of the Restoration, the Exclusion crisis, and the Glorious Revolution, Locke had laboured incessantly to demolish the intellectual credentials of absolute monarchy and secure the claims of political Liberalism and constitutional government. At the centre of his philosophical system was the axiom that the property rights of the individual exist by nature—not by dint of sovereign approval. This principle was the foundation on which Locke's defence of civil liberties against the infringement of absolute power had been constructed and the ideological basis of the new regime of constitutional government. There was no question that money—self-evidently one of the most important of all classes of property—could be exempted from this reasoning.

The theory of money had to be retrofitted to this, the new philosophy of politics. Lowndes' premise—and the teachings of the schoolmen—that the value of an Englishman's money was nothing but an artefact of the sovereign's authority implied that the private individual "lives merely at the Mercy of the Prince, is Rich or Poor, has a Competency, or is a Beggar, is a Free-man, or in Fetters at his Pleasure."[26] Locke's entire philosophical system had been devised to prove that the existence of such absolute and arbitrary power of the sovereign over his people was not just unjust, but unnatural. The power of his arguments had convinced the age, and with the Glorious Revolution and the Bill of Rights they had transformed the English constitution. Lowndes' proposal to debase the coinage

was a Trojan Horse that could not on any account be allowed to
enter the ideal city of political Liberalism.

The foundation of the Bank of England only made it all the
more urgent that these potentially seditious monetary doctrines be
stamped out. The financial revolution had already demonstrated as
never before that the bankers' mysterious art of credit creation was
a source of great political power. The Great Monetary Settlement
which the Bank represented was poised to deliver to that power the
Holy Grail of the sovereign's approval. It was a moment at once of
great promise and high danger. With the correct understanding of
money, the Bank might be the dream instrument for co-ordinating
the balance of power between the sovereign and his subjects—a
financial counterpart to the ingenious political concept of King-in-
Parliament. If, however, the delusions of men like Lowndes and Barbon were allowed to convince people that the value of money was
nothing but what the sovereign—and now his bankers—said it was,
financial and political tyranny surely lay in wait. The only way to
make the Great Monetary Settlement safe for constitutional government was by committing unswervingly to a fixed monetary standard,
impervious to interference from the sovereign, the bankers, or any-
body else. The possibility of a free monetary order had to be sacrificed to ensure that a free political order could be guaranteed victory.

As we saw earlier, the practical results of the new policy of a fixed
monetary standard were not immediately encouraging. And within
a generation, rigid adherence to the silver standard even resulted
in its euthanasia: so much silver disappeared from circulation that
gold came to displace it in practice as the precious-metal standard.
Yet the tight connection established by Locke between his monetary
doctrines and the fundamental principles of political Liberalism
meant that despite these initial hiccups they not only survived, but
prospered. That the pound sterling simply was a definite weight of
gold became the conventional view of money: thus it was by nature,
and thus it was Parliament's duty to confirm it to be. "Largely as a
result of Locke's influence," as the great historian of the English currency, Sir Albert Feavearyear, put it, "£3 17s 10½d an ounce came to

be regarded as a magic price for gold from which we ought never to stray and to which, if we did, we must always return."[27]

The question of how the Great Monetary Settlement would adjudicate the ancient dilemma of how to manage the standard was closed. Since money was just precious metal, nature demanded that its standard be fixed—just like the standard for length, or weight, or time. The monetary policies of the medieval sovereigns had been exercises in daylight robbery whereby they had stolen their subjects' property by abusing their uncivil authority. Money was precious metal: the standard simply a shorthand for weight. On these solid intellectual foundations, the Bank of England could be allowed to mint its new public–private money without danger of infringing the new constitution. Meanwhile, the new school of political economists could finally deliver what money's inventors, the ancient Greeks, had never managed: an intellectual framework that could explain and justify monetary society.

ENTER THE DRONE: THE APOTHEOSIS OF MONETARY SOCIETY

Eleven years after the foundation of the Bank of England and a year after Locke's death, Bernard Mandeville—a Dutch physician who had moved to London in 1699—published a satirical poem entitled *The Grumbling Hive, or, Knaves turn'd Honest.*[28] It described a "Spacious Hive well stock'd with Bees, That lived in Luxury and Ease" and explained that the root of its prosperity was nothing other than the venal appetites of its inhabitants. The lawyers drum up disputes in order to generate work; government officials take bribes; doctors look for fees rather than their patients' well-being; and soldiers fight for money and titles rather than love of King and Country; but the result is a vigorous and prosperous community. Then disaster strikes: the bees get it into their heads that they should convert to the path of virtue. Greed, ambition, and dishonesty are denounced. The politicians and generals are upbraided for being slaves to self-interest rather than servants of patriotism. And the ironic result of this conversion is that everything stops working: the economy deflates, the population shrinks, and the bees are reduced to the primitive condition of living in a hollow tree. The moral of the poem is that "Fools only Strive, To Make a Great an Honest Hive. To Enjoy the World's Conveniencies . . . Fraud, Luxury, and Pride must live, Whilst we the Benefits receive."

Mandeville's doggerel was intended to rebut Tory criticism of the ongoing military campaigns on the Continent, and in particular of its chief protagonist, John Churchill, the Duke of Marlborough. The Tories disliked the fact that Marlborough and his Whig supporters had grown rich and powerful as a result of the long war. They had long suspected that the new system of public finance—and especially its most prominent innovation, the Bank of England—was little more than a corrupt machine concocted by the Whig money interest and its cronies like Marlborough for personal gain. With his parable of the libidinous bees, Mandeville sought to show that venality in politics, business, and war were the price of an economy wealthy enough and a polity powerful enough to confront its enemies. The age of chivalry, he warned, was long gone. Men like Marlborough would not fight for glory alone—and it was important to have men like Marlborough on your side rather than the other. The puritanical alternative for which the Duke's critics argued would leave England enfeebled, poor, and vulnerable to attack.

Mandeville quickly realised, however, that his throwaway polemic contained the seed of a more profound and timeless idea. The particular case of the rapacious Marlborough could be generalised. Not just some, but all actions which are superficially wicked are, perversely, actually for the best. Mandeville republished his poem in 1714 in an expanded edition. The title of this new version—*The Fable of the Bees, or, Private Vices, Publick Benefits*—went straight to the paradoxical point. The very existence of human community relies on "neither the Friendly Qualities and kind Affections that are natural to Man, nor the real Virtues he is capable of acquiring by Reason and Self-Denial." Instead, it depends upon "what we call Evil in this World, Moral as well as Natural." It is to the encouragement of Evil that we owe "the true Origin of all Arts and Sciences, and . . . the Moment Evil ceases, the Society must be spoiled, if not totally dissolved."[29] The best—indeed, the only—way of achieving an optimal outcome at the level of the community as a whole is by encouraging the pursuit of ambition, avarice, and raw self-interest at the level of the individual. The satirical poet and partisan had become a serious political economist.

Mandeville's thesis provoked outrage: philosophers and divines rushed to refute his abominable proposition and his poems and essays were proscribed. But as the financial revolution given wing by the foundation of the Bank gained momentum, it became clear that Mandeville's paradoxical argument had captured the spirit of the age. Money was everywhere. Every year, new companies were founded. Even country ladies talked about nothing but stock-jobbing. The new world being forged by this corporate and financial revolution clamoured to be explained and justified—and Mandeville's outrageous hypothesis appeared to do both at once. When it was taken up by one of the Enlightenment's morning stars, the Scotsman Adam Smith, it became the basis of a fully fledged theory of monetary society that has survived to this day.

In his *Inquiry into the Nature and Causes of the Wealth of Nations*, Adam Smith formulated the first systematic theory linking individual behaviour with the organisation of the economy, and presented the first cogent synthesis of earlier thinkers' ideas of how the financial revolution had transformed traditional society. The growth of commerce and money, he argued, had "generally introduced order and good government, and with them, the liberty and security of individuals."[30] It was Smith who recognised the historical irony in the accumulation and paying-out of this political dividend. The feudal lords who had been the prime beneficiaries of traditional society had been bewitched by the magic of money. Their love of luxury had made them encourage the monetisation of their feudal rents: "thus, for the gratification of the most childish, the meanest and the most sordid of all vanities, they gradually bartered their whole power and authority."[31]

Smith's metaphor for Mandeville's paradoxical process—the

"invisible hand" which ensures that "by pursuing his own interest [the individual] frequently promotes that of the society more effectually than when he really intends to promote it"—is so famous that it has long ago taken on a life of its own.[32] Smith also emphasised that this pleasing outcome is a feature not so much of the individual's decisions, as of the system itself: the individual "generally, indeed, neither intends to promote the publick interest, nor knows how much he is promoting it."[33] Smith articulated a vision of society in which economic value had become the measure of all things, and static traditional social relations were being replaced by dynamic monetary ones. It was a vision of monetary society as an objective system which would tend towards an equilibrium that was both economic and political. For once traditional society had been thrown over, once "the tenants in this manner [were] independent, and the retainers dismissed . . . a regular government was established in the country as well as the city, nobody having sufficient power to disturb its operations in the one any more than in the other."[34] Smith had achieved something unprecedented in the history of monetary thought: a thoroughgoing justification of monetary society in both economic and political terms.

It was an historic accommodation on the intellectual and moral planes to match the Great Monetary Settlement on the practical level. The founders of the Bank of England believed that their marriage of private banking and sovereign money had unleashed the greatest force for economic and social progress in history. The economists had now proved that they were right. And the father of political Liberalism himself had decreed that—so long as one kept to the correct understanding of money, and did not stray from the immutable, natural standard of economic value that it entailed—it was all perfectly consistent with the new gospel of constitutional government. Money had achieved its apotheosis.

There was, however, a problem.

9 Money Through the Looking-Glass

THE ACHILLES' HEEL OF MONETARY SOCIETY
That problem was debt—and specifically, its tendency to accumulate
to unsustainable levels. Today, we are only too aware of the vulnerability of monetary society to what is euphemistically known as
"financial instability." But the global financial crisis that began in
2007 is just the last of a long list within recent memory—from
international sovereign debt crises like the Argentinian default of
2002 and the Russian default of 1998, to domestic financial crises
such as the collapse of the boom in U.S. technology stocks in March
2000, the U.S. Savings and Loans crisis of the early 1990s, or the
October 1987 stock-market crash in the U.K. But the unusual persistence of the current crisis has provoked a deeper interest amongst
economists in the longer-term incidence of debt crises. Readers
rushed to consult the great financial historian, Charles Kindleberger.[1]
To learn of his discovery that "financial crises have tended to appear
at roughly ten-year intervals for the last 400 years or so" was either
disturbing or comforting, depending on one's perspective.[2] Within
a couple of years, however, the economists Carmen Reinhart and
Kenneth Rogoff had published an even more comprehensive investigation into the history of financial crises. Its ominous subtitle
warned the reader to expect not just four but "Eight Centuries of

Financial Folly."³ And as Tactitus' account of the credit crunch under
the Emperor Tiberius shows, monetary society has been prone to
the problem of growing indebtedness ending in a crisis of solvency
for much longer even than that.

The reason is that this instability is intrinsic to money's miraculous promise to combine security and freedom. The distinctive claim
of money was that it could combine social stability and social mobility
in a way that traditional society, with its immutable social structure,
never could. It was this promise that made it so revolutionary and so
irresistible an invention. And to be sure, the spread of money proved
again and again to be extraordinarily effective at licensing ambition
and innovation where previously society and the economy had been
hidebound by tradition. Money had indeed been the agent of vigorous and pervasive social change on an undreamt-of scale—to say
nothing of the political revolution that its chief accomplice, banking,
had fomented. Not without reason did two well-known sceptics of
its benefits, Karl Marx and Friedrich Engels, complain of the highly
developed monetary society of the mid-nineteenth century that
"[a]ll fixed, fast-frozen relations, with their train of ancient and venerable prejudices and opinions, are swept away, all new-formed ones
become antiquated before they can ossify. All that is solid melts into
air, all that is holy is profaned."⁴

The trouble was that it had never been quite as simple as the
sceptics claimed. Social fluidity was only one half of the bargain.
The other half was the paradoxical promise of continued stability.
Monetary society did not promise anarchy—that would never have
caught on. Instead it promised a rule for anarchy: both mobility and
stability, both freedom and certainty. And the feature of money that
delivered this second part of its promise was the fundamental axiom
of the fixed nominal value of credit and debt. Wherever social obligations were destroyed, financial obligations—debts—were heaped
up in their place. And the whole point of debts was that unlike the
obsolete social obligations they had just replaced they were not going
to be "swept away." Smith and his school had constructed a theory
that purported to show how both parts of money's promise could

hold—how objective laws governing monetary society would so choreograph things that the fixed financial obligations would not themselves fall foul of money's indefatigable promotion of social change. But the reality of monetary society is—and has always been—strikingly at odds with this idea.

This failure of the economists' new framework to engage with the central problem of monetary society was not just a cosmetic shortcoming. As we have rediscovered in the aftermath of the global financial crisis, the unsustainable accumulation of debt can present not just incidental, but existential, challenges to monetary society. Money's intrinsic tendency to generate instability, in other words, is a danger not only to the victims of crashes and recessions—but ultimately to money itself. When a financial crisis results in half the youth population being out of work, or in civil servants facing the sack to free up funds to pay foreign bondholders, then conventional remedies available within the current economic system can begin to look unappealing. Central bankers and finance ministers work on the assumption that monetary society itself works fine. Its rules must be respected, they counsel, and any injustices that result should be remedied by more progressive taxation or transfusions from wealthy benefactors abroad. But the mood of those at the sharp end of the debt crisis is less business-as-usual. Why respect the rules of the system, ask the Occupy protestors in New York and the *indignados* in Madrid, if the system consistently generates crises?

The idea that, left unchecked, monetary society's tendency to generate unsustainable debt burdens is its own worst enemy is not new. In June 1919, John Maynard Keynes resigned from the British delegation to the Versailles peace negotiations. The Allied powers, hell-bent on extracting massive recompense from the defeated Germans, had imposed grievous reparations payments on them. Only thus, they had argued, would the lessons of aggression be learned and future peace assured. Keynes realised that Germany's new financial obligations were unrealistic, however—and that attempting to enforce them would end in disaster. In *The Economic Consequences of the Peace*—the sensational exposé of the negotiations that he published in December 1919—he implored the Allies to find a way to reduce the debts they had rashly imposed. His plea was refused as dangerous nonsense: an immature attempt to play fast and loose with the rules of international finance that were the most basic guarantors of stability and peace. But his prognosis proved sound. Unable to revive its crippled economy or to extract sufficient revenues as a result, and racked by civil strife, Germany drifted towards total economic collapse—including the most extreme hyperinflation ever recorded. In 1923, the default that Keynes had publicly predicted arrived, and the Allies were forced to rewrite the reparations settlement.

By then, Keynes was ready with a piercing analysis of the more general lessons of this policy error. The spectre of Versailles haunted his *Tract on Monetary Reform*, published that year. It is not just craven politicians at peace negotiations who create unsustainable debts, he wrote—the problem is intrinsic to monetary society: "The powers of uninterrupted usury are great. If the accretions of vested interest were to grow without mitigation for many generations, half the population would be no better than slaves to the other half."[5] So those who set up respect for contract as an idol while forgetting the higher law that all financial contracts must be fair to be sustainable—the victors at Versailles, the followers of Locke—will ultimately be the authors of their own frustration. "[S]uch persons," wrote Keynes, "by overlooking one of the greatest of all social principles, namely the fundamental distinction between the right of the individual to repudiate contract and the right of the State to control vested interest, are the worst enemies of what they seek to preserve. For nothing can preserve the integrity of contract between individuals except a discretionary authority in the State to revise what has become intolerable."[6] Locke's monetary doctrines lead, in other words, to a profound irony. Not only is respect for contract alone insufficient for the survival and prosperity of monetary society, but "[t]he absolutists of contract . . . are the real parents of revolution."[7]

Keynes was right. The true nature both of debt crises and of the ways that they can be resolved reveals a fundamental flaw in the reasoning of Smith and his school. Money promises to organise society in a manner that combines freedom and stability. This it will achieve first by transforming social obligations—traditional rights and duties that are fundamentally incommensurable with one another—into financial obligations—assets and liabilities all measured in the same units of abstract economic value; and then by making these financial obligations liquid—allowing them to be transferred from one person to another. The trouble is that the world is an uncertain place. Liquidity evaporates, solvency is reassessed: the network of indebtedness that a moment ago was sustainable is suddenly not. The network must adapt—but there's the rub. Money has created interests vested in the network as it stands. What happens next is the key question; one to which Smith and his school offered no answer.

How was it that the new discipline of economics managed to miss the problem of debt and the financial instability it causes? Why did it not notify the grateful new inhabitants of the ideal city of these flaws in its foundations? Given subsequent financial history, it was a rather dramatic oversight. One obvious answer has enjoyed much popularity through the ages: that monetary thought, and indeed economics more broadly, is simply a corrupt discipline. On this view, Nicolas Oresme set the tone: orthodox economists are in the pay of vested interests, and their allegedly objective theories are little more than special pleading for the moneyed classes. The title of U.S. director Charles Ferguson's Oscar-winning documentary on the role of economics in the global financial crisis sums it up. Modern finance theorists, Ferguson's film argues, were not the impartial scientists they made themselves out to be. They were just cheerleaders for the banking lobby, handsomely remunerated to produce an elaborate intellectual justification for an immoral commercial enterprise. The debt crisis was an *Inside Job*.

But there is another possibility—one which is, in the end, even more alarming. What if the real reason for the chronic failure of economics to engage with the reality of monetary society is not due to vested interests? What if it is the consequence of a mistake on the level of ideas? What if, in other words, no warning of the structural failings of monetary society was ever issued because the theorists honestly believed that there were no problems to report? The real culprit for the gargantuan blind spot in the theory of Smith and his school is not a set of vested interests, but an idea—none other than the conventional understanding of money promulgated by John Locke.

MONEY THROUGH THE LOOKING-GLASS

The problem was that John Locke's well-intentioned effort to make money safe for constitutional government came with a significant hidden cost. As the great recoinage debate had revealed, Locke's understanding of money represented a complete reversal of perspective from the vantage point occupied by Lowndes and his practitioner friends. It was obvious to them that the pound was just an arbitrary standard of economic value. It had lost value against silver—there had been inflation, and the price of silver had risen. The coinage had lost its silver content because the pound had lost value. Locke, by contrast, thought this was getting it completely the wrong way round. A pound was nothing but a definite weight of silver bullion. The pound had lost value because the coinage had lost its silver. The old understanding had been that money is credit, and coinage is just a physical representation of that credit. The new understanding was that money is coinage, and that credit is just a representation of that coinage. Lowndes and his ilk had believed that the Earth went round the Sun. Locke had explained that the Sun in fact revolves around the Earth.

The consequences of looking at the universe from standing on the Sun turned out to be dramatic. It was as if money had gone, with Alice, *Through the Looking-Glass*, to a world in which what had for centuries been the central dilemmas of money were now nowhere to be seen. To begin with, there was the question of what was the appropriate scope of monetary society, and how extensive a role its central concept of economic value should play in co-ordinating social life. This was a dilemma, as we saw, that had troubled philosophers since the time of money's invention by the Greeks. In the Looking-Glass world of the conventional understanding of money, however, things are different. Economic value

Through the Looking-Glass: where the conventional
view of money leads . . .

is just a property of the natural world, like length, or weight, or
volume. One might just as well complain that it is unethical to
measure the distance between Pyongyang and Seoul as start asking whether it's right to put a price on human life.

Then there was the question of the monetary standard. For centuries, this had been the subject of the most heated political contention. It was the fulcrum on which the scales weighing the competing
claims of the sovereign and his subjects were balanced, and where
that fulcrum should sit was one of the quintessential questions of
political justice. In the Looking-Glass world of Locke, however,
money was a thing, value was a natural property, and the monetary
standard was therefore an objective fact. The fulcrum of the scales
had to be fixed—otherwise, how could it generate consistent mea-
surements? In the old world, respect for contract and for the monetary standard had been understood to be operational principles;

but the morality of breaching contract or the monetary standard by debt restructuring, devaluation, or inflation was understood to be a quintessentially political question. In the Looking-Glass world of Locke's understanding of money, however, respect for contract and for the monetary standard became a matter not of fairness, but of accuracy.

The truth, of course, is that this Looking-Glass world—like the one that Alice visited—is just a dream. Far from being a natural property of the physical world, there was a time, as we have seen, when the concept of economic value simply didn't exist—because money had not yet been invented. And far from there being any objectively true standard against which economic value must necessarily be measured, the choice of monetary standard is always a political one—because the standard itself represents nothing but a decision as to what is a fair distribution of wealth, income, and the risks of economic uncertainty. As a result, the triumph of Locke's understanding of money led not to a new age of objectivity in economic affairs but, perversely, to just the opposite. It opened the way to the dominance of particular, quite arbitrary, prejudices—and even worse, it covered their tracks with a veil of apparent scientific objectivity.

For the new understanding did not mean that there was no ethical debate to be had about money; not a bit of it. It was just that the ethics of money now meant something completely different. The old dilemmas disappeared from view. If money was a thing and value a physical property, to discuss either in ethical terms no longer even made sense: to call the monetary standard unjust made about as much sense as calling the weather unfair. But in their place, the Liberal shibboleths of the free pursuit of self-interest and respect for contract became the overriding focus of moralising attention. Morality in monetary society now meant whether or not you submitted unquestioningly to the philosophy of laissez-faire, and whether or not you paid your debts. Money's commandments, like those of the law, had to be obeyed: it was disobedience that constituted unethical behaviour. Perhaps *Through the Looking-Glass* is too light-hearted a literary analogy. Perhaps it would be fairer to say that money had been transported to the Prague of Franz Kafka's *The Trial*, or the Paris of

Anatole France's *The Red Lily*, in which the cynic Choulette applauds "[t]he majestic equality of the laws, which forbid the rich and the poor alike to sleep under the bridges, to beg in the streets, and to steal their bread."[8]

It is here, in the ascendancy of Locke's understanding of money, that the curious inability of orthodox economic thought to engage with the social and political roots of the instability of monetary society has its roots. The highest hidden cost of Locke's mission to make money safe for democracy was what it implied not for the topics that remained within the province of economics, but for those which it left out. It was the licence that his concepts of money and economic value provided to the economists—indeed, the imperative it urged on them—to treat respect for the unimpeded action of the market as the moral duty of every rational person that was in the end its most baleful consequence.

The immediate aftermath of the great recoinage itself served ominous notice of the human tragedies that this self-inflicted ethical blind spot could result in. Yet it was a mere shadow of catastrophes to come. The more widespread that belief in the economists' story of monetary society's miraculous ability to regulate itself became, the greater became the capacity for moral disaster when policy-makers succumbed to the simplistic charms of its Looking-Glass world. The story of one of the most shameful episodes in the history of economic policy-making testifies to quite how bad things could get.

THE INVISIBLE HAND IN ACTION

In 1845, Ireland had been a full constituent nation of the United Kingdom for more than four decades, and an accessory of the British economy and polity, if often by force, for several centuries before that. Yet in its religion, politics, and language, Ireland retained a quite distinct culture from its neighbour: economically and socially speaking, it was almost of another era. By the early nineteenth century, Britain was the greatest manufacturing economy in the world, while Ireland was one of the most backward in Europe. The most telling evidence of its poverty was the near-total reliance of the rural economy and population on a single crop: the potato. So when the first reports of a disastrous failure of the Irish potato crop began to emerge in September 1845, they were brought at once to the attention of the government in Westminster.

The government's initial response was quick. A scientific fact-finding mission was dispatched, the gravity of the situation was ascertained, and a Relief Commission established. At its head was Sir Randolph Routh, who had been the senior logistics officer at Waterloo. Meanwhile, the mastermind of government policy was to be the young Assistant Secretary at the Treasury, Charles Edward Trevelyan. Trevelyan was a prodigy—one of the most brilliant of the new breed of modernising progressives then beginning to dominate the British civil service. With a team combining such unimpeachably noble principles and such long practical experience in charge, Ireland was surely in the safest possible hands.

Those praying for a merciful policy from Trevelyan's Treasury should, however, have been forewarned by the very first sentence of an editorial shot across his bows from *The Economist* magazine in late November 1845. It opened with a chilling warning: "[c]harity is the national error of Englishmen."[9] There was no question that the impending Irish famine was an economic disaster and a human tragedy. But simply sending aid was absolutely the wrong way to help. It would violate two central principles of economic theory. The first was the need to avoid moral hazard. Send aid, and one might alleviate the immediate problem—but at the cost of reducing the Irish to a state of permanent dependency. The second was the hallowed principle of non-intervention in the operation of the market. Adam Smith had proved that it was allowing private self-interest to operate as freely as possible that most efficiently achieves the social good. For the government to interfere with the operation of the market in solving the crisis would therefore be a foolish error.

A second editorial in *The Economist*, published in March 1846, captured the consensus which dominated the views of the British Establishment. Proactive intervention by the government, the editors warned, would be futile: "To feed the Irish, to attempt which it is now practically driven, . . . is for the legislature physically impossible."[10] To attempt it therefore risked jeopardising the authority of government: it would "only damage the interfering, unthinking lawmaker . . . arms against him all the unsatisfied desires of the people, and must in the end destroy his power."[11] Ultimately, it would do more harm than good: "The legislature therefore cannot effectively help Ireland . . . [I]t can no more relieve the wants of the Irish, than a man can cure *delirium tremens* by swallowing daily increasing quantities of ardent spirits."[12] Above all, to deny these self-evident truths was proof not of an alternative political or moral disposition—but of wilful ignorance of objective, scientific fact. Appealing to the British people to send assistance to Ireland, the editors of *The Economist* wrote, "appears like calling on us to unlearn the first rules of arithmetic, and do our sums by the assertion that two and two make five."[13] Within seventy years of its publication, Adam Smith's theory of monetary society had attained the status of scientific—indeed, mathematical—truth.

Since virtually every official and politician dealing with Ireland was a devoted acolyte of these doctrines, they dictated British policy. Sir Robert Peel managed to have Parliament authorise a lone consignment of £100,000-worth of American maize before his government collapsed and with it any further hope of significant relief. The consequences of this inaction were catastrophic. Throughout the winter of 1845 and the spring of 1846 there was famine on a scale unprecedented in Ireland's history. By the summer of 1846 large bands of the poor were to be found roaming the countryside, living off weeds and nettles. The country was close to a breakdown of civil order: military rule was installed in all but name. Yet worse was to come. In August, to universal horror, the potato crop failed for a second year. None of this was secret; all of it was widely and vividly reported—on 2 September, a leader-writer in *The Times* of London described the situation simply but clearly as "total annihilation."[14]

Incredibly, the policy debate in London continued at the level of abstract principles. Smith and his followers had proved that interference with the natural operation of monetary society can only be bad: it was essential not to heed the siren song of those calling for government intervention. "We have no knowledge of any theoretical or scientific deduction whatever, so amply confirmed as this of Smith," thundered the editors of *The Economist* on 2 January 1847. Morality had nothing to do with it: it would be a travesty of reason itself if the government were to "turn back to the old discredited principles of interference, and adopt practices the most unscientific and the most decried."[15] This editorial was published less than a fortnight after the following account of conditions in the district of Skibbereen had been submitted in desperation by Nicholas Cummins, a magistrate of Cork, to the Duke of Wellington, and published in *The Times*:

> My Lord Duke, Without apology or preface, I presume so far to trespass on your Grace as to state to you, and by the use of your illustrious name, to present to the British public the following statement of what I have myself seen within the last three days . . . I was surprised to find the wretched hamlet apparently deserted. I entered some of the hovels to ascertain the cause, and the scenes which presented themselves were such as no tongue or pen can convey the slightest idea of. In the first, six famished and ghastly skeletons, to all appearances dead, were huddled in a corner on some filthy straw. I approached with horror, and found by a low moaning that they were still alive—they were in fever, four children, a woman, and what had once been a man. It is impossible to go through the detail . . . The same morning the police opened a house on the adjoining lands, which was observed shut for many days, and two frozen corpses were found, lying on the mud floor, half devoured by rats . . . A mother, herself in a fever, was seen the same day to drag out the corpse of her child, a girl about twelve, perfectly naked, and leave it half covered with stones. In another house, within 500 yards of the cavalry station at Skibbereen, the dispensary doctor found seven wretches lying unable to move, under the same cloak. One had been dead many hours, but the others were unable to move either themselves or the corpse.[16]

There could be no more searing indictment of a mistaken policy and of the terrible intellectual error that had led sensible and humane people to persevere with it unquestioningly. And unlikely as it may at first seem, it is from Locke's revolution in monetary thinking that the awful failings of economic thought that were on display in this shameful episode originated. It was only once money had gone, with Locke's assistance, through the Looking-Glass, that the traditional ethical dilemmas over monetary society had magically disappeared. Foremost amongst these was the question of the extent to which money should really be the co-ordinating mechanism for social life. This question was rendered obsolete by the new view of money as a thing—a harmless fact of nature. The new discipline of economics boldly claimed to reduce what had once seemed vital questions of moral and political justice to the mechanical application of objective scientific truths. The complicity of this new worldview in ethical disaster was not lost on all contemporary observers. It was Nassau Senior—the Drummond Professor of Political Economy at Oxford and one of the government's chief advisers on Irish economic policy—whom Benjamin Jowett, the great Master of Balliol College, Oxford, had in mind when he said years later: "I have always felt a certain horror of political economists since I heard one of them say that he feared the famine of 1848 in Ireland would not kill more than a million people, and that would scarcely be enough to do much good."[17]

Fortunately, the conventional view of money is not the only one. There is, as we saw earlier, another tradition in monetary thought that never stepped through the looking-glass—a tradition that never flinched from interrogating the ethical consequences of the concept of universal economic value and the political and economic realities implied by the choice of the monetary standard. And it is a tradition that started right back when money was first invented, with the Greeks.

10 Strategies of the Sceptics

The brilliantly counter-intuitive notion that the pursuit of money
for its own sake could actually be good was an idea alien to the
Greeks. For them, money was still new and strange. They understood
it quite accurately as a competing ideology of social organisation,
and subjected it to critical evaluation. Their attention focused on
exactly that aspect which the advent of the conventional understanding of money some two thousand years later was to brush under
the carpet: money's central idea, the revolutionary notion of universal economic value. Their experience of this concept as a novel
idea for the organisation of social life allowed them to discriminate
its good and bad effects with a clarity not available to the jaded eyes
of thinkers who have lived with monetary society for centuries.
Their misgivings were brilliantly summarised in one of the Greeks'
most enduring and popular stories: the myth of Midas.

Midas was the king of Phrygia, and the proprietor, it was said,
of a beautiful garden in which, without cultivation, "roses grew
of themselves, each bearing sixty blossoms and of surpassing fra-
grance."[1] One day, Midas found the satyr Silenus, who had become
detached from the retinue of the god Dionysus, gambolling amongst

these lovely roses.[2] Midas captured the nature deity, and forced him to reveal his ancient wisdom. What, he asked, is the best that man can attain to? The satyr at once recognised him for what he was—a shallow and greedy despot. So as satyrs are wont to do, he poked fun at Midas' ephemeral outlook and responded with the disappointingly philosophical answer that the best thing for a man is never to have been born; and the second best, to die as soon as possible. This was hardly what Midas had in mind, of course, and he made no secret of it. "Well, then," replied Silenus, "have it your own way. If you let me go, I shall grant you one wish—and if you are so wise, you can choose whatever it is that you think is the best thing of all!" Believing, naturally, that wealth is the best thing a man can have, Midas chose that everything he touched should turn to gold.

The mischievous god granted his wish, and at first Midas was delighted. He broke off a twig, and it turned to gold! He picked up a clod: it turned to gold too! He picked an apple—and all at once it became as golden as the famous apples of the Hesperides! So intoxicated was the avaricious old king with his amazing new power that "his mind could scarcely grasp its own hopes, dreaming of all things turned to gold."[3] He ordered up a splendid banquet to celebrate his good fortune. But here, things started to go wrong. He grasped a crust of bread to eat—but it turned to solid gold. He mixed wine to drink—but as it passed his lips, it turned to molten gold. In later versions of the myth, Midas even made the fatal mistake of kissing his dear daughter—and turning her to cold and inert gold. Cursing his foolish error, "rich and yet wretched, he sought to flee his wealth, and hated what he but now had prayed for."[4] He begged the gods to take back their terrible gift—and, luckily for him, Dionysus took pity on him. He instructed Midas to go to the source of the River Pactolus in Lydia, and plunge his head and body into the water to wash away his powers. This Midas did, and so lost his now-detested gift. In doing so he transferred it to the river itself, which thereby became the source of the gold and silver alloy from which the earliest coins were made—the source, in other words, of the questionable invention of coined money for the rest of mankind.

The central theme of this myth is money's intrinsic tendency to reduce everything to a single dimension by weighing it in the balance of universal economic value. Like the money he craves, Midas' touch reduces the enormous variety of life and nature—the twig, the apple, his bread, his wine, even his fellow human beings and his family—to a single, lifeless substance. Where in nature there is variety of substance—and in traditional society, many dimensions of social worth—monetary society imposes an artificial monotony. The inexorable logic of money, the Greeks realised, was to put a price on everything, and to make everyone think of everything first and foremost in terms of a single dimension. By itself, a universally applicable concept of economic value was in one sense exhilarating, just as it is today. A single metric that can serve as the criterion for any decision does wonders for the organisation of a complex economy. But for the Greeks it was also a source of unease. Could it really be right for money to solve not only the humdrum problem of how many chickens to bring to market, but also the social dilemma of whom one's daughter should marry—let alone the cosmic question of whether one was living in accordance with the divine order of the universe? Aristophanes tried the traditional method of disarming discomfort with comedy when he had the old hand Heracles explain to Dionysus that these days crossing the River Styx to enter Hades required payment up front, in cash.[5] Even in the Underworld, money had become the organising power.

The myth of Midas is less ambiguous, however. The universal application of the new concept of economic value brings with it a major problem: the lack of any intrinsic limit to consumption, accumulation, and the quest for status. Midas did not just want some gold. He wanted everything he touched to turn to gold, because only then could he be sure that come what might he would be richer than anyone else: the best that a man can attain in life. Traditional society had intrinsic limits—limits defined by the immutable social obligations owed by peasants to chieftains, chieftains to priests, and so on. Monetary society, the Greeks feared, had none. There is no intrinsic limit to the accumulation of wealth; and since status in monetary society is by its nature relative, not absolute, monetary society constantly risks degenerating into an unending one-upmanship. "No one ever gets their fill of you," says Aristophanes' hero Chremylus to the god Wealth: "There can be too much of everything else"—from an abstract virtue like manliness to something as earthily concrete as humble lentil soup—"but no one ever gets his fill of you. If someone gets his hands on thirteen talents, he hankers all the more to get sixteen; and if he achieves that, he wants forty, or else he says life isn't worth living."[6] And what is even worse, the Greeks feared, the lack of a limit to the imperative to get money may lead to a lack of limits to what people will do to get it. In this respect, Midas was a special case—opportunity fell into his lap. But in the real world, where passing satyrs do not grant wishes, the incentives to try anything to get unlimited wealth would surely, the Greeks feared, be unlimited as well.

The impact of excessive accumulation, consumption, and competition for status remains a widespread concern today. Contemporary thinkers identify a number of potential culprits. "Today, the logic of buying and selling no longer applies to material goods alone but increasingly governs the whole of life," laments the American philosopher Michael Sandel in his meditation on *What Money Can't Buy*: "[i]t is time to ask whether we want to live this way."[7] Markets, in other words, are the problem—and we must consciously decide the parts they should and should not reach. *How Much Is Enough?* ask the British thinkers Robert and Edward Skidelsky in the title of their recent book, before arguing that only a substantive ethical conception of what a good life consists of can answer that eternal question; hoping that the market mechanism will impose limits on itself is a pipe dream.[8] What we need is to be specific about what we think is good and bad, and then have the moral fibre to stick to our judgement. Neuroscientists, and the economists who follow their research, explain that both Sandel's and the Skidelskys' questions are futile. Markets and ethics are froth. Competition for status is hard-wired into the human brain—a physical trait evolved to give us an edge in a world where the best mates and the most food mean the survival of one's genes. Evolution is the problem—and there is hardly much point in worrying about that.[9]

The Greek suspicion of the lack of limits to acquisitiveness, to ambition, and to what people will do to fulfil them, shows that this debate is not modern at all. And the Greeks' greater proximity to the invention of money gave them a different perspective on it. It is neither markets, morals, nor man himself that is the problem: it is money. It is the particular set of ideas and conventions that make up the most precocious social technology ever invented that is the source of this lack of limits. Life in monetary society, the Greeks understood, inextricably involves a commitment to the idea of universal economic value, to conventions of calculating that value, and to the possibility of its decentralised transfer from one person to another. It is precisely these ideas which distinguish it from earlier ways of organising social and economic life. And once these ideas have been admitted, the rest follows automatically. Since there is no intrinsic limit to economic value, there is no fixed point of reference in monetary society. It is from this set of ideas that the constant imperialism of markets, the ceaseless carousel of status competition, and the insatiability of the desire for money flow.

From this prognosis of the inevitable consequences of allowing money free rein flowed the Greeks' conclusion that far from being a viable—even an ideal—mode of organising society, money was in fact self-contradictory. Aristotle adduced the story of Midas as the mythical expression of nominalism: the fact that economic value is a social contrivance rather than a natural property. Monetary wealth, he argued, differs from an abundance of real, useful, physical things like food or firewood precisely in this respect: it only has value—indeed, it can only exist—in society. Take away its social context and one would quickly discover that money is wealth "of such a kind that a man may be well supplied with it and yet die of hunger, like the famous Midas in the legend."[10] But the myth is also a cautionary tale. Money and its value rely on other people: but it is precisely Midas' ability to turn everything to gold—the universal application of the idea of economic value—which ends up isolating him from everyone else. So there is a paradox at the heart of money. It is a social technology which depends on other people. Yet it is a social technology which isolates us from other people, by transforming the rich and varied ecology of human relationships into the mechanical and monotonous clockwork of financial relationships.

The tragedies of Aeschylus, Sophocles, and Euripides—which form the pinnacle of classical Greek art and thought—are endlessly absorbed with exposing the flaws in this extravagant undertaking. Time and again, the tragedians present protagonists who yearn for, and achieve, money and power—but at the cost of isolation from their community and their family. On some of the most terrible occasions, the connection to money's inexorable logic is made explicit. When, in Aeschylus' treatment of the famous myth of the *Seven Against Thebes*, the protagonist Eteocles finally resolves to go out and fight his own brother for their inheritance, the chorus beg him not to. It will be, they warn, a duel to the death between flesh and blood—"a sin against the natural order that will never fade"—and all for the sake of money.[11] "Cast out the root of this evil desire!" they plead.[12] But Eteocles explains he cannot help himself. The curse of his father, he says, is whispering in his ear a piece of advice—advice that captures everything that the Greeks most feared about monetary society: "profit first, the natural order afterwards."[13]

Money's ability to deliver personal freedom—from traditional social obligations, even from family obligations—was an exhilarating prospect. The Greeks knew that as well as anyone today who has had to endure the wrong end of the class system or the miseries of a stifling family hierarchy. Its promise to do so without destroying the stability and security created by these ancient institutions of political and personal security sounds almost too good to be true. And in the end, as the self-destructive heroes of the classical tragedians and the foolish Midas alone amidst all his gold testify, it is.

THE SPARTAN SOLUTION

In ancient Greece, this scepticism about money was not just idle philosophising: it was the stuff of live political debate. In the immediate aftermath of money's invention, the contrast between monetary and traditional society was a stark one. Where money's negative social and political consequences were felt to outweigh the positive ones, dissatisfaction spilled out from the symposium and the academy to the council chamber and the battleground. And although it was the exquisitely cultured artists and thinkers of Athens who articulated the most sophisticated critique of monetary society, the most visceral and negative practical reaction came from Athens' great ideological opponent, Sparta. In one sense, this was no surprise: Sparta was a martial, totalitarian state, clearly made of sterner stuff than the self-proclaimed "school of Greece."[14] Indeed, to some contemporaries Sparta's constitution seemed dangerously fanatical. This was a state, after all, in which special officials exterminated babies deemed insufficiently strong to cope with Sparta's militaristic ethos, and then subjected the survivors to strict indoctrination from the age of seven. Children were separated from their families from the age of twelve and the institution of the family was actively suppressed in favour of communal living in military-style messes and unquestioning obedience to the state for both men and women. There was, most unusually for the ancient world, legal equality of the sexes; but there also existed a rigid caste system in which an underclass of peasants were subject to the most barbaric terrorisation by the true-born elite.[15]

But to many ancient thinkers it was precisely this ultra-disciplined civic life, steeped in convention, tradition, and blind prejudice, that made Sparta what one eminent historian has called "the most important historical model of an ideal society."[16] The Spartans themselves certainly thought so. The fact that their constitution had survived, allegedly unchanged, for more than four centuries was in their eyes irrefutable evidence—evidence amply corroborated by their victory over Athens in the defining war of the late fifth century BC. It is hardly surprising, then, that Sparta's reaction to the undesirable aspects of money was more extreme than that of her democratic rival. After all, what use could the ideal state have for a social innovation like money? Was not the truest freedom the sort guaranteed by membership of one's mess, one's tribe, and, ultimately, the Spartan state? And what was stability if not a constitution unaltered for four hundred years? The conclusion was obvious: the ideal state had no need of this invention. Confident in the perfection of its traditional social architecture, Sparta eschewed the use of money. So when, at a critical juncture in the Peloponnesian War, the Spartans won a decisive victory over Athens' ally, democratic Mantinea, they added a third and novel humiliation to the usual ancient practices of razing the defeated city to the ground and forcibly resettling its surviving inhabitants. They abolished the use of money. In a sense, this strategy of obliteration was the most enlightened part of their policy. Eradicating money was merely bringing Mantinea into line with the ideal state that had just defeated it: perhaps the earliest known example of post-conflict international development assistance.

The Spartans believed that the only real way to master money's defects was to get rid of it and to revert to traditional society. It is a strategy for dealing with money's shortcomings that has proved periodically popular over the centuries. In the ancient world, even Athens' greatest philosopher, Plato, expressed his admiration. Whilst he stopped short of abolishing money altogether in his utopian *Republic*, he ordained that money should be strictly regulated, subject to rigorous exchange controls, and should not be used at all by the highest caste of citizens.[17] But on its own terms the rationale for the Spartan strategy has always made perfect sense. If society's non-monetary institutions were well enough designed then money would be obsolete. Of course, it is always possible that, no matter how perfect a state's institutions, its irritatingly imperfect human citizens might mess everything up. As a result, the Spartan strategy has proved most popular in those traditions which believe mankind to be fundamentally good—with the Western, socialist tradition foremost amongst them.

In the sixteenth century, Thomas More had the inhabitants of his island of Utopia bring their goods to shared warehouses and then take in turn whatever they needed, "living in common, without the use of money."[18] The seventeenth-century Quaker and economic pamphleteer John Bellers, meanwhile, acknowledged that money had its uses and attractions—but also looked forward to a world without it. "Money in the body politick is what a crutch is to the natural body, crippled," he explained, "but when the body is sound, the crutch is but troublesome."[19] And in the nineteenth century Karl Marx and Friedrich Engels were swift to point out that what had been troublesome in the early days of the commercial economy was positively dangerous in the era of fully fledged industrial capitalism. To them, money meant economic freedom—but in the capitalist sense of bourgeois entrepreneurs being free to exploit proletarian workers rather than the socialist sense of everyone fulfilling their human potential. Money meant the impersonal and inhumane relations that hold together the economic machine in bourgeois society—leaving "no other nexus between man and man than naked self-interest, than callous 'cash payment'"—in place of the natural and human relations that would characterise the socialist paradise.[20] Money as it existed in capitalist economies was antithetical to the ultimate objectives of the communist project—and in the coming socialist paradise, money, therefore, would serve no purpose.

Like Plato, however, the one communist regime of the twentieth century that actually tried to implement the Spartan solution to money found it rather harder than expected. As a result, they adopted a second generic strategy instead: a strategy not of abolition, but of containment.

THE SOVIET SOLUTION

Ostap Bender, the roguish hero of Ilya Ilf and Evgeniy Petrov's 1931 satirical novel *The Golden Calf*, is a desperate man. The first decade of the Soviet Union has left him distinctly nonplussed. He has discovered that he is constitutionally unsuited to the new order. "I have had some serious differences with the Soviet regime over the last year," he confides to a fellow con-artist: "They want to build socialism. I don't. I'm bored by building socialism."[21] Bender's ambitions in life are much simpler, and more mundane. He just wants to get rich, and, if at all possible, move to Rio de Janeiro. To do so, he needs to find a millionaire and defraud him of his wealth. If only he lived in

the West this would be a cinch. "There, millionaires are popular figures," Bender muses: "Their addresses are known. They live in large
houses somewhere in Rio de Janeiro. You go straight to see them in
their house and there, in the hall, after the initial greeting, you take
their money."[22] The trouble is, he lives in the Soviet Union, where
"[e]verything's hidden, everything's underground."[23] Still, where
there is money, there must be millionaires: "[s]ince there are currency notes in circulation," he reasons, "there must be people who
have lots of them."[24] The challenge is simply to locate one.

With the help of a motley band of associates, this is what Bender
proceeds to do. A suitable black market tycoon is quickly identified—a
tight-fisted old railway clerk called Koreiko who has accumulated
an impressive fortune through schemes ranging from speculation
in government medical consignments during a typhus epidemic to
siphoning off food supplies destined for famine-ravaged regions.
Koreiko turns out, however, to be a shrewd operator himself, so that
actually extorting the money involves a long series of preposterous
adventures. In the end, having endured an unspeakably long railway
journey into the heart of Soviet Central Asia, Bender succeeds in confronting the old miser at the grand opening of the new trans-USSR
railway. There, he threatens to reveal Koreiko's crimes to the Party
unless he pays a cool million roubles. Koreiko finally concedes defeat
and hands Bender a suitcase filled with banknotes. It is the moment
for which the con man has waited all his life: he is ecstatic. Koreiko's
reaction, ominously, is more sanguine.

Bender soon finds out why. He offers to treat the demoralised
Koreiko to dinner at the finest restaurant in Moscow, but when they
try to catch the train back to the capital, they are refused seats because
they are not part of the official delegation. Undeterred, the newly
minted millionaire Bender heads for the local airfield, where he has
spotted a plane about to leave. This, too, is not available, however: it
is a "special flight" reserved for use according to the Plan. In the end,
a group of passing Kazakh nomads are the only ones who will take
their roubles, and the two plutocrats are reduced to travelling back
by camel. They have no more luck with lodgings. In one town, they

are told that all hotel beds are already allocated to a congress of visiting soil scientists; in another, to the construction workers building a new power station. Eventually, Bender is forced to resort to "what he used to do while the possessor of empty pockets. He began assuming false identities, such as engineer, medical officer, or tenor . . . to get a room."[25] The million roubles he lusted after for so long have turned out to be virtually useless—since in the command economy, there is virtually nothing for them to buy. Everything he dreamt of—smart transport, luxurious accommodation, fine food—is allocated by the Party and the Plan.

Ilf and Petrov's frustrated hero was a victim of the second generic strategy for fixing money's failings: the strategy of containment. In the period of so-called "War Communism" immediately following the socialist revolution in Russia, the young Soviet Union had attempted the more radical Spartan solution of abolishing money completely.[26] "In a socialist society," the Commissar for Finance had explained in a bashful apology made to the inaugural All-Russian Congress of the Council of the National Economy in 1918, "finance is not supposed to exist, and therefore I beg to be excused for its existence and for my own appearance here."[27] The new regime had lost no time in working to spare the Commissar any further blushes. Within two months of the revolution, all banks had been nationalised; within three, all public debts annulled. In June 1919, the All-Russian Central Executive Committee ordered the Commissariat of Finance "to endeavour to establish moneyless settlements with a view to the total abolition of money."[28] By the end of 1920, the Commissariat reported that it was well on its way. In financing the ongoing civil war between the Reds and the Whites, the Commissariat boasted, it had been solicitous in making "free use of the money system."[29] Its officials therefore looked forward confidently to the ancillary benefit this was sure to produce of "a progressive depreciation and finally a complete disappearance of money."[30]

More pragmatic elements were sceptical, however. No less an authority than Vladimir Ilyich Lenin warned against the Spartan strategy. Even Marx and Engels, he pointed out, had advised that the achievement of true socialism would take time—and that during the transition, money, the greatest weapon of the bourgeois class, would remain necessary as the means of co-ordinating activity and trading with those benighted countries not yet blessed by revolution. "When we are victorious on a world scale," he had reassured the Party, "I think we shall use gold for the purpose of building public lavatories in the streets of some of the largest cities of the world."[31] But in the meantime, he warned, money would have to be retained. "When you live among wolves," he reminded his audience, "you must howl like a wolf."[32] Belatedly, the new regime had grasped the wisdom of this advice. The most noticeable result of the Commissariat of Finance's well-intentioned efforts to debauch the currency was a spectacular collapse in agricultural and industrial output. By early 1921, a dramatic reversal was under way. A completely revised monetary policy was unveiled at the 9th All-Russian Congress of Soviets in December of that year. Its first priority, it soberly announced, was the "transition to a stable monetary unit, which is absolutely essential for the trade turnover among the smaller units of the economy."[33] Banks were back. Money was not to be abolished after all.

The world's first communist society was skewered on the horns of a fundamental dilemma. A socialist economy organised by capitalist money and finance was an oxymoron. But the experience of War Communism had proved that the abolition of money was, at least for the time being, a pipe dream. It would be necessary to devise some kind of compromise. Money would have to continue to exist—but with strict limitations imposed on its powers. This was to be the essence of the Soviet strategy: achieving the containment of money by reducing its ability to deliver freedom and increasing its commitment to ensure stability. It was a strategy that sought, in other words, a partial reversion from monetary to traditional society. Of course, the values and hierarchy to be protected from money's assault, and given priority over it, were not those of the feudal Russian society that had come to an ignominious end in October 1917. They were the political priorities of the revolution. Money was to be dammed and canalised so that rather than flooding indiscriminately into every corner of society as it did in capitalist countries, it would henceforth flow only along those channels beneficial to the progress of socialism. Money would become, as Lenin's successor Stalin put it, "an instrument of the bourgeois economy which Soviet power has taken into its own hands and adapted to the interests of socialism."[34] The result was the financial hall of mirrors in which Ostap Bender found himself trapped.

In practice, this Soviet strategy of containment was achieved in two ways, both of which gathered momentum from the end of the 1920s. The first was the relegation of money and finance to second place in all economic decision-making. Priorities were set by the Plan, and neither it, nor the system of centralised management introduced to implement it, were defined in monetary terms. It was physical quantities and technological coefficients that occupied first place. The role of money was to keep account, not to control. The annual company budget was known, significantly, as its *techpromfinplan*—its technical, trade, and financial plan—with finance deliberately bringing up the rear. The leading place in the company was to be occupied by an engineer or technician. The finance function in enterprises was little more than an exercise in bookkeeping, and the powerful figure of the Western CFO was unknown. The emasculation of the financial sector itself was even more extreme. The job of banks was not to screen projects for financing and monitor loans once granted. It was simply to create money to order as soon as a payment instruction had been issued from an engineer's desk. The process was automatic. The ultimate aim was to ensure that by starving it of personnel and denying it responsibility, money could interfere with the Plan's organisation of the economy as little as possible.[35]

The inevitable result of this relegation of money to a passive role was an explosion in its issuance. The engineers were in charge, and there was no incentive to listen to the irrelevant bankers' whining about financial viability. The bankers might issue periodic pleas for enterprises not to demand so much new money by continually increasing production which they, by law, had to fund; but since it was production and not money that mattered, who cared? One exasperated banker characterised the prevailing attitude of com-

"The Power of the Dollar" to circumvent all legal constraints and
transport the wealthy capitalist up to take control of the political
machinery, as illustrated in this Soviet poster: it was this subversive
power that Soviet monetary policy was designed to curb.

pany chiefs as follows: "let's build our factories, let's make our
goods: victors are not judged, after all."[36] The resulting flood of
money increased the need for the second part of the Soviet strategy: the imposition of ever stricter limits on what it could be used
for, and when. With the introduction of the first Five Year Plan
in 1928 and the related Credit Reform of 1930, money, even in its
passive form, was gradually removed from more and more parts
of the economy. As Ostap Bender discovered, money became less
and less the organising technology: pulling the strings in its place
was the Plan, and an ever more elaborate system of vouchers and
privileges assigned to particular classes of worker or members of
specific unions. Even money's most basic component—the concept

of universal economic value—ceased to exist. A whole plethora of goods and services had no monetary price, since they could not be bought and sold for money; and as for those that could, their prices were administered and access was rationed, so money's role as a universal comparator was no more than a empty charade.

The Spartan solution of abolishing money and the Soviet solution of attempting to contain it both focus on restraining or eliminating the applicability of money's core idea: the concept of universal economic value. Whilst advocates of the abolition of money are a rare breed today, the idea of constraining money is undergoing a rebound in popularity: the philosopher Michael Sandel was even invited to address the annual conference of the U.K.'s main opposition party on the subject in September 2012. But practical methods of implementing it remain as elusive as ever.[37]

Yet there is a third historic strategy for managing money's contradictions which concentrates not on trying to limit or extinguish the use of money, but on a novel solution to the age-old question of what its standard should be. It is a strategy that is reappearing today not in the visions of revolutionaries or the public outreach lectures of philosophers, but in the discussions of politicians and regulators at the heart of the world's financial system. It is the strategy of innovation: the structural reform of money.

11 Structural Solutions

THE SCOTSMAN'S SOLUTION

"Some men are born great," reads Malvolio, the vain antagonist of Shakespeare's *Twelfth Night*, "some achieve greatness, and some have greatness thrust upon them." In the case of the Scotsman John Law, it was most definitely the last of the three. By 1705 and the age of thirty-four, Law had certainly had an exciting career—but not one that could be called conventionally distinguished. The son of a prominent Edinburgh goldsmith, he had a brilliant natural talent for numbers, but his commercial education in the Projectors' London of the 1690s had been cut short when he was convicted of murder in April 1694 as the result of a duel in Bloomsbury Square.[1] Somehow, he had escaped from prison on New Year's Day, 1695 and fled to the Continent, where he had spent the next eight years deploying his unusual mathematical skills as a professional gambler from Venice to the Low Countries. By 1703, however, he had tired of travelling, and contrived to return to his native Edinburgh—only to discover, to his dismay, that all the talk was of a mooted Union of Scotland with England. Whatever the political and economic merits of this proposal, it was quite obvious that for Law it would be a disaster. While Scotland remained an independent state, Law was a free man—there were no extradition treaties in those days—but Union would almost certainly mean arrest and trial. The trouble was that many enterprising men in the Scottish Parliament were dazzled by the success of England's financial revolution and ashamed of their own failed efforts to replicate it.[2] Joining forces, they believed, was the only way to catch up. Law's best hope was to convince them they could stand on their own two feet. Scotland's problem was not that it needed to import the new system of English finance wholesale, but that it needed a proper monetary system of its own. If Law was to save his skin, he had to explain why and how it could get one. The result, published in 1705, was one of the most profound and far-sighted economic treatises of his or any other era: *Money and Trade Considered, with a Proposal for Supplying the Nation with Money.*[3]

Law had witnessed at first hand the prodigious effects that modern banking and finance could have, and he had followed assiduously the great dispute between Locke and Lowndes. But Law's analysis significantly superseded either of these more eminent authorities in both its clarity and its depth. He started from an understanding of money summarised in a concise formula: "[m]oney is not the value for which Goods are exchanged, but the Value by which they are Exchanged."[4] To see the true nature of money—and its true potential for good or ill—one must look beyond tokens to the underlying system of credit and clearing. "Gold, Silver, Copper, Bills, Shells mark'd and strung," he explained, "are only representative Riches, or the Signs by which real Riches are Transmitted."[5] Even so solid and substantial a thing as a gold coin, one had to remind oneself, is just a "Sign of Transmission": "I look upon a Crown-Piece it self," he boldly explained, "as a Bill drawn up in these terms."[6]

If money is simply transferable credit, Law reasoned, then the debate between Locke and Lowndes had really been missing the point. They had not in fact been arguing about the nature of money itself, but about what the standard of abstract economic value should be. This, Law believed, was the single most important question in all economic policy, for two reasons. The first was that for an economy to prosper, the choice of standard must be such as to ensure a sufficient supply of money—an objective that had been acknowledged as important by monetary pamphleteers all the way back to Nicolas Oresme.[7] The second was that the choice of standard also determines the distribution of wealth and income. This, too, was an old topic in monetary thought, insofar as seigniorage—the ability of monetary policy to redistribute wealth to the sovereign from his subjects—was concerned. But Law realised that in the new world in which money and finance were beginning to pervade the private sector, the economic significance of inflation and deflation was increasingly that it shifted the balance of financial power between private creditors and debtors as well. A healthy commercial economy, he explained, requires the primacy of the entrepreneurial classes. Monetary credit that never circulates, but reverts to a bilateral mortgage of the rentier over the entrepreneur, is a recipe for economic stagnation. One might as well return to the static feudal obligations of traditional society.

The trouble, Law explained, was that money would not generate healthy conditions by itself. The more people use money to preserve their security, the less that money generates wealth and facilitates mobility. And nothing, Law argued, exacerbates this incipient flaw at the heart of money like the tendency to mistake the representative token for the technology itself. Economic slumps occur, he explained, when "[s]ubjects . . . hoard up those Signs of Transmission as a real Treasure, being induced to it by some Motive of Fear or Distrust."[8] These psychological urges, nurtured by this conventional misunderstanding of money, "I always call blind," Law wrote, "because it stops a Circulation that puts a State to a loss, and which is more likely than any Thing else, to bring that Poverty which they fear, both upon others and themselves."[9] Without appropriate intervention, money's seductive promise is self-defeating.

Here was the problem with money, analysed in detail for the first time. What was the solution? The answer, Law reasoned, was simple. The sovereign issuer of money must have the ability to vary the supply of money to match the needs of private commerce, public finance, and the balance between private creditors and debtors. The central choice, therefore, is over the monetary standard: it must be one which allows discretion in the issuance of money. This immediately ruled out a precious-metal standard. Indeed, if one lived in a country without significant gold and silver mines, "it would be contrair to Reason," Law argued, "to limit the Industry of the People, by making it depend upon a Species [that] is not in our power, but in the power of our Enemies."[10] Law's economics pointed in a much more radical direction. To achieve both a sufficient supply and a healthy distribution, money must be managed. To be managed it needs a flexible standard. Gold or silver "species" therefore will not do. Fortunately, Law informed the Scottish Parliament, "we have a Species of our own every way more qualified."[11]

The world would have to wait another thirteen years to discover exactly what the Scots Projector's tantalising alternative was. Law failed to convince the Scottish Parliament that independence under his scheme would be better than Union with England. In 1706 he therefore returned to the Continent and resumed his itinerant lifestyle. In addition to his gambling he now had a second vocation, however—the attempt to win political backing for his economic ideas. If Edinburgh would not listen, perhaps Turin, or Venice, or some other less prestigious principality would. Yet despite the Scotsman's tireless angling, none would bite. As irony would have it, that opportunity finally presented itself a decade later in the largest, wealthiest, and most powerful European country of all: the Kingdom of France.

By the beginning of 1715, France had been embroiled in one major war or another for almost half a century. The cumulative effect on the finances of its long-reigning absolute monarch, Louis XIV—the "Sun King" of Versailles—had been disastrous. Every acre of the royal domain had been mortgaged, and every tax hypothecated. An entire system of public finance and an entire social structure had grown up around the king's endless campaigns. Some of the wealthy advanced money to the crown in return for long-term bonds—*rentes*—and lived off the income as *rentiers*, while others purchased feudal offices which enjoyed the right to collect various fees and duties from a particular population. The masters of this elaborate machine were not the king and his court, but a small club of bankers in Paris—through whose networks private money could be raised and to whose clients sinecures and sovereign paper would flow back in return. These grand financiers were the greatest tycoons in France: men like Samuel Bernard who had funded the War of the Spanish Succession; his friends, the banker brothers Antoine and Claude Paris; and Antoine Crozat, who personally owned the concession over the whole of French North America.

Like most tycoons, and especially those who make their money conspicuously from pilfering the public purse, these men were not universally popular. Indeed, they were known proverbially as *sangsues*—bloodsuckers—and almost the only feeling common to both the nobles at court and the peasants in the provinces was that these vampires should themselves be periodically subjected to a painful *saignée*—a bloodletting—in order to relieve their stranglehold on the nation. When complaints reached a sufficiently fevered pitch, the king would typically declare the creation of a special court, the Chamber of Justice, which would proceed to dole out swingeing-sounding punishments. But the host was too heavily dependent on its parasites. Once a little red meat had been tossed to the most disgruntled taxpayers and the bloodsuckers had lain low for a few months, the machine would crank into action again, and the forced transfusions would resume.

On 1 September 1715, everything changed. Louis XIV, by then the longest-reigning monarch in France's history, died after seventy-two years on the throne, and his nephew, Philip, Duke of Orleans, was confirmed as Regent. France's new ruler's first priority was to consolidate his power and gain control of the calamitous state of the public finances. An essential first step was an unequivocal show of strength. A gala version of the Chamber of Justice was therefore announced in March 1716 and put in charge of an orgy of recrimination. Tax evasion was to be investigated as far back as 1689. Anyone unable to prove correct payment was to be subject to the most extreme punishments—the galleys, exile, seizure of assets, even public execution. Generous inducements were offered to informers. France's commercial class, and her commerce, was petrified. Law saw his chance.

France, in Law's eyes, was a special case—the greatest policy challenge, but also the greatest policy opportunity, in Europe. Like Scotland, he believed, France was in the grip of a chronic monetary crisis.
Simply put, it had a shortage of money, as a result of its medieval
reliance on the worst possible combination of a precious-metal monetary standard and an almost exclusive reliance on coins. But France
also had a public debt problem, driven by decades of war expenditure.
In theory, an innovation like the Bank of England might have served
to meet both challenges, as it was doing across the Channel. But
the situation in France, Law believed, was well past that point. The
accumulated debt of the crown was simply unsustainable with the
tax base represented by the existing economy. What was needed therefore was both a monetary revolution and a radical reordering of the
public debt. Fortunately, Law's theories equipped him with a plan that
could achieve both.

The first part of his plan was designed to address France's lack
of a money supply sufficient to the needs of its economic potential.
Barely had the Chamber of Justice put the old financial interests to
flight than Law persuaded the Regent to allow him to establish a
General Bank—the first in France's history with the power to issue
notes. Initially, the General Bank adopted a conventional, precious-
metal standard, and its notes were convertible to specie on demand.[12]
Law activated a network of foreign correspondent banks so that
the General Bank's notes could be used to settle foreign trade, and the
Regent announced that taxes would be payable using its notes. The
Bank proved a conspicuous success—its notes began to circulate
widely and to stimulate trade, as Law had predicted. But this initial
stage was only a warm-up act. No one familiar with Law's fierce
invective against the restrictive effects of a precious-metal monetary
standard just over a decade previously could have doubted that. Sure
enough, in December 1718 the Bank was nationalised: the General
Bank became the Royal Bank, with all the added authority that this
implied. Far more consequentially, it was announced that the number of banknotes it could issue was to be delinked from its holdings
of gold and silver. Henceforth, the rate of note issue was to be regu-

lated by decision of the King's Council alone. Law's alternative standard had been unveiled. France's monetary standard now consisted of nothing other than the sovereign's own judgement. If money-users trusted the King's Council to issue prudently, all would be well; and better by far, according to Law's theory, than under a restrictive metallic standard. There was no safety net if they did not: no guarantee from now on that notes could be exchanged for a standard quantity of precious metal. Just in time for Christmas 1718, John Law had introduced France and the world to "fiat" money.

Not content with furnishing France with an all-new system of paper money, Law also began to attack the second part of France's economic problem—its parasitic system of public finances and the unsustainable level of the public debt. The tried and tested solution was to take a scythe to the sovereign's creditors' claims by devaluing the monetary unit or announcing an outright default. But Law's plan was to play not on creditors' fears, but on their greed. In 1717, with his prestige buoyed by the success of his Bank, he had convinced the Regent to allow him to form a joint-stock company, the Company of the West, and to award it the rights to develop French North America, which had until then been held by the arch-bloodsucker Antoine Crozat. These vast and virgin territories were sure, Law publicly predicted, to yield gigantic profits for the new company—and all of it with the endorsement of the French crown. Holders of sovereign bonds were invited to swap their debt claims on the crown for equity shares in the Company of the West. Instead of government debt, savvy investors could henceforth enjoy a type of government equity.

The response was decisive. Sovereign creditors deluged the new company's offices hoping to exchange bonds for equity shares, and the new company was heavily oversubscribed. Its business model—or at least, its ability to raise finance—now proven, the Company of the West embarked on an impressive trail of mergers and acquisitions. One by one, the corporations that owned the trading rights in every one of France's possessions were swallowed up. The Company of Senegal went first; then the Company of the East Indies; then the China Company and the Africa Company as well. Each acquisition was funded in the same way. Investors turned in their sovereign bonds and bills at Law's office in the Rue Quincampoix in return for equity shares in the ever-expanding Company. By the middle of 1719—now officially renamed the Company of the Indies, but known popularly after its most glamorous asset as the Mississippi Company—Law's giant corporation had subsumed every major joint-stock company in France.

In August 1719, Law put the final phase of his plan into action. The Company acquired the rights to collect all the indirect taxes in France. It no longer represented only the crown's foreign interests; its revenues now derived from the French economy as a whole. At the same time, it announced its intention to buy up the entire remaining part of the sovereign debt. To finance these mammoth transactions, it issued huge new tranches of equity. Such was the euphoria surrounding Law's "System," as it was now known, that it was more a matter of repelling than attracting investors. The Company's share price rose from 500 livres in May to over 10,000 livres in December—and the higher it went, the more public debt was absorbed by new equity issues. With the transaction complete, Law had finally achieved an unprecedented and never-to-be-repeated feat: a comprehensive swap of government debt for government equity. Meanwhile, by successive decrees of the sovereign before the end of the year, gold and silver lost their status as legal tender in the Kingdom of France, and the notes of the Royal Bank acquired it. The supremacy of bank money and the fiat standard was complete.

Law had used the window of opportunity provided by the Chamber of Justice to superlative effect. The Royal Bank was solving the monetary crisis, and the economy was booming. The Mississippi Company was reaping the profits, and using them to solve the public debt crisis. And the remaining rigidity in the system—the link between the Bank, with its certain notes, and the Company, with its risky assets—had been solved as well by the greatest innovation of all. The monetary standard was now the exclusive creature of the sovereign—so that if the economy, and thereby the Company, fell on hard times, the value of the Bank's money could fall to reflect this.

Accolades for Law's spectacular achievements flooded in from all sides. The Regent and his court were entranced. "[T]he construction was admired by everyone in France and was the envy of our neighbours, who were really alarmed by it," wrote a wistful contemporary two decades afterwards: "It was a type of miracle that posterity will not believe."[13]

With all the essentials of the System now in place, Law's underlying reasoning was becoming clear. The problem with conventional sovereign money was that it consisted of financial claims of certain value backed by revenues whose value was intrinsically uncertain. Sovereigns might promise, and subjects believe, whatever they liked—and these promises and beliefs be solemnly inscribed in bonds and *rentes*. But there was only one ultimate source of sovereign revenue: the industry and commerce of France. If the economy prospered, the sovereign's tax revenues grew, his credit improved, and his bonds would pay as promised. If not, the opposite applied. Since this is the reality of public finance, why not be honest about it? asked Law. Rather than pretending to his subjects that he can magic away the uncertainty inherent in economic activity, better for the sovereign to give them access to its proceeds directly—and by the same token, make them bear the risks. With government equity—shares in the Mississippi Company—this could be done directly. With transferable sovereign credit on a fiat standard—notes issued by the Royal Bank—it could be done at one remove.

On 5 January 1720, John Law was appointed Controller-General of the Finances of France. A few weeks later, he crowned his extraordinary ascent to power with the final merger of the Company and the Bank into a single, vast conglomerate. But his moment of triumph was short-lived. Almost immediately, cracks began to appear in the System. The long shadow of the Chamber of Justice had finally begun to fade: the bloodsuckers of the old financial system were beginning to stir again. When Law sent a memorandum to the Regent proposing a drastic simplification of the tax system, the Regent expressed concern that the old financial oligarchy might finally revolt. Law brushed away the Regent's concerns: "[w]hat will become of the rats that live in my barn if I remove the grain so as to transport it to a safe location?" he coolly responded.[14] But Law had underestimated his opponents, and the fragility of his success.

Wily old financiers that they were, Law's enemies knew that his System—like any monetary system—was vulnerable to a collapse of confidence. With so brief a track record to fall back on, even the slightest suspicions about the value of the Company shares and the Bank's fiat money might be fatal. The rumour mill was set to work. It had plenty to work with. The laughing colonists who had been seen processing to the docks to cross the Atlantic were not toiling prosperously on their French–American homesteads. Half had died of malaria; the other half had been hired stooges, and never made the crossing. Louisiana was not, as Law had given out, a commercial Promised Land to rival British North America. It was an irretrievable swamp that would never yield a profit. But above all, there were simply too many monetary claims chasing too little real activity. Regardless of whether they were debt or equity, notes of the Bank or liabilities of the Company, the value of the System's outstanding claims on the cash flow of the French economy were unsustainably large. No matter how optimistic one was about its prospects, they were never going to pay.

The smart money began to sell. Word got out that senior members of the Regent's court had converted their banknotes to gold the previous December. Panic set in. Law tried to engineer a controlled reduction in the value of the System's shares and banknotes. New and more draconian measures were introduced to discourage, and finally to outlaw, the ownership of gold and silver. The market crash intensified. At the end of May, with the System disintegrating, Law was arrested. Two days later he was at liberty again, but only because the Regent, one of his councillors reported, had realised that "the only man capable of taking him out of the labyrinth in which he found himself was Mr. Law."[15] In the confusion, Law's credibility was destroyed. With sage shakes of their heads, the resurrected *sangsues* regretfully advised the Regent that the only viable policy was retreat, at haste. On 1 June, gold and silver were restored as legal tender.

Two days later the old system of annuity finance was relaunched. By October the notes of the Bank had been abolished. By December, Law had fled France in fear of his life.

So unlikely was the rise, and so precipitous the fall, of the System that it has always been easy to dismiss the whole affair as a typical tale of unscrupulous financial chicanery, with Law in the role of an eighteenth-century Bernie Madoff. The English writer Daniel Defoe painted Law's career sarcastically as an excellent model for a young man seeking his fortune. "The Case is plain," he advised, "you must put on a Sword, Kill a Beau or two, get into Newgate, be condemned to be hanged, break Prison, IF YOU CAN,—*remember that by the Way,*—get over to some Strange Country, turn Stock-Jobber, set up a Mississippi Stock, bubble a Nation, and you may soon be a great Man."[16]

Such assessments are too superficial. Law's System was an experiment in harnessing the power of money of major historical significance, the archetype of a third generic strategy for harvesting the benefits of monetary society while avoiding its undesirable drawbacks. The Spartan and the Soviet strategies were fundamentally distrustful of money—and attempted to abolish or restrict its application. John Law, by contrast, believed that money's capacity to unleash ambition and entrepreneurship was its most valuable quality. The Scotsman's scepticism was reserved instead for the second leg of money's promise: its ability to combine this social mobility with the security and stability provided by fixed financial obligations. His strategy therefore aimed not to restrain the use of the concept of universal economic value, but to square the circle instead by making the standard by which is it measured intrinsically flexible. This was the ultimate objective of the System: a new financial settlement in which the risks inherent in money's contradictory promise were borne fully and explicitly by all money-users, rather than hidden behind the veil of unfulfillable promises by the sovereign to pay.

By merging the single state holding company with the single state bank, Law made explicit what he believed to be obscured in a decentralised system of money and finance. All income and wealth flows in the end from the productive economy—and it is claims on

John Law, before his fall (left, front view)—
and after it (right, rear view).

this income alone that money ultimately represents. That income is, however, uncertain, because the world is an uncertain place—so the value of those claims is in reality uncertain too. The simplest way to acknowledge this fact of life is to transform the fixed financial claims that are generally used as money—otherwise known as debt—into variable ones—otherwise known as equity. That required something that did not exist in Holland or England, and has not existed since: a corporation that owns all the assets of the state, including its rights to collect taxes, in which citizens can own shares. This equity-money, of course, would provide much less security than conventional money, since its value could go down, as the System's investors found out in 1720. But by the same token, it would provide a lot more mobility. For those who could not stomach such thoroughgoing transparency, the System also furnished a less powerful option: the notes issued by the Royal Bank. These had a fixed value in terms of the standard monetary unit. But that standard itself was now flexible, determined by the King's Council at the level they felt most appropriate from an economic and a fiscal perspective. The only difference, in other words, was that for the notes it was the sovereign, rather than the market, that would set the value of money.

Law's System was ingenious, innovative, and centuries ahead of its time. It was even to prove prophetic two hundred and fifty years later, when the international gold exchange standard finally disintegrated in 1973 and fiat monetary standards became the worldwide norm. Yet it failed spectacularly. Where was the flaw? There were of course plenty of circumstantial problems that bedevilled Law's ambitious scheme. He overestimated his own abilities, and underestimated the vested interests that his System would disenfranchise. The plan attempted far too much in far too short a time. And Law's particular idea of offering the public government equity rather than government debt was indeed so far ahead of its time that its like has not been seen again since.[17] But far outweighing these incidental challenges, the Scotsman's solution suffered from a much more fundamental flaw. It was a bug for which another neglected monetary genius had discovered the fix more than two millennia earlier.

THE WISDOM OF SOLON

While Sparta's reaction to the invention of money might have been the least ambiguous in the ancient Greek world, it was certainly not the only one. In many other Greek city states, money was embraced with enthusiasm—despite the widespread scepticism about its drawbacks.[18] Such openness was, according to Aristotle, a particular characteristic of democratic city states, in which "[p]ayment for services, in the assembly, in the law courts, and in the magistracies, is regular for all."[19] Athens was the canonical example and had become, by the fifth century BC, a uniquely monetised society—"a salary-drawing city," in which virtually every aspect of civic life was mediated by money.[20] Somehow or other, the citizens of classical Athens—whose poets, philosophers, and playwrights were the source of so much of the profound scepticism about money—had devised a means of harnessing their precocious and potentially dangerous invention. They owed this priceless discovery to one of their greatest philosophers, poets, and statesmen whose heyday had coincided, as luck would have it, with Athens' very first financial crisis.

In the Athens of the late seventh century BC, money and its spread was the social problem of the age.[21] Until recently, Athens had still been organised along traditional lines with a small class of land-owning aristocrats leasing land to sharecroppers in return for a portion of their harvest. In the days when the aristocrats had supplied the ranks of the army, there had been a compact of mutual aid with their tenants. But in the competitive, atomising world of monetary society, the peasant farmers, with the prospect of social mobility now opened to them and the requirement to fight now imposed on them, resented the aristocrats' traditional rents. The aristocrats, meanwhile, saw their land-holdings not as hereditary estates to which they owed a duty of care but as potential sources of financial gain. Money was tearing the social fabric apart. "The citizens themselves in their wildness wish to destroy this great city," lamented the poet Solon, "trusting as they do in wealth."[22]

It was a situation ripe for a financial crisis if ever there was one. As the creditor class of aristocrats attempted to maximise their profits, they met with increasing resistance from their insubordinate clients. Disputes multiplied, but there was no such thing as property or contract law to adjudicate them—only customs and taboos that were fast disintegrating. As for a property registry, there were nothing but worn and faded marker stones to settle arguments over ownership. The transition from traditional to monetary society was provoking a messy class war, driven by a debt crisis fuelled by the very shortcomings that the Greeks knew to plague money's fantastic promise: financial obligations cannot fulfil every role that social obligations can; there is no intrinsic limit to ambition in monetary society; and, left unchecked, the exhilarating independence that money promises becomes destructive isolation. "The leaders of the people . . . are ripe to suffer many griefs for their great arrogance," warned Solon, "for they know not how to restrain their greed."[23] Something had to be done to defuse the situation.

As it happened, there was a precedent. The great command economies of Mesopotamia may never have assembled all the components of money—but they did have the institution of interest-bearing debt. As a result, they were no strangers to the crises that this could generate and were as concerned as the Greeks with the potential of debt to disable the martial capacity of their cities by demoralising a vital class of fighting men through foreclosure and therefore disenfranchisement.[24] They understood this problem, and therefore its solution, in terms of their traditional and religious cosmology: it was the responsibility of the king, who was heaven's divine representative on earth, to restore social balance by cancelling some or all of the debts. The earliest known examples of this Mesopotamian practice of proclaiming a clean slate when the burden of debt became socially unsupportable are almost as old as the earliest evidence for interest-bearing debt itself—dating from the reign of Enmetana of Lagash in around 2,400 BC.[25] It was a tradition that survived in the Ancient Near East into biblical times, in the form of the institution of the jubilee, which the Book of Leviticus enjoined the Hebrews to declare every fifty years.[26]

There was, however, a fundamental problem with the application of this tried and tested oriental remedy in Athens at the turn of the sixth century BC. Athens was a society in the throes of scientific enlightenment. The religious cosmology of traditional society no longer cut the mustard as the definitive guide for the distribution of power on earth. "Man controls his destiny" was the spirit of the age.[27] So man himself must determine the fair distribution of wealth and power by money. Once again, an oriental practice—this time, the institution of debt cancellation—was imported into Greece. And once again a critical innovation, peculiar to the distinctive political culture of the Greeks, was made. An ulterior ideal of social order would indeed be imposed upon the uncontrolled excesses of monetary society. But this ideal would not be a simulacrum of the divine order in heaven. It would be a human notion of fairness in society hammered out by man. It would be determined, in short, through politics.

The man who introduced this radical idea was none other than the one who had done most to diagnose the problem: the statesman-poet Solon. Elected chief magistrate of the city in 594 BC, Solon proceeded to enact a series of social reforms known from then on as the "Shaking-off of Burdens." Chief amongst these was a cancellation of debts—but one which differed fundamentally from the oriental practice of the jubilee. For the central decision of any debt relief—who should gain and who should lose—was a matter of political compromise. The leadership of a gifted politician was of course crucial. "In great matters, it is hard to please all," wrote Solon in defence of his greatest legacy years later, but "[i]n between the two opposing sides, I stood like a boundary-stone."[28] Poet that Solon was, his choice of metaphor conveyed brilliantly the essence of the revolution he had wrought. If monetary society was to function, the old system of fixed boundary stones—the system that had regulated traditional society, with its immutable social obligations—would have to go. In its place would be a new system, in which the boundary markers—the standard of social justice—would have to be adaptable to the social change that money by its nature brings. And in the world in which mankind controlled its destiny, there could be only one source of legitimacy for that new standard of fairness: democratic politics.[29] The Shaking-off of Burdens did not stop there. Sharecropping was abolished, taxation by economic category rather than class introduced, and the right to trial by jury guaranteed. More than two centuries later, Aristotle argued that this last reform was "said to have been the chief basis of the powers of the multitude . . . for the people, having control over the courts, thereby have control over the government."[30]

But another aspect of Solon's reforms was more important than any single measure. For the critical role to be played in future by political decisions regarding what was and was not economically fair called for a new and more formal system of recording such decisions and assessing compliance with them. What was required—and what Solon therefore supplied, inscribed on a famous set of rotating wooden tablets—was a comprehensive body of law.[31] With Solon's achievement of a democratic state under the rule of law, the formula for making money work was complete.

SETTING THE STANDARD: DIVINE, DESPOTIC, OR DEMOCRATIC MONEY?

Scepticism about money has a distinguished pedigree—stretching all the way back to its invention—and radical strategies such as the Spartan or the Soviet have their supporters even today. The oldest sceptical strategy, however, is one which tries to remake money, rather than reduce it or remove it. It is the strategy that sees money as fundamentally a force for good—but one which left unmanaged will inevitably get out of hand. It is the strategy which superimposes on monetary society a periodic recalibration—as dramatic as a one-off jubilee or unilateral default, or as humdrum as a gradual depreciation of the monetary standard—or even, in the unprecedented experiment of John Law, attempts a structural fix by withdrawing money's promise to deliver stability entirely. The focus of these strategies—the Scotsman's strategy, and Solon's long before him—is on the flexibility of the monetary standard. They require, therefore, an answer to a question that the others do not: on what grounds should adjustments to the standard be made?

It is in their answers to this question that the historical adherents of this strategy of managing money have diverged. The civilisations of the ancient Orient had their clean slates and their jubilees. For them the answer was given by divine law. Let money do what it will for fifty years, says Leviticus, and then "proclaim liberty throughout all the land unto all the inhabitants thereof: it shall be a jubilee unto you."[32] But this is the very view of the world as governed by divine law that the scientific revolution of the Greeks superseded—and it is that revolution whose children we are today. Nobody in today's world would suggest to the participants at the next IMF board meeting or central-bank policy committee that they start to make their decisions based on their religious convictions. To the great innovator John Law, all this was quite clear. It is man, he argued, not God or nature, who must decide. This was the meaning of his great innovation, the fiat money standard: a regime in which the issuance and value of money became at all times a matter of deliberate policy, not of arbitrary chance.

But here too lay hidden the fundamental flaw in Law's version of the strategy. For Law believed that an absolute monarch should make this policy. He believed that the king should determine the standard conducive to economic efficiency and social justice, and that money-users would trust him to do so. Indeed, he thought only an absolute monarch could do all this. Democracies and republics, he believed, could never manage money properly—they would always be arguing about who should win and who should lose, and no one would ever trust them to keep their word. Absolute monarchs were different. "A wise Prince infinitely shortens all these Difficulties," wrote Law,

> a King is always in a better Capacity to remedy them, than a Sovereign Council, whose Debates and Delays must of necessity take up Time before a majority of Votes can be obtain'd upon the most urgent Affairs . . . a King acting by himself, is capable of reducing the whole to one View, and of giving his Kingdom a general Credit, as the only one that can procure even the Confidence of Foreigners.[33]

It is an old and tempting trap—the belief that only the strong arm and single mind of "Despotick Power" can really generate loyalty in politics and credibility in finance. The reality, as history was beginning to show even as Law was writing, was exactly the opposite. In time, his contention that "Kings have never fail'd, and never will fail in the Payment of their Debts" would come to seem as quaint and obsolete as absolute monarchy itself.[34]

Rather, it was Solon who had seen how the strategy might work, all the way back at the beginning. Only the compromises of democratic politics can durably decide what is fair; and only the promises of democratic governments can reliably last. This was the secret of the recalibration of the standard—the secret of harnessing money's benefits while avoiding its flaws. The tribal society of Dark Age Greece knew the fundamental equality of the individual. This was the invaluable idea that furnished a universal standard of value, which, combined with the Eastern technology of accounting and the scientific revolution in archaic Greece's intellectual worldview, led to the invention of money. From the beginning, however, the Greeks were sceptical of money's prodigious claims—and the earliest experience of monetary society seemed to confirm their fears. The contradictions inherent in money's promise to combine freedom and stability threatened to overwhelm Athens' newly enlightened state. Solon showed the way to square the circle. The original standard of economic value—the standard that had allowed money to serve, not only as a device for organising one line of trade or one part of the bureaucracy, but the entire economy and the whole of society—expressed a political ideal: the equal social value of the individual member of the tribe. But by its nature, money permits social mobility and the accumulation of wealth and power over others. Any fixed standard of monetary value will therefore necessarily become obsolete—and that obsolescence spells mortal danger, for it is the root of civil strife. Instead, the state must be always vigilant to ensure that the architecture of financial obligations reflects what society believes to be fair. Only politics—democratic politics, in constant activity—can furnish such an evolving standard. And only law—its debate, codification, and rule—can enact it.[35]

It is a strategy for harnessing money's potential as relevant today as it was two and a half millennia ago. But the entire sceptical tradition in monetary thought has been thoroughly eclipsed by the conventional understanding of money and the new discipline of economics that was constructed on its foundations. We have already discovered the blind spot in moral reasoning that this unfortunate neglect has generated. In the immediate aftermath of the global financial crisis, it is the shortcomings of practical economic policy that are the starkest evidence of the problem. So it is to investigate the consequences of the conventional understanding of money for our current economic predicament that we turn next.

12 *Hamlet* Without the Prince: How Economics Forgot Money . . .

THE QUEEN'S QUESTION

On 5 November 2008, Queen Elizabeth II was at the London School of Economics to conduct the official opening of a £71 million extension to the world's oldest academic institution devoted to teaching and research in economics.[1] After a tour of the magnificent new building, the Queen was presented to the School's faculty. The ceremony had been arranged months before—but a mere seven weeks previously, the leading U.S. investment bank Lehman Brothers had collapsed into bankruptcy, sparking a global economic crisis of unprecedented severity. It was an instance of serendipity too good to pass up. The Queen asked the international aristocracy of economists assembled before her an obvious question: why had none of them seen the crisis coming?

The question struck a chord. The popular press took it up. Why was it that all those brilliant economists and highly paid bankers, with their elaborate theories and their computerised models, had failed to foresee such an enormous catastrophe lurking at the heart of the economic system? The British Academy convened a conference to formulate an answer, and in July 2009, sent a response to the Queen.[2] It described a by now familiar litany of problems, including global macroeconomic imbalances, failures of risk management in banks, general over-exuberance due to a long period of low inflation, and lax regulation. It admitted that none of the main interested parties had grasped the fact that they might precipitate such a cataclysmic crash. And it identified the reason for this—the answer to the Queen's question—in the failure of anyone to take a sufficiently broad view of things. "[I]n summary, Your Majesty," wrote the Academy's representatives, "the failure . . . while it had many causes, was principally a failure of the collective imagination of many bright people, both in this country and internationally, to understand the risks to the system as a whole."[3] The British Academy's diagnosis was that in isolation, "[e]veryone seemed to be doing their own job properly on its own merit."[4] The problem was rather that nobody had seen the big picture: that whilst "[i]ndividual risks may rightly have been viewed as small . . . the risk to the system as a whole was vast."[5]

History does not relate what the Queen made of this answer. What is certain is that it would not have satisfied the Committee on Oversight and Government Reform of the United States House of Representatives, which had held its fourth hearing into the crisis a fortnight before the Queen posed her question at the London School of Economics. It was hardly going to be satisfied with the answer that no one saw the big picture. After all, seeing the big picture is

This time it was not the Emperor—at least, not the Queen—
who had no clothes.

exactly what macroeconomists, central bankers, and other financial regulators are meant to do. It was therefore no surprise that one of the witnesses called before the Committee was Alan Greenspan—the longest-serving Chairman of the Federal Reserve in history and indisputably one of the most important world economic policy-makers in the two decades leading up to the crash. Unlike the British Academy, Mr. Greenspan did not fudge responsibility. He did not deny that his job had been precisely to understand how the economy worked as a whole. The problem was, he explained with admirable honesty, that his understanding had simply been wrong. "I found a flaw . . . I have been very distressed by that fact," he testified. "I found a flaw in the model that I perceived is the critical functioning structure that defines how the world works."[6]

The multitrillion-dollar question was what the flaw in the model being used by Mr. Greenspan was—and how it had crept into his thinking. Economics is not a young discipline. Central banks are not new. How could the most influential social science of the last two centuries have fallen into such catastrophic error? A third verdict was delivered in April 2011, by Lawrence Summers—recently retired as the Director of President Obama's National Economic Council, a former Chief Economist of the World Bank, and one of the leading academic economists in the United States. Asked at a conference in Bretton Woods whether he believed that the crisis had exposed the failure of orthodox macroeconomics and financial theory to understand the economic reality, Summers made an astonishing admission. In the breach, Summers explained, the "vast edifice" of orthodox economic theory constructed since the Second World War had been virtually useless.[7] It had proved to have almost nothing to say about why the economy was nose-diving and what could be done to stop it.

But, Summers said, there had been other traditions—much less heralded ones—that had come to his assistance. As the American financial system had teetered on the edge of oblivion in late 2008 and early 2009, Summers nominated a trio of economists as his chief guides during the desperate policy-making in the White House: Walter Bagehot, Hyman Minsky, and Charles Kindleberger.[8] This was a selection of economic thinkers, he admitted, from well beyond the pale of orthodox economics and from some time ago. Hyman Minsky was a economist whose unconventional theories of how a monetary economy functions were largely spurned by the core of the profession, and who died in 1996. Charles Kindleberger was an economic historian—economic history being widely considered the poor cousin of theory by most academic economists—whose best known work was published in 1978. Walter Bagehot—who is barely considered an economist at all by the modern profession—was a British finanical journalist who died in 1877 and whose major work dates from 1873. Yet it was to the understanding of banking and finance of these obscure and unfashionable thinkers that Summers had turned in the heat of the crisis. And as for the medium-term policy response, once the most acute phase of the crisis had passed, there had been Keynes. Whilst the core research programme of modern academic macroeconomics "was not something that informed the policy-making process in any important way," Summers said, "I was heavily influenced . . . by the basic Keynesian . . . framework."[9]

So what was it about this alternative tradition of economic thought that made its theories so much more useful, and so much more realistic, than the "vast edifice" on which so much effort had been spent in the post-war period? How could a book like Walter Bagehot's *Lombard Street*—an account of the London money market in the early 1870s—have had more to say to the Director of the Council of Economic Advisers in the midst of the biggest financial meltdown in history than the most up-to-date and technically accomplished productions of the finest minds in twenty-first-century economics? As Summers put it: "I think economics knows a fair amount; I think it has forgotten a fair amount; and it has been distracted by an enormous amount."[10] The questions are, What has it forgotten? What was it distracted by? And, perhaps the biggest mystery of all, How on earth did all this happen?

"THE MODEL INSTANCE OF ALL EVIL IN BUSINESS"
It is a commonplace that the market has a short memory. It had been only a few years since the last financial crash had threatened to

destroy the banking system, the economy, perhaps even capitalism itself, and yet it had all been forgotten in the subsequent boom. And this time there really did seem a reason why it might all be different, for both the world economy and finance itself seemed to be in the throes of an epochal transformation. The previous decade had witnessed unprecedented growth and innovation in the capital markets. The leading actors in the creation of credit for the new globalising economy were no longer the traditional banks but a new breed of dealers that originated and distributed tradable debt securities. Individually, these novel forms of credit seemed risky and perhaps illiquid—but another class of firms had appeared that specialised in parcelling them up into well diversified, and hence low-risk, bundles. Those who doubted the wisdom of all this were dismissed as economic Luddites—until the pyramid of credit developed the odd crack when interest rates spiked and a few of the smaller firms went under. Then came rumours that a really big fish was in trouble. It seemed inconceivable that the regulators would let it go: everyone knew that it was "too big to fail." Yet the sanctimonious talk of the dangers of moral hazard emanating from the central bank was far from reassuring. And then, taking everyone by surprise, it happened. There was a full-blown run, and the central bank let it fail. All hell broke loose: a panic the like of which hadn't been seen for decades. As financial markets tanked, credit seized up, and the economy capsized, moral hazard was suddenly the last thing the central bankers were worrying about. The policy-makers realised that the time had come to run the printing press at full tilt and bail out the financial sector before it disintegrated completely.

This, of course, is the story of the crisis of 2008–9 in which Lawrence Summers played such a critical policy-making role. What is perhaps less well known is that it is also exactly the story of another great financial crisis—one that occurred more than a hundred and forty years earlier, in 1866.

In the two generations following the publication of Adam Smith's *Wealth of Nations* Britain underwent an economic and technological transformation so thorough that it was almost immediately christened the Industrial Revolution.[11] Like all good revolutions, it had a vanguard; albeit a rather unexpected one. For an astonishing number of the entrepreneurs who created Britain's industrial supremacy were members of one marginal Protestant sect: the Religious Society of Friends, or, to give them their more familiar name, the Quakers.[12] Jealous contemporaries often ascribed the conspicuous success of Quaker businessmen to nothing more than a greater capacity to tolerate the hypocrisy of Christian money-making. Their pious brethren, it was whispered, not only "Grip'd Mammon as hard as any of their Neighbours," but even "call Riches a Gift and a Blessing from God."[13] Yet there was a great deal about the Quaker way of life that was conducive to success in the new world order. Central to the Quaker ethos were personal honesty, hard work, and conservatism. The Society placed great emphasis on education. And above all, the movement stressed the importance of solidarity amongst the Friends, reinforced in everyday intercourse by distinctive dress and language, and over the generations by the strong encouragement of marriage within the faith. All these features of Quakerism were ideally suited to the burgeoning commercial economy, based as it was on reliability, personal trust, literacy, and numeracy.

In no sector of the economy were these traits more valuable than in banking. An exclusive commercial club, knit together by implicit trust and bound to an ulterior ideology, is the dream environment for private monetary networks to flourish in. So it is hardly surprising that in banking, even more than in other fields, Quakers were unusually pre-eminent. Even today, two of Britain's four high street banks—Lloyds and Barclays—were originally Quaker firms.[14] But the greatest of all the mid-nineteenth-century Quaker banks no longer exists. In the days when Lloyds and Barclays were still little more than provincial counting houses, one bank ruled the City like no other before or since. This was the famous Quaker firm of Overend, Gurney and Co., or the "Corner House" as it was known to a generation of Victorian financiers, because it stood as a rival to the Bank of England itself, not only metaphorically in the financial markets, but in hard reality on the corner of Lombard Street and Birchin Lane in the heart of the City of London.

The Gurney family had begun as wool merchants in the prosperous farming district of East Anglia, and had evolved naturally into merchant bankers by borrowing on their good name in London and lending to the local sheep-farmers. As Britain's economy grew and diversified, the opportunity to capitalise on this generic line of business—connecting the local capitalists in need of credit at the base of the pyramid to the London banks in its higher echelons—became more and more attractive. Eventually, the Gurneys of Norfolk decided to seed a London operation, and in 1807 they acquired the small London firm of Richardson, Overend. In the beginning, the firm's business was brokerage pure and simple. A potential borrower in the provinces would bring his bills to Overends for scrutiny. If Overends liked the credit, they would find a London commercial bank that would lend against security of the bill—a procedure called "accepting" it. The more practised in this art brokers like Overend, Gurney became, the more readily were their recommendations accepted by the banks. Bill-broking became big business, and the market in debt securities that they intermediated became the governing mechanism of the Industrial Revolution.

As time went on, the bill brokers began to act not only as agents of the commercial banks, but as finance houses in their own right. Banks would deposit their excess funds with the brokers on demand, and the brokers themselves would discount the provincial or foreign entrepreneur's bills.[15] The risk now resided on the brokers' balance sheets—and they would reap any profits: in modern terminology, they had ceased to be just brokers and had become dealers. By the middle of the nineteenth century, the London bill brokers were the merchant bankers at the very heart of the global financial system—the direct heirs of the Italian exchange bankers of medieval Europe, but lords and masters of an estate incomparably more international, more complex, and more wealthy. When Parliament established a committee to investigate the London capital markets in 1857, the reaction of its members to an account of the bill brokers' role was nothing short of astonishment. Did the Governor seriously mean to say that "[a] man cannot buy . . . tea in Canton without getting credit from Messrs Matheson or Messrs Baring?" they asked. "That is so," came the reply matter-of-factly. Even six thousand miles away, it was the name of a bill broker in Lombard Street that was wanted to persuade a merchant to part with his goods. It was via the bill brokers that "English credit supplies the capital of almost the whole world."[16]

By the 1830s, Overend, Gurney was the greatest bill broker in all of Europe. By the 1850s, it was the greatest in the world, turning over £170 million a year, taking deposits from every bank in the City, and discounting bills of industrialists and merchants from Lancashire to Lahore. The firm returned annual profits of more than £200,000 to its partners, and had a balance sheet ten times larger than those of the two biggest banks in Britain combined.[17] Never in history had there been so uniquely important a banking house or one whose name and credit were so synonymous with the credit of the nation's—even of the world's—economy. As Walter Bagehot attested, the reach of the credit of the greatest bill broker in London was such that "[n]o one in the rural districts (as I know by experience) would ever believe a word against them, say what you might."[18] It was "the most trusted private firm in England": so great was public confidence in its acumen at screening borrowers that "[p]robably not one-thousandth of the creditors on security of Overend, Gurney and Co., had ever expected to rely on that security, or had ever given much real attention to it."[19] It is just such unquestioning confidence in credit that is the essential ingredient of liquid financial markets, as the Governor of the Bank of England knew: "[b]anking . . . depends so much on credit," he concluded, "that the least blast of suspicion is sufficient to sweep away, as it were, the harvest of a whole year."[20]

This was a lesson that had been learned time and time again in the course of the preceding half-century. The year 1825 had seen the first financial crisis of the industrial era, following a speculative bubble generated by the over-expansion of the new country banks. When it burst, it had brought the country to "within twenty-four hours of a state of barter."[21] Thereafter crises had occurred with alarming regularity. In 1836, a bubble in railway bonds burst. A decade later, there was another boom and bust; and in 1857 the end of the Crimean War sparked an investment boom that again ended in distress and panic. Many a bank had been laid low by one or other of these successive crises; but Overend, Gurney and Co. had survived them all, and prospered. The crisis of 1857 forced two momentous changes to the "Corner House," however.

The first was a regulatory development. Ever since their transformation into dealers carrying risk on their own balance sheets after the crisis of 1825, the bill brokers had enjoyed access to loans from the Bank of England in times of crisis. But in the Bank's view, the crisis of 1857 had exposed a tendency to rashness amongst the bill brokers: the Directors had noticed that the lion's share of the Bank's emergency lending had for the first time gone to the bill brokers rather than the banks.[22] There was much talk of the fact that access to the emergency facilities was encouraging the brokers to invest in over-speculative bills. The Bank's Directors therefore resolved in March 1858 to end the bill brokers' access.

At the very same time that its business environment was changing in this way, the house of Overend, Gurney and Co. faced a second challenge. The original managing partners retired, and a younger generation took the reins. It quickly became apparent that they lacked some of the distinctive Quaker qualities of their illustrious forebears. In contrast to the stern solidity of the fathers, the sons were precipitous in their decision-making, ambitious for the trappings of wealth, and—the most dangerous flaw of all in a banker—credulous. If the 1690s had been the decade of the Projector in London, it was the company promoter who was ubiquitous in the 1860s; and where the former had been famous for his amazing, if sometimes hare-brained, inventions, the latter was a byword for little more than the main chance—if not outright fraud. The new managing partners of Overend, Gurney and Co. quickly attracted a strong following amongst such characters; indeed, as one of their own clients put it, "a miniature court of Louis XIV."[23]

The intention of the Bank's withdrawal of its lender of last resort facility from the bill brokers had been to discourage the riskier end of their discount business. At Overend, Gurney, however, it had exactly the opposite effect. The new partners lost no time in filling the firm's portfolios with a succession of speculative, long-term, and high-risk investments. Early on, their own appetite for the famous Quaker virtue of hard work began to flag, and they started to delegate much of the firm's investment strategy to a newly recruited lieutenant, a certain Edward Watkin Edwards. As a former partner in a well-known firm of accountants and an ex-assignee of the bankruptcy court, he was "regarded at the 'Corner House' as a great mathematician and a high financial authority."[24] His true calling was less elevated: "[m]y vision," he told a prospective borrower, "is to become a very rich man."[25]

The combination of all these changes proved disastrous. In the space of two years, Overends' annual profit of £200,000 had turned to a loss of £500,000. The new managers attempted to regain profitability by taking more risk. They made a bold foray into emerging market bonds, financed a port development in Ireland, and made a host of other long-term, speculative investments, the only unifying feature of which was that every one was funded, as was the way with the bill brokers' business model, by deposits from the commercial banks that could be withdrawn on demand. If, heaven forbid, there was to be a market panic, and the banks were to demand those deposits back, there was now no question that without support the firm would be exposed as insolvent.

By April 1865, the situation was becoming desperate, and the partners met to weigh up the options. It was clear that new capital was needed to make good the losses and supply the means to rebuild the firm's fortunes. The question was where it should come from. New partners could be allowed to buy in; or the old partners could put up more money; even a merger with a rival bill broker was considered. But in the end, it was the oldest trick in the City's books that was chosen: an initial public offering that would transform the partnership into a public company and thereby offload the problem on to that perennial saviour of the City insider's bacon—the general public.[26] Those in the know were suspicious. *The Economist* went as

far as the libel law would allow when it welcomed the fact that a public offering of shares would oblige Overends "to publish an account
of the nature of their business" which "[f]or many years it has been
a matter of public notoriety . . . [has been] of a sort different from
those conducted by bill-brokers 'pure and simple.' "[27] But as the partners well knew, such subtle admonitions sailed miles over the heads
of most prospective investors. "Needless to say," wrote one eminent
historian of the episode, "the public did not read the prospectus, and
in consequence the issue was a great success."[28]

For the first few months of its existence, shares in the new limited liability company, Overend, Gurney and Co. Ltd., traded at a
premium. But late in the year, the Bank felt it needed to put another
squeeze on the market. Bank Rate was raised to 8 per cent, and at
the beginning of January 1866 the first sign of distress appeared
in a most unfortunate quarter. A middling boutique railway bond
arranger went into default on liabilities of £1.5 million. As bad luck
would have it, the name of this quite unrelated firm was Watson,
Overend and Co. Now the ignorance of the market worked against
Overends. A connection was assumed, and—just as a precaution—
withdrawals began. It became known that the old partners were having to sell assets. The withdrawals accelerated. In two months, £2.5
million worth of deposits streamed out of Overends, even as loans
continued to go bad and the general panic spread. In a final gamble,
on 9 May, the management made an urgent and humiliating appeal
to the Bank of England for emergency support. But a general crisis
was in prospect, and to bail out one firm alone would open the Bank
to unanswerable charges of encouraging moral hazard. The Governor's response was therefore swift and unequivocal. There would be
no lifeboat. At 3:30 p.m. on Thursday, 9 May 1866, Overend, Gurney
and Co. Ltd. suspended payment.

The effect of Overends' failure was catastrophic. "It is impossible
to describe the terror and anxiety which took possession of men's
minds for the remainder of that and the whole of the succeeding
day," reported the *Bankers' Magazine*. "No man felt safe. A run immediately commenced upon all the banks, the magnitude of which can

hardly be conceived."[29] The next day—the day that was to become known in City folklore as Black Friday, the ancestor of many a Black day since—was worse. "[A]bout midday the tumult became a rout," reported *The Times*. "The doors of the most respectable Banking Houses were besieged . . . and throngs heaving and tumbling about Lombard Street made that narrow thoroughfare impassable."[30] It was a classic financial crisis: "Not long ago, men trusted everybody; it would almost seem that now they will trust nobody."[31] All liquidity had evaporated. No broker would deal. Only the Bank of England continued to discount bills at the punitive interest rate of 9 per cent. Over the preceding week, its reserves had already fallen by half. Now, in a single day, it lent £4 million. The Directors were transfixed. As the Governor put it afterwards, "I do not think that anyone would have thought of predicting, even at the shortest period beforehand, the greatness of those advances."[32]

By Saturday, everything was confusion. In the morning, the Chancellor of the Exchequer, William Ewart Gladstone, reassured the House of Commons that although there was "panic and distress . . . without parallel in the recollection of even the oldest men of business in the City of London," he had "not the least reason to suppose" that the Bank would ask him to suspend the Act stipulating the strict upper limit to the note issue.[33] He then returned to the Treasury to find the Bank's Governor telling him that with only £3 million left in its reserve, the Bank could not withstand another day like Friday, and asking just that. Gladstone acceded, signing a letter of suspension like the ones that had been needed in 1847 and 1857, on the condition that Bank Rate be further raised to 10 per cent. As in previous crises, the mere word that the Bank's firepower was no longer limited was enough to quell the panic. The acute phase of the crisis began to subside, and though the demand for sovereign money remained unusually high for months following the crisis, the focus shifted to counting the casualties in the post-Overends era. These were considerable. Three English and one Anglo-Indian bank had been forced into liquidation—at a time when there was no deposit insurance. Dozens of bill brokers and finance companies had gone under.

But as always, the real ramifications of the crisis were felt far beyond the medieval wards of the City of London and long after the acute panic had subsided. All over the country, the credit crunch resulting from the damage to confidence brought a severe contraction of business. More than a hundred and eighty bankruptcies were recorded in the three months following Black Friday.[34] Unemployment rose from 2.6 per cent in 1866 to 6.3 per cent in 1867, and rose again in 1868 before a proper recovery took hold. Sectors that relied particularly heavily on credit, such as the global shipping industry operating from the wharfs of London's East End, were especially badly affected: the annual report of the Poplar Hospital, a charitable institution for dockers, recorded that "there has never been a year so pregnant with disaster both public and private."[35] All in all, it had been the greatest financial crash since 1825—indeed, if only by virtue of the far more advanced development of the City and its international importance compared with that time, the greatest crash of all. Little wonder, then, that the editor of one contemporary journal, surveying the wreckage seven years later, called the collapse of Overend, Gurney which had sparked the catastrophe, "the model instance of all evil in business."[36]

WHAT ECONOMICS FORGOT

That journal was *The Economist*, and its editor was none other than Walter Bagehot—the first of the thinkers that Lawrence Summers identified as representatives of an invaluable, but neglected, tradition in economic thought. Bagehot occupies a singular place in the history of economics. He was born in 1826, and so had no formal training in economics: he used to refer to himself as "the last man of the ante-Mill period," referring to John Stuart Mill's 1848 *Principles of Political Economy*, the first real textbook of economics which organised the subject to be taught in schools and universities.[37] Bagehot had learned everything he knew on the job—first as a banker, working for an uncle who controlled the largest bank in the West of England, and later as a financial journalist. Yet the profound influence of his writings after he became editor of *The Economist* in 1860 on both economic thought and economic policy was without precedent. "Bagehot's position amongst English economists is unique," wrote Keynes in 1915, summing up the conundrum. "Some of his contributions to the subject are generally acknowledged to be of the highest degree of excellence. And yet in some respects it would be just to say that he was not an economist at all."[38]

Close familiarity with actual developments in the commercial and financial worlds was, however, of far greater worth than any amount of abstract theorising. Never was this more so than in the case of the crisis of 1866. When Overend, Gurney failed, Bagehot had already lived through three financial crises and their attendant economic slumps. These crises, he had come to realise, were an intrinsic feature of the modern monetary system as it had evolved over the previous century. The received economic wisdom on how to manage and prevent them, however—the wisdom of Adam Smith and John Stuart Mill—was hopelessly out of touch with reality. The potential consequences of this mismatch, Bagehot believed, were disastrous—and he had devoted many pages of journalism in the previous decade to attempting to correct it. After the Overends crisis Bagehot resolved to write a simple statement of his case—something that could be understood by the politicians who would need to introduce the reforms. The result, published in 1873, was his masterwork— *Lombard Street, or, a Description of the Money Market.*

Lombard Street deliberately set out to be short, polemical, and lively—"a piece of pamphleteering, levelled at the magnates of the City and designed to knock into their heads, for the guidance of future policy, two or three fundamental truths," as Keynes called it.[39] Yet it was also a brilliant work of economic exposition and analysis. Two features in particular distinguished it from the works of Mill and the classical school. The first was that Bagehot's economics started explicitly from money, banking, and finance—which Bagehot saw as the governing technology of the modern economic system. The second was that Bagehot insisted that theory should be constructed to fit the reality of the monetary economy, rather than the other way round. The very title and opening sentences of *Lombard Street* proudly advertised these departures from the abstract economics of Bagehot's classical forebears. "I venture to call this Essay 'Lombard Street,' and not the 'Money Market,' or any such phrase," wrote Bagehot, "because I wish to deal, and to show that I mean to deal, with concrete realities."[40]

And what Bagehot saw as the most basic reality to be grasped about the modern monetary economy was that the conventional understanding of money as gold and silver—the understanding adopted by habit by the man in the street, and the one promoted by the academic economists of the day—was confused. The slightest acquaintance with Lombard Street revealed that the money overwhelmingly used by businessmen was by and large private transferable credit: above all, bank deposits and notes. "[T]rade in England," he explained, "is largely carried on with borrowed money."[41] This simple and apparently innocent fact, Bagehot argued, had profound ramifications for understanding the modern economy's cycles of boom and bust, and how to moderate them. If money is in essence transferable credit—rather than a commodity medium of exchange, as the academic economists insisted—then fundamentally different factors explain the economy's demand for it. Meeting demand for commodities is a simple matter of ensuring a sufficient supply on the market. When it comes to transferable credit, however, volume alone is not enough: the creditworthiness of the issuer and the liquidity of the liability come into play. And both these factors are determined not technologically or physically but by the general levels of trust and confidence. "The peculiar essence of our banking system," wrote Bagehot, "is an unprecedented trust between man and man: and when that trust is much weakened by hidden causes, a small accident may greatly hurt it, and a great accident for a moment may almost destroy it."[42]

It was from this starting point alone that a proper understanding of the modern economy could be constructed, Bagehot argued. The central importance of the intrinsically social properties of trust

Walter Bagehot, the supreme explainer of the
"concrete realities" of the money market.

and confidence called for a quite different focus for economic analysis
than that of Mill and the classical school. "The main point on which
one system of credit differs from another is 'soundness,'" wrote
Bagehot. "Credit means that a certain confidence is given, and a certain trust reposed. Is that trust justified? And is that confidence wise?
These are the cardinal questions."[43] And the answers to these cardinal questions were, he was sorry to disappoint his academic elders,
not amenable to mechanical theorising. "Credit is an opinion generated by circumstances and varying with those circumstances," so
that genuine insight into the functioning of the economy requires an
intimate familiarity with its history, its politics, and its psychology—
"no abstract argument, and no mathematical computation will teach
it to us."[44]

   This simple change of perspective on the fundamental nature of
money, Bagehot argued, implied not only a different understanding

of how the economy worked, but alternative policies to avoid crises and recessions. The first step here was to understand that although all money is transferable credit, there is one issuer of money whose obligations are, under normal circumstances, more creditworthy and more liquid than all the rest: the sovereign, which in the modern financial system had delegated its monetary authority to the Bank of England. This dominant role of sovereign authority in the monetary system was no fluke, Bagehot warned. Money depends on social trust, and "[c]redit in business is like loyalty in government," wrote Bagehot in a famous comparison, "[it] is a power which may grow, but cannot be constructed."[45]

This clear view of how sovereign money is, in normal circumstances, qualitatively different from private money, allowed Bagehot to explain the continuing importance of the Great Monetary Settlement and its practical implications for the modern economy. Though the modern monetary system, he explained, was now vastly expanded from the day of the Bank of England's establishment, it continued to work on the identical principle. The Bank had married the commercial acumen of one privileged set of private bankers with the public authority of the sovereign to render the Bank's money both creditworthy and universally transferable. And in the subsequent century and a half, the Bank itself had struck the same marriage time and time again with an ever-widening harem of other private bankers. Just as the sovereign had lent its unique authority to the Bank, so the Bank had over time got into the practice of lending its authority to the universe of other banks; and, until the policy reversal of 1858 that had heralded the beginning of the end for Overends, to the bill brokers as well. The result was a modern monetary economy in which "[o]n the wisdom of the directors of one Joint Stock Company, it depends *whether England is solvent or insolvent* . . . [a]ll banks depend on the Bank of England, and all merchants depend on some banker."[46]

Here was the reason, Bagehot explained, that Lombard Street was the money market of the entire global economy: the place where more banks were able to issue more money than ever before in the history of the world. Just as the Bank's money had originally gained its currency from its settlement with the sovereign, so now the moneys issued by the banks and bill brokers of Lombard Street gained theirs from the Bank, and the moneys of the country banks gained their currency from the banks and brokers of Lombard Street. Country and London banks attracted deposits from the savings of entrepreneurs and rentiers; merchant banks and bill brokers sourced investment opportunities from company promoters in which to place them. Modulating, and thereby enabling, the constant flux and reflux of payments to and from depositors and entrepreneurs was the great bill broker at the apex of the pyramid—the Bank of England, the first modern central bank. In a crisis, its pivotal role was clear for all to see. The Bank became all of a sudden the bill broker and banker of last resort, because it alone was always able to discount bills even if no one else would.

This remarkable monetary infrastructure was, Bagehot explained, the operating system of the Industrial Revolution, and what distinguished Britain from every other country in the world. That was the good news. But by the same token, if it was allowed to malfunction, the effects could be catastrophic. And the greatest temptation of all—the temptation for which the abstract economics of the classical school showed an insuperable weakness—was to forget that the central bank, as the delegate of the sovereign, is uniquely able to support the trust and confidence on which the monetary system depends; and is therefore uniquely responsible for the health not just of the City, but of the entire economy, in both normal and crisis times. "We must not think," wrote Bagehot, "that we have an easy task when we have a difficult task, or that we are living in a natural state when we are really living in an artificial one. Money will not manage itself, and Lombard street has a great deal of money to manage."[47] The crisis of 1866 had ruthlessly exposed the governance and policy of the Bank of England as an anachronistic relic at the heart of what had become the largest financial centre in the world. The time had come for reform.

Bagehot had two sets of proposals—both of which remain at

the heart of modern central-banking practice. The first concerned reforms of the governance and status of the Bank itself. The Bank of England remained a private company, and the agreement according to which it topped the monetary pyramid was implicit, intermittent, and entirely at the whim of its privately appointed management. Despite the facts that "[t]he directors of the Bank are . . . in fact, if not in name, trustees for the public . . . so far from there being a distinct undertaking on [their] part . . . to perform this duty, many of them would scarcely acknowledge it, and some altogether deny it."[48] And as for higher political oversight, "[n]ine-tenths of English statesmen, if they were asked as to the management of the Bank of England, would reply that it was no business of theirs or of Parliament at all."[49] This situation was no longer tenable. The central bank was an essential element—*the* essential element—of the modern monetary system. This fact should be acknowledged in the open, rather than honoured in the breach.

So much for the institution of the central bank. Even more important was its policy. In the crises of 1847, 1857, and after Overends itself, it had ultimately deployed its unique powers to save the financial system from disaster. But on each of these occasions, the Bank had acted only when catastrophe was imminent. As Winston Churchill once said of the United States, it could always be counted on to do the right thing—after it had exhausted all other possibilities. A large part of the problem, Bagehot argued on the basis of the testimony of the Bank's directors following the Overends crisis, was simply that they had no properly articulated principles of monetary policy. So Bagehot supplied them—and he kept them simple enough for policy-makers to grasp.

His first and most basic prescription was that the central bank's role as the lender or broker of last resort should be made a statutory responsibility, rather than left to the directors' discretion. When faith in the safety or liquidity of private money faltered, the Bank of England should stand ready to lend sovereign money without any specified limit. By offering to exchange its own obligations for those of the now discredited banks and businessmen, the Bank could and should

stay a panic before it becomes self-fulfilling. Bagehot therefore established the rationale for a proactive monetary policy, and his first rule
explained what the essential substance of this policy should be: "in
time of panic [the Bank] must advance freely and vigorously to the
public out of its reserve."[50]

Bagehot's second and third rules then set out two important
aspects of how such a policy should be applied. The second was that
in its role as lender of last resort, the bank should not try to make
nice distinctions between who is insolvent and who merely illiquid in
the heat of a crisis. It should lend "on all good banking securities, and
as largely as the public ask"; with a good banking security being any
that "in ordinary times is reckoned a good security."[51] The point of
the operation is "to stay alarm, and nothing therefore should be done
to cause alarm. But the way to cause alarm is to refuse some one who
has good security to offer."[52] There is always the risk, if a lender of last
resort is waiting in the wings to assuage a panic, that private banks
and merchants will become over-exuberant in their speculation—
that there will arise a problem of "moral hazard" as insurers and
economists call it. Bagehot therefore proposed his third principle to
ward off this risk. Emergency lending "should only be made at a very
high rate of interest . . . [to] operate as a heavy fine on unreasonable
timidity, and . . . prevent the greatest number of applications by persons who do not require it."[53]

Why was it that these ideas of Bagehot's were so controversial?
Why was it that Bagehot felt the need to apply himself so zealously
to such a polemical tract? If all this was so obvious to the practitioners, then why all the fuss? The reason was that there was in wide
circulation a quite different view of the nature of money and of how
the economy worked. This was the view of the dominant, classical school of economics—the school that had been inaugurated by
Adam Smith's *Wealth of Nations*, refined by men like David Ricardo
and Jean-Baptiste Say, and systematised by John Stuart Mill in his
great 1848 textbook, *The Principles of Political Economy*. Bagehot was
simply bringing logical rigour to the folk wisdom of the money market and the rules of thumb of the central bank. In the background,

however, remained the orthodox church of classical economics, with clear doctrines and a precise catechism on matters monetary and economic. And the disparity between its teachings and Bagehot's could not have been starker, both in their understanding of the economy and in their implications for policy.

At the root of these differences between Bagehot and his classical forebears was the way they conceived of money and finance. For there was a ghost haunting the pages of Smith and his classical followers: the ghost of John Locke and his monetary naturalism. Money, the classical economists held with unswerving devotion to Locke, was nothing but gold or silver. As such, it was a commodity subject to the same laws of supply and demand as every other commodity. "[M]oney, or specie, as some people call it," wrote the French economist Jean-Baptiste Say in 1803, "is a commodity, whose value is determined by the same general laws, as that of all other commodities."[1] "Money," pronounced John Stuart Mill forty-five years later, "is a commodity, and its value is determined like that of other commodities."[2] Private credit instruments, by contrast, were not money—they were just substitutes for money, and had value only insofar as there was real gold or silver available to redeem them.

The conventional understanding of money led the classical economists to diverge dramatically from the views of Bagehot in three areas. The first was the correct principles for monetary policy in a crisis. If the classical conception of money was correct—if money was gold and silver alone—then although everyone might want it in a crisis, there was only so much to go round. The Bank of England should therefore protect its hoard by refusing access, or raising the rate of interest at which the Bank would lend out its gold. Such was the policy recommended by the classical economists—a policy which Bagehot had no hesitation in calling "a complete dream," "a delusion," and "too absurd to be steadily maintained."[3] In reality, he explained, this was the very worst policy to pursue, because it was the one most likely to exacerbate the panic. What was in short supply in a crisis was not gold, but trust and confidence—which the central bank had a unique ability to restore by standing ready to swap the discredited bills of private issuers for its own sovereign money. Such was the solution to which the Bank Directors always in the end groped their way reactively in any case. Grasp once that money is not a commodity but credit, and the rationale for making it explicit policy was clear.

These diverging views of appropriate policy in a banking crisis were put in the shade, however, by a broader disagreement over the need for government policy, and especially monetary policy, to manage the macroeconomy more generally. The conventional view of money as a commodity medium of exchange was one of the pivotal assumptions behind perhaps the single most famous proposition associated with the classical school—an alleged economic law of nature as practically important as it was counter-intuitive, articulated by Jean-Baptiste Say in his *Treatise on Political Economy* in 1803. If money was a commodity, Say wrote, then there was no real distinction between sovereign and private money: gold is gold, whether minted or not. What is more, since the choice of commodity which serves as the medium of exchange is quite arbitrary, there can never be any danger of a shortage of money, since the enterprising mercantile class will always be able to improvise an alternative.

So far, so familiar. But combine these acknowledged facts with Smith's theory of the market and one had a key that unlocked the canonical question of macroeconomics: what is the origin of slumps? Smith had shown how the interaction of supply and demand will, in the absence of interference, generate a price that will clear the market. Since money is just a commodity subject to the same laws as other commodities, Say explained, this argument about how individual markets work can be generalised across all markets at once—including the market for money. Grant the conventional view of money, in other words, and Smith's theory implies that the uninhibited market mechanism will generate a set of prices that will clear all markets in the economy at once, so that everything which is produced is consumed. This in turn implies, as Say put it, "a conclusion that may at first sight appear paradoxical, namely, that it is production which opens a demand for products"; or in the more familiar modern version, that supply creates its own demand.[4]

This result, known as Say's Law, became enormously influential as a central organising principle of classical macroeconomics. If Say's Law holds, then recessions cannot be caused by a shortfall of demand. They must instead derive from problems on the supply side: natural disasters that wipe out harvests; unexpected factory outages; striking workers; the discovery of disruptive new production technologies; and so on. The popular explanation—indeed, the evidence of first appearances—that it is a shortage of money that causes a downturn must be an illusion. The fact that buyers do not have enough money with which to buy can only mean that they do not have enough produce to sell. Supply creates its own demand: so naturally if there is an interruption to aggregate supply, then—and only then—aggregate demand will flag to the same extent. The result will be a fall in the overall value of the economy's output; in other words, a slump.

So Bagehot's monetary economics implied a radical divergence from the precepts of the classical school not just over the correct policy to stem financial crises, but over the correct policy to prevent recessions. The basic policy implication of Say's Law was that there is no point in attempting to boost aggregate demand per se. Since the origins of recessions must necessarily be on the supply side, it is on policies to improve supply that anti-recessionary policy should concentrate—if it should do anything at all. Regulations that hinder hiring should be repealed; taxes and tariffs reduced; and so on. Attempting to bolster national output through monetary policy, however, would be putting the cart before the horse. It is because production increases that more money is demanded and will be supplied—not the other way round. And in fact, given that most recessions creep up on the economy unawares, and are over fairly rapidly, the policy that Say's Law really recommends for the government finding itself in the teeth of a recession is even simpler. Since supply-side conditions generally can't be changed much over the short term, it is really best to do nothing at all.

Bagehot's economics, by contrast, implied that the commonly held view that recessions are the result of people not having enough money was, to be blunt, quite right—and that Say's Law, therefore, was the economics of clever fools. When the economy fell into a crisis, the demand for sovereign money did not obey the same rules as the demand for commodities. It did not collapse as output flagged and confidence wilted. Quite the opposite: sovereign money's unique character meant that the demand for it increased. The paradox had been understood by practitioners at least since the crisis of 1825, when the prosperous Newcastle timber merchant and economic pamphleteer Thomas Joplin had summed it up concisely: "[a] demand for money in ordinary times, and a demand for it in periods of panic," he had written, "are diametrically different. The one demand is for money to *put into* circulation; the other for money to be *taken out* of it."[5] The correct remedy for an incipient recession is therefore not the policy fatalism implied by Say's Law. It is a larger supply of sovereign money to meet the excess demand and restore confidence. And fortunately, as Bagehot pointed out, the supply of sovereign money is in the real world a matter of central-bank policy.

There was one final consequence of the haunting of classical economics by Locke's view of money that was to prove in the long run even more influential than its implications either for central-bank policy in a financial crisis or for the right macroeconomic policy to combat a recession. Indeed, it was this consequence of the conventional view of money that would ultimately lead to the great distraction to which Lawrence Summers referred. For the intellectual debt the classical economists owed to Locke was much larger than just the idea that real money is gold and silver. It also included the most fundamental feature of Locke's understanding of money: the idea that economic value is a natural property, rather than a historically contingent idea.

This proposition had a profound consequence for the nature of classical economic analysis. In essence, it vastly simplified the task of understanding the economy. For if it was possible to take the concept of economic value for granted then economic analysis could, indeed should, proceed without worrying about money at all. Economic value had, after all, existed in the state of nature, long before the invention of money, or banks, or any of the other complications of modern finance. Money itself is simply one out of the universe of commodities which has been chosen to serve as a medium of exchange and so minimise the inconveniences of barter. As such, no one wants money itself: what is really wanted is the commodities that can be bought with money. This being the case, the simplest and best method of analysis is to begin by ignoring money. Economic analysis should proceed in what economists learned to call "real" terms. Money can then be added on afterwards, if it is a subject of interest for its own sake—or not, if it isn't.

This was the attractive invitation generously made by Locke's monetary naturalism, and the classical economists eagerly accepted it. Modern finance may look as though it is of great economic importance, conceded Smith. But in reality "what the borrower really wants, and what the lender really supplies him with, is not the money, but the money's worth, or the goods which it can purchase."[6] The economics of production and the distribution of income can therefore safely be analysed in terms of those goods alone. Of course it was true that almost every sale and purchase in a modern economy is settled with money, admitted Say. But when one really thinks about it, "[m]oney performs but a momentary function in this double exchange; and when the transaction is finally closed, it will always be found, that one kind of commodity has been exchanged for another."[7] But as usual, it was the great systematiser John Stuart Mill who stated the implications most clearly. "Great as the difference would be between a country with money, and a country wholly without it, it would be only one of convenience; a saving of time and trouble," he wrote, "like grinding by water power instead of by hand."[8] As a result, money was relegated to the middle of the third book of Mill's standard textbook and banished to the exotic fringes of the discipline. Since the quintessential economic topics of production, distribution, and exchange are all governed by the key concept of value, which is logically prior to money, everything worth knowing about them could be discovered by the analysis of the "real" economy. "There cannot, in short," Mill concluded, "be intrinsically a more insignificant thing, in the economy of society, than money."[9]

Nothing captures more succinctly the difference between the economics that the classical economists built using the conventional understanding of money, and the economics which Bagehot sought to popularise with the publication of *Lombard Street*. And nothing, in light of the crises of either 1866 or 2008–9, could be more patently absurd.

HOW ON EARTH IT HAPPENED

An observer innocent of the subsequent history of orthodox economics would no doubt assume that the consequences of Bagehot's devastating assault on the unrealistic apparatus of the classical school were swift and deadly. It is hardly surprising, she would think, that Bagehot would be the first name on Lawrence Summers' list of authorities to whom the leadership of the greatest economy on the planet would turn in the midst of the worst financial crisis in history. Bagehot, after all, finally threw off the intellectual shackles of the classical school and brought analytical rigour to the practical business of how money works in the real world. He explained how the principles of central-banking policy could be deduced from a proper understanding of a monetary economy. And he showed why the classical insistence that a slump cannot be due to a shortage of sovereign money was wrong—and how it derived from the mistaken view of money as a thing. Surely the abstruse and irrelevant doctrines of the classical school, with their bizarre blind spot for the world of money and finance, collapsed like a house of cards in the face of the terrible hurricane of 1866. Presumably, Bagehot's alternative perspective went on to become the foundation for all subsequent macroeconomics.

The innocent observer would be forgiven for shortening her odds still further, given the dazzling efforts of another member of Summers' alternative canon: the dominant economic thinker of the first half of the twentieth century, John Maynard Keynes. Money and finance were central to everything Keynes wrote. In the early 1920s he became "absorbed to the point of frenzy" in an attempt to discover the ultimate origins of finance in ancient Mesopotamia—an episode he would later mock as his "Babylonian madness" and admit had been "purely absurd and quite useless."[10] In 1923, however, he published *A Tract on Monetary Reform*, in which he argued that the monetary turmoil of the period during and immediately after the First World War demonstrated the central importance of inflation and deflation for both economic growth and the distribution of wealth and incomes. The stability generated by the nineteenth-century orthodoxies of the Gold Standard and laissez-faire, which the classical economists had alleged to be a scientific necessity, had been exposed as a special case entirely contingent upon the particular social compact of the pre-war world. The post-war experience had revealed the general rule to be that deliberate management of the monetary standard was needed to meet challenges of growth and distribution. It was an argument for putting money at the centre of economics and economic policy— and one of which John Law, for one, would have heartily approved.

These ideas were already far beyond the pale of classical economics; indeed, they were barely even comprehensible in terms of its moneyless doctrines. In characteristic fashion, Keynes decided that if his ideas could not be made to fit with the orthodox theory, then the theory would have to be made to fit with his ideas. He therefore resolved to rewrite the classical theory wholesale. The result, published in 1936, was his *General Theory of Employment, Interest, and Money*—the work that was to animate macroeconomics and macroeconomic policy-making for the rest of the century.[11]

In *General Theory*, Keynes took Bagehot's criticism of the classical economists a step further. A realistic view of money, he argued,
implied the necessity of deliberate management of not only monetary but fiscal policy. Like Bagehot, he located the root of the classical school's failings in its erroneous infatuation with Say's Law. The
nub of the matter, Keynes argued, was that in a monetary economy
Say's Law need not hold. There is no guarantee that, in the aggregate, supply will always equal demand, for the simple reason that in
a monetary economy, rather than having to buy goods and services
with their income, people can hold money instead. When prospects
look grim, that is exactly what people choose to do in spades—and
only the safest and most liquid money, the money of the sovereign,
will do.

The experience of the extended international depression of the
interwar period had taught Keynes something that was beyond even
Bagehot's broad experience. Proactive policy to boost demand indi-
rectly by ensuring that there is sufficient sovereign money available
to quell panic and meet an elevated demand for safety and liquidity is indeed a necessary condition to fight a slump. But when the
private sector's confidence is being constantly eroded by the down-
ward pull of excessive debt, it may not be enough. When that stage is
reached, it is time for the direct approach. The government will have
to spend if the private sector will not. This was the "basic Keynesian . . . framework" that Summers explained had come to the aid of
policy-makers in the immediate aftermath of the 2008 crash.[12] The
hour of expansionary fiscal, as well as expansionary monetary, policy
will have arrived.[13]

Once again, events seemed to have exposed the classical school
and the conventional theory of money as flawed: just as the crisis of
1866 had refuted the classical theory of crisis management, the monetary instability and mass unemployment of the 1930s had proved
the inadequacy of laissez-faire monetary and fiscal policy. And once
again, a brilliant thinker and irresistible communicator had been
on hand to explain how an alternative framework, founded on a
realistic understanding of money and finance, could inform bet-

ter policy. But history is replete with records of the extraordinary resilience of intellectual orthodoxies—and the conventional theory of money and the classical economics built on it proved to be an especially robust example. Like many a modernising church, the reaction of the classical school to these troubling practical setbacks and irritating theoretical critiques was not capitulation, but adaptation and abstraction. Money was no longer claimed literally to be a commodity—it was just right to think of it as if it were one. Value was no longer held explicitly to be an intrinsic property of things— though it was still treated as a natural fact. It had to be admitted that sovereign and private money were not, in light of experience, perfect substitutes—but there was no need to abandon the approved creed in favour of dangerous monetary heresies like Bagehot's or Keynes' in order to explain this. The moneyless economics of the classical school emerged from the Second World War battered, discredited, and apparently overshadowed by a new and persuasive set of ideas. But emerge it did. And within a decade of the war's end it received a powerful new tonic—a tonic which not only revived it, but gave it a whole new lease of life.

The classical school had not had to subsist without spiritual nourishment of its own in any case. Only a year after the publication of *Lombard Street*, the French economist Léon Walras had presented a mathematically rigorous formulation of the classical theory of price formation in his *Elements of Pure Economics*.[14] In 1937, the British economist and future Nobel laureate John Hicks had alleged that the central ideas of Keynes' *General Theory* could in fact be reconciled with classical orthodoxy.[15] It was in 1954, however, that a paper appeared that was, to those who believed, the discovery of a fifth gospel. The American economist Kenneth Arrow and the French mathematician Gerard Debreu published a formal proof that, given certain assumptions, a market economy would indeed tend to gravitate towards a "general equilibrium" in which a unique set of prices would ensure that there could be no excess demand or supply across all markets taken together.[16] It was, in other words, a knock-down argument in favour of the canonical classical doctrine—a formal proof of Say's

Law. What had long been suspected, and disputed back and forth in woolly, literary treatises, had now been proved with stark, mathematical precision. Almost immediately, however, an objection was raised: namely that it could only be proved for an economy without money.[17] The devotees of the new, general equilibrium theory could barely contain their amusement. Problem? That was the whole point. Arrow and Debreu's famous proof showed once and for all that money was extraneous to worthwhile economic analysis. Everything important could be logically proven in a model with no money at all.

Arrow and Debreu's proof of the existence of a general equilibrium rapidly became a fundamental tool for all mainstream research in macroeconomics over the next sixty years. It was true that reality kept butting in. Everyday experience continued to suggest that money and banking were important independent factors in the economy, rather than things that could be blithely ignored. Heretics continued to appear and preach the need to repent and heed alternative visions that took money seriously. But most were marginal figures— dismissed by the mainstream as eccentric cranks like Hyman Minsky, or safely defused as mere purveyors of historical colour like Charles Kindleberger. Once in a while, a savvy operator such as Milton Friedman would emerge and go straight to the policy-makers or even the public to champion the importance of money in economic analysis. But Arrow and Debreu's tonic proved a potent one: their recasting of the classical framework proved almost limitlessly flexible. It was complained of their original theory that it neglected the fact that the economy is not static, but evolves through time. A dynamic version was developed. It was said that it was overly deterministic, and ignored the fact that the real world is an uncertain place. The tools of classical probability theory were adduced to incorporate the possibility of what statisticians call "stochastic," or random, developments. It was pointed out that, even then, many of the assumptions required to prove the result required unbelievable assumptions concerning how rational and knowledgeable people are, and how universally and perfectly markets function. Generations of researchers spent countless hours delicately relaxing each of these assumptions one by one—some of the more reckless even took to relaxing several of them together—and exploring the consequences. There was no objection, it seemed, which the new orthodoxy of so-called dynamic, stochastic, general equilibrium models could not meet.

There was only one fly in the ointment. Everyday central-banking practice remained annoyingly ambivalent towards the so-called "neoclassical" theory. The academic profession might spend its time in transcendental meditation on the mystical abstractions of a general equilibrium theory of the economy, devoid of money, banks, and finance. Policy-makers, however, had to make do with the real world, where these things continued to make as much of a difference as ever and the central bank's interest-rate policy remained the most important tool available to discipline or encourage the private sector. For several decades there was, as a result, "not much fruitful interaction between economists from the central bank and academics," as one leading monetary economist put it with charming understatement.[18] This was clearly an untidy—even potentially an embarrassing—situation. How could modern, orthodox macroeconomics hold its head up as queen of the social sciences if it could not even win over its own policy-makers? Further doctrinal flexibility was required. By the late 1990s, an acceptable way to justify a limited role for monetary policy was at last identified—without, of course, recourse to such heretical notions as credit or liquidity risk.[19] The coup de grâce was to christen this latest version of the classical theory "New Keynesian"—to suggest that after the latest revamp it represented an adequate formalisation of all the wisdom that the *General Theory* contained. This heady mixture proved irresistible even to central bankers. Their defences were finally breached, and New Keynesian, dynamic, stochastic, general equilibrium models rapidly came to dominate the policy planning of the world's leading central banks. But at a fundamental level, all these modifications had been mere mopping-up operations. The real battle fought by Bagehot and Keynes had long ago been lost. The elephant in the room—the fact that the primary analytical workhorse of academics and policy-makers was not a theory of a monetary economy and "lacks an account of financial intermediation, so money, credit, and banking play no meaningful role," as the Governor of the Bank of England put it in 2012—had, as Lawrence Summers lamented, long since been forgotten.[20]

Such was the Lazarus-like destiny of the moneyless economics of the classical school. The fate of Bagehot's original concerns with the central importance of money, banking, and finance was initially less happy. Once their second coming in the hands of Keynes had been rebuffed by the mainstream, they languished in the backwaters of economic thought. Until, that is, they too were revived by a magic elixir—though one which also proved to have alarming transformative powers—when the worlds of banking and finance embarked on an era of deregulation after the Second World War. The growing importance of the equity and bond markets generated a demand by their participants for a framework in which to think cogently about their investing and trading activity. Theorists with a genuine interest in money and finance therefore discovered a private intellectual reservation opening up in which they could exercise themselves safe from inquisition by the orthodox church of macroeconomics. Unfortunately, enforced seclusion often makes for its own breed of dogmatism. All too quickly this new discipline of academic finance became just as detached from the economic realities that had obsessed Bagehot, Keynes, Minsky, and Kindleberger as post-war macroeconomics was. In its case, the problem was definitely not a lack of attention to the economics of financial claims. Quite the opposite: academic finance elected to concern itself with nothing else. It chose as its exclusive focus of investigation the pricing of financial securities on the private capital markets—the equity shares and bonds that were becoming ever more important as the liberalising policies of the post-war period picked up steam. Its major innovations—the theory of portfolio balance, the Capital Asset Pricing Model, the theory of options pricing—were eagerly adopted by financial practitioners, since investors and their agents were naturally interested in making sense of what they were doing.[21] Yet by focusing exclusively on the pricing of securities on private markets, academic finance developed an exact mirror image of the flaw of neoclassical macroeconomics. By ignoring the essential link between the financial securities traded on the capital markets and the monetary system operated by the sovereign and the banks, academic finance built a theory of finance without the macroeconomy just as neoclassical macroeconomics had built a theory of the macroeconomy without finance.

What was critically missing was the insight of Bagehot, and Joplin and Thornton before him, of the importance of liquidity as a distinct property of credit—the property which makes it money when it exists, and inert bilateral credit when it does not. This was the crucial link between finance and the real economy that Bagehot and Keynes had sought so hard to emphasise, and the rationale for macroeconomic policy—because the sovereign's liabilities enjoy a degree of liquidity to which no private issuer can aspire. Post-war academic finance, however, gladly abandoned to the macroeconomists the theologically fraught topic of whether and how the sovereign might need to provide liquidity support, and concerned itself only with unlocking the secrets of how the creditworthiness of financial claims traded on private markets affected their price. As such, it felt no need to complicate things with the additional dimension of liquidity, and before long, as one leading scholar has summed it up, "[i]n the . . . new formulation, it became impossible to conceptualize liquidity risk as a separate category of risk."[22] Just as modern, orthodox macroeconomics had ended up as a formal, mathematical theory of the moneyless doctrines of Say, Ricardo, and their classical followers, so modern, academic finance had ended up as a formal, mathematical theory of money in Utopia: a world with an infinite array of substitutable claims, with no mention of sovereign money.

WHY IT IS A PROBLEM: THE ANSWER TO THE QUEEN'S QUESTION

Most people are not that interested in the fine details of what academic economists get up to—and had these abstruse theoretical developments in macroeconomics and finance remained cloistered in the ivory towers, they would be right to be indifferent. But that is not what happened at all. It is a rare faith that does not at some point become so convinced of its own rectitude that it sets out to convert the world at large. By the late 1990s, the disciples of both modern, orthodox macroeconomics and modern, academic finance were proudly marching out under their respective banners to fight the good fight and evangelise their gospels.

The case of finance has become more notorious. In its early days, the older and more worldly of its proponents did wonder about the relevance of it all. In 1969, for example, the Nobel laureate James Tobin saw it as evidence of a worrying lack of realism that in the world depicted by academic finance "[t]here would be no room for monetary policy to affect aggregate demand" and that "[t]he real economy would call the tune for the financial sector, with no feedback in the other direction."[23] These features, he dared to suggest, showed that it must need careful handling before being used to guide policy in the real world. As the capital markets grew in size and scope, as innovation accelerated, and as the theory developed, however, newer proponents argued that Tobin's qualms were irrelevant, since what they were doing was showing the marvellous way the world could be, even if it wasn't that way yet. The pitch that such zealotry reached was demonstrated by the verdict delivered in 1995 by Fischer Black, one of the founding fathers of options theory, on the cornucopia of new financial instruments that his models had helped to create. "I don't see that the private market, in creating this wonderful array of derivatives, is creating any systemic risk," Black argued; "[h]owever, there is someone around creating systemic risk: the government."[24]

The manner in which anti-authority fantasies of this sort, and the automatic presumption in favour of practical financial deregulation which they supported, were rudely interrupted by reality during the crash of 2008 needs no rehearsal. Perhaps less well known are the practical consequences of the conversion of the policy-making world to the doctrines of the orthodox, New Keynesian macroeconomics on the other side of the schism. The most important of these concerned the correct objectives of monetary policy. The sole monetary ill that had been permitted into the New Keynesian theory was high or volatile inflation, which was deemed to retard the growth of GDP.[25] The appropriate policy objective, therefore, was low and stable inflation, or "monetary stability." Henceforth, governments should therefore confine their role to establishing a reasonable inflation target, and then delegate the job of setting interest rates to an independent central bank staffed by able technicians.[26] On such grounds, the Bank of England was granted its independence and given a mandate to target inflation in 1997, and the European Central Bank was founded as an independent, inflation-targeting central bank in 1998.

There is little doubt that under most circumstances, low and stable inflation is a good thing for both the distribution of wealth and income, and the stimulation of economic prosperity. But in retrospect, it is clear that "monetary stability" alone was far too narrow a policy objective as it was pursued from the mid-1990s to the mid-2000s. Disconcerting signs of impending disaster in the pre-crisis economy—booming house prices, a drastic underpricing of liquidity in asset markets, the emergence of the shadow banking system, the declines in lending standards, bank capital, and liquidity ratios—were not given the priority they merited, because, unlike low and stable inflation, they were simply not identified as being relevant. As the Chairman of the U.K.'s Financial Services Authority admitted bluntly in 2012, central banks had "a flawed theory of economic stability . . . which believed that achieving low and stable current inflation was sufficient to ensure economic and financial stability, and which failed to identify that credit and asset price cycles are key drivers of instability."[27]

Indeed, the fruits of a decade's devoted worship at the shrine of monetary stability were more damaging even than this. The single-minded pursuit of low and stable inflation not only drew attention away from the other monetary and financial factors that were to bring the global economy to its knees in 2008—it exacerbated them. The heretical Cassandra Hyman Minsky had warned of this baleful possibility many years before.[28] The more successful a central bank is in mitigating one type of risk by achieving low and stable inflation, the more confident investors will become, and the more they will willingly assume other types of risk by investing in uncertain and illiquid securities. Squeezing the balloon in one place—eliminating high and volatile inflation—will simply reinflate it in another—causing catastrophic instability in asset markets. Monetary stability will actually breed financial instability.

Not all policy-makers were unaware that the orthodox theory might be leading them into error—and why it might be doing so. In 2001, Mervyn King—an internationally renowned macroeconomist and future Governor of the Bank of England—was to be found lamenting the fact that while "[m]ost people think that economics is the study of money," it was in fact nothing of the sort. "Most economists," he explained, "hold conversations in which the word 'money' hardly appears at all."[29] "My own belief," he warned, "is that the absence of money in the standard models which economists use will cause problems in the future . . . Money, I conjecture, will regain an important place in the conversation of economists."[30] The global financial crisis has shown his belief to have been prophetic, though precisely because his conjecture was not.

What was it in the end that frustrated the dream of Bagehot and of Keynes for an economics that takes money seriously? The ultimate answer lies in the powerful influence of Locke's monetary doctrines. By the time Bagehot launched his assault it was too late. Money had already gone through the Looking-Glass. The conventional understanding of money as a commodity medium of exchange was already in place—and neither evidence nor argument to the contrary was even intelligible any longer to anyone under its spell. As a result, the crisis of 1866 and Bagehot's famous reaction to it was not, it turned out, the point at which two ways of thinking about money and the economy converged—but the one from which they parted ways.

From the moneyless economics of the classical school there evolved modern, orthodox macroeconomics: the science of monetary society taught in universities and deployed by central banks.

From the practitioners' economics of Bagehot, meanwhile, there evolved the academic discipline of finance—the tools of the trade taught in business schools, used by bankers and bond traders. One was an intellectual framework for understanding the economy without money, banks, and finance. The other was a framework for understanding money, banks, and finance, without the rest of the economy. The result of this intellectual apartheid was that when in 2008 a crisis in the financial sector caused the biggest macroeconomic crash in history, and when the economy failed to recover afterwards because the banking sector was broken, neither modern macroeconomics nor modern finance could make head nor tail of it. Fortunately, as Lawrence Summers pointed out, there were alternative traditions to fall back on. But the answer to the Queen's question—Why did none of the economists see it coming?—is simple. Their main framework for understanding the macroeconomy didn't include money. And by the same token, the question that many were keen to put to the bankers and their regulators—Why didn't they realise that what they were doing was so risky?—also turned out to be simple. Their framework for understanding finance did not include the macroeconomy.

It would all have been comical—or just irrelevant—had it not ended in such a cataclysmic economic disaster. At the end of his speech at Bretton Woods, Lawrence Summers noted how economics had lost track of finance over the previous two decades—and acknowledged that the crash showed how it, and thereby the world, had suffered as a result. But as Keynes, Bagehot, and indeed William Lowndes before them, would have been eager to explain, the divergence was much older than that. And at the root of it all was a deceptively simple change of perspective: the difference between two conceptions of money.

14 How to Turn the Locusts into Bees

CAN WE AVOID THE ISLAND OF DR. MOREAU?
In November 2004, the Chairman of Germany's governing Social Democratic Party, Franz Müntefering, made a famous speech attacking the culture of modern financial capitalism. He launched a vitriolic tirade against contemporary financiers, describing them as "irresponsible locust swarms, who measure success in quarterly intervals, suck off substance, and let companies die once they have eaten them away."[1] It was a metaphor that struck a chord with the public all over Europe—and one that stood in ironic contrast to the analogy of the enterprising and co-operative beehive which the Dutchman Bernard Mandeville had employed to convince sceptics of the benefits of monetary society in the early eighteenth century.[2]

At the time, Müntefering's invective seemed the nadir of finance's public reputation in Europe. Nine years later, the stock of banks and bankers across the globe had sunk infinitely lower still. The immediate catalyst was the global financial crisis of 2007–8. It was in the banking sector, after all, that the macroeconomic disaster that left millions out of work and societies deeply fractured began; and to add insult to injury, the general public was forced to bail out the very institutions which caused the crisis. In Southern Europe, popular resentment found a target in "the dictatorship of the bankers."[3] Even in the centres of global capitalism, banking's reputation took such a battering that by mid-2012 the house magazine of the global financial elite, *The Economist*, required only one word to summarise its assessment of contemporary finance professionals: "Banksters."[4]

The crisis and its aftermath reactivated the old suspicion—perfectly captured in Müntefering's rhetoric—that banking is basically a parasitic rather than a productive activity. Banking has always been difficult for outsiders to understand, but the last decade and a half has seen an exponential increase in the rate of innovation and sophistication in finance. When many of these same innovations were implicated in the crash and it was taxpayers rather than bankers who were stuck with the bill, old doubts resurfaced. What was the point of the CDOs and CDSes, the ABCP and the SPVs, that the 1990s and 2000s gave us? It was not just brassed-off account-holders and exasperated taxpayers who expressed their doubts, but some of the leading lights of the financial industry itself. Adair Turner, Chairman of the U.K. Financial Services Authority, put it diplomatically in August 2009 when he said that at least some of the previous decade of financial innovation had been "socially useless."[5] Paul Volcker, the grand old man of global financial regulation, was more direct. The only financial innovation of the previous two decades that had added any genuine value to the broader economy, he said with withering contempt, was the ATM.[6]

The result of this powerful and widespread reaction to the crisis is that today, for the first time in decades, there are serious campaigns in progress in virtually all of the world's most developed economies to reform banking, finance, and the entire framework of monetary policy and financial regulation. There has been a slew of investigations, reports, panels, and legislation—all of which have come on top of other, ongoing, and international efforts.[7] The politicians and regulators, it appears, have been eager to heed the well-known motto of the ex–White House chief of staff Rahm Emanuel: "Never let a serious crisis go to waste."[8]

Or have they? If the unauthorised biography of money we have unearthed tells us something about what went wrong with economic theory and policy before and after the crisis, does it also have something to contribute to the very live debates over the more structural questions of whether the monetary and financial system can be fixed so that a repeat of today's economic and social catastrophe can be avoided? Is there anything we can learn from the neglected tradition of monetary scepticism that would help solve this pressing policy problem? And might it be rather more radical than the reforms currently working their way through the parliaments and regulators of the world's financial capitals? The stated aim of all these processes is to make banking and finance serve the real economy and society again—to turn Franz Müntefering's locusts into Sir Bernard Mandeville's bees. But as connoisseurs of the horror genre, from H. G. Wells' 1896 novel *The Island of Dr. Moreau* to David Cronenberg's 1986 film *The Fly,* know only too well, genetic engineering is a risky business. Get it wrong, and you can end up with a monster.

FROM QUID PRO QUO TO SOMETHING FOR NOTHING

On 14 September 2007, the U.K. Chancellor of the Exchequer announced that he had authorised the Bank of England to provide a "liquidity support facility"—effectively, a larger than normal overdraft—to Northern Rock, a medium-sized British bank that specialised in residential mortgages.[9] Northern Rock had run into trouble because it funded a large part of its book of mortgage lending—by its nature, a collection of very long-term promises to pay—by selling short-dated bills and bonds to investors; that is, short-term promises to pay. When problems emerged in international financial markets in the course of 2007, this short-term funding disappeared. And when Northern Rock's depositors saw the way the wind was blowing, they also began to pull out their money. A run on the bank in the so-called "wholesale" funding markets—the markets for its bills and bonds—had become a run on the bank in its "retail" funding market—its deposits from individuals and companies. All of a sudden, Northern Rock was in the throes of a classic liquidity crisis. The "run on the Rock," as it soon became known, had begun.[10]

This was hardly a novel problem in the world of banking. As we have seen, the purest essence of banking is the business of maintaining the synchronisation of payments in and out of the balance sheet.[11] The generic challenge is that the assets which banks hold—the loans they have made—are typically to be repaid relatively far in the future, while their liabilities potentially come due much sooner—indeed, on demand, in the case of many kinds of deposits. There is, in other words, an intrinsic mismatch—the bank's "maturity gap" as it is called—that cannot be eliminated from a banking system like the one that exists today. Most of the time, the maturity gap is not a problem. Indeed, its very existence is in one sense the whole purpose of the banking system. The bank's depositors get the freedom of being able to withdraw or make payments with their deposits at a moment's notice, while they get interest that can only be generated by risky and illiquid loans. But it makes synchronising payments a particularly delicate art. If, for one reason or another, depositors and bondholders lose confidence in a bank's ability to meet its commitments to them as they come due, and they therefore withdraw their deposits and refuse to roll over their lending en masse, the maturity gap presents an insuperable problem for the bank if it can only rely on its own resources.

Fortunately, however, modern banks have friends in high places. Under the terms of the Great Monetary Settlement, a bank's liabilities, unlike the liabilities of normal companies, are an officially endorsed component of the national money supply. And since money is the central co-ordinating institution of the economy, any impairment of its transferability would impose grave costs on the whole of society—not just on the particular bank that issued it. Money must therefore be protected from suspicions concerning any one of the banks that operate it. Just as electricity is delivered through a network for which the failure of a single power station can be disastrous, the vast majority of modern money is provided and operated by a network of banks in which the failure of one can disrupt the system as a whole. In fact, even greater vigilance is required in the case of the banking system. Disruption of the electricity grid at least requires the malfunction of physical infrastructure. In the banking system, a mere loss of confidence in one of the parts can be fatal to the whole.

Preventing liquidity crises in banks has therefore long been recognised as an important responsibility of the sovereign: as we saw earlier, it was Walter Bagehot who formalised the rules for how to cure a crisis when it occurs. If panic strikes and a bank's depositors and bondholders withdraw their funding, he taught, the correct remedy is for the sovereign to step into their shoes. As bondholders and depositors demand payment, the bank should be permitted to borrow from the Bank of England in order to pay them out in sovereign money. More and more of its balance sheet will be funded, in effect, by the central bank, and less and less by private investors. And by the same token, private investors will hold fewer and fewer claims on the private bank and more and more claims on the Bank of England; or cash, as it is more commonly known. Bagehot's solution became standard practice throughout the world. Even the U.S., a latecomer to the wonders of modern central banking, installed the system in 1913. This was the time-honoured palliative being deployed in September 2007 by the Bank of England—for the first time, it was said, since the collapse of Overend, Gurney a hundred and forty years earlier.[12]

As the months went on, it became clear that Northern Rock's problem was not just one of liquidity, however. Many of the loans it had made were no good. This was no longer a problem of synchronising payments that were going to be made as agreed. It meant that no matter how good the synchronisation, the sums might not add up. The total value of Northern Rock's liabilities, it seemed, was larger than the value of its assets—regardless of when one or the other was coming due. Under normal circumstances—if it has been doing its job properly—the value of a bank's assets will be larger than its liabilities. The difference between the two is the bank's equity capital. When it is positive, the bank is said to be solvent, and the more positive it is, the larger the decline in asset values that the bank can withstand without becoming insolvent. Northern Rock, it seemed, had been sailing too close to the wind. It had operated with a small amount of equity capital. When the housing market had deterio-

rated and the economy gone into recession, the value of the mortgages that made up much of its assets had started to fall. The value
of the bank's liabilities, on the other hand, had stayed the same—as
liabilities awkwardly do. The bank's equity capital had quickly been
eroded. The market price of a share in that equity had collapsed in
response. From a high of over £12 in the halcyon days of February
2007, it had already fallen to around £7 in late August, and then to £3
two days after the announcement of the Bank of England's liquidity
support operation. Now it dropped to below a pound a share. In the
absence of external assistance, it was clear that the market believed
Northern Rock to be not just illiquid, but insolvent.

Luckily for Northern Rock—or at least for its bondholders, depositors, and other customers—external assistance was at hand for the
second time. Once again, the U.K. sovereign stepped in, but this time
into the shoes not of the bank's lenders, but of its shareholders. New
equity capital was required in order to make good the gap between
the value of the bank's assets and its liabilities—and to provide an
adequate buffer against potential further declines. The liquidity support operation had consisted of the sovereign merely agreeing to
give one fixed promise to pay—a claim on the Bank of England—in
return for another fixed promise of supposedly equal value—a claim
on Northern Rock. What was now required, however, was something quite different. The sovereign would give its fixed promises to
pay in return for equity: a residual claim on the uncertain difference
between the value of Northern Rock's assets and its liabilities. The
liquidity support, at least in principle, had involved no risk of profit
or loss—just a transfer of liquidity risk from private investors to the
sovereign. This new operation would involve, by contrast, a transfer
of credit risk. If losses ceased to mount on Northern Rock's mortgages, the sovereign might not lose money. But if they did not, the
sovereign, as equity owner, would be on the hook. This was not a job
for the Bank of England—the monetary authority. If the sovereign is
deliberately going to put taxpayers' money at risk, better to ensure
that it is its democratically elected government that is doing so. The
purchase of Northern Rock's equity was therefore made by the U.K.

Treasury—the fiscal authority. On 17 February 2008, the bank was nationalised.[13]

Amongst the general public, the initial reaction was one of mystification, even indifference. The bank had failed and had been bailed out—by which arm of the state and how was frankly much of a muchness. Policy-makers and financial professionals, however, recognised the U.K. Treasury's decisive action as a radical new policy—one which spoke ominously to the potential scale of the crisis ahead, and which set a radical precedent for the policy response to it. By nationalising Northern Rock, the U.K. sovereign had revealed that it felt it necessary to provide not just liquidity, but credit, support to the banking sector. The Bank of England's lending from September to February had kept depositors, bondholders, and the bank's existing equity-holders unscathed—on the assumption that there was some value in the bank's equity. Once the bank's equity capital had been eroded by losses, the luck of its shareholders had run out. In the normal order of things, its bondholders would have been next in line. Instead, it now transpired, they were able to call on a second line of defence: the U.K. Treasury's previously undeclared insurance of bank investors against credit losses. Courtesy of the Chancellor of the Exchequer, the British taxpayer was on hand to assume the risk of further losses that would otherwise have had to be borne by Northern Rock's bondholders.

What, observers asked, could have prompted the U.K. sovereign to such extraordinary generosity? Liquidity support was one thing—it had been official policy at least since Bagehot's day and unofficial policy even before that. But credit support and bank recapitalisation with direct costs to taxpayers—these were clear and controversial policies historically reserved for the direst circumstances. They were the stuff of the Great Depression—when a special government-funded body, the Reconstruction Finance Corporation, had been established to recapitalise banks in the U.S.—or of the near-collapse of the U.K. economy in the 1970s, when the government had stepped in to provide capital to the secondary banks when private investors would not. Moreover, credit support was historically shunned for good reason. If moral hazard presented a dilemma for the central bank's role as lender of last resort, how much more of a dilemma did it present for the National Treasury's role as shareholder of last resort? If every banker—and, just as important, every investor that funded his bank—knew that the sovereign stood ever-ready to cover his losses should things go wrong, what possible discipline could there ever be on lending standards and volumes?

The market began to suspect that there was something terribly wrong. Why else should the line between liquidity and credit support have been crossed, and the natural political reluctance to have tax-payers bail out banks have been trumped? The policy-makers knew only too well the gravity of what they had done, and tried furiously to dispel what they knew would be the fatal impression that no one need any longer watch their backs. "Banks," announced the U.K. Parliament's Treasury Select Committee in a desperate attempt to shut the stable door, "should be allowed to 'fail' so as to preserve market discipline on financial institutions."[14]

But the horse had already bolted. Only the most terrifying warning might chase it back in again. So it was that when Bear Stearns, the fifth-largest U.S. securities dealer, ran into trouble in March 2008, the U.S. authorities made it clear that liquidity support alone would be forthcoming. When it emerged that Bear Stearns was on the brink of failure, it was a private investor—the universal bank, J. P. Morgan—that stepped in to buy its equity. The policy-makers were encouraged. Perhaps the horse had been scared back into its stable. When a second major U.S. investment bank, Lehman Brothers, began to suffer a catastrophic run almost a year to the day after the run on Northern Rock, the emboldened U.S. authorities held their nerve. Alas, the horse was not back in the stable after all. "They can shoot a Bear," was the gag doing the rounds in the financial markets on Friday, 12 September 2008, "but they can't shoot the Brothers." Despite the stand on Bear Stearns, bankers and their investors remained convinced that the policy-makers would fold. The strength of their conviction was measured by the sheer panic which ensued when on Monday, 15 September, credit support from the sovereign was refused, and Lehman Brothers filed for bankruptcy.

The collateral damage to the financial sector and the real economy caused by the failure of Lehman Brothers was beyond all expectations. The heroic attempts of the policy-makers to deny the doctrine of blanket credit insurance disintegrated. What, after all, was the point of trying to preserve market discipline when the markets themselves were no longer functioning? The End of the World—or at least the End of the Banks—was nigh, and had to be prevented at any cost—or at least, any cost to the taxpayer.[15] In an instant, the nationalisation of Northern Rock became not an embarrassing aberration, unmentionable in polite society for fear of giving the bankers unsuitable ideas, but the model of good policy. The result was a level of sovereign credit support for the world's banking sectors unlike anything ever witnessed before. Twenty-five countries experienced major banking crises between 2007 and 2012: two-thirds of them resorted to providing credit support to their banks.[16] The sheer scale of some of the interventions was unprecedented. The U.S. spent 4.5 per cent of GDP recapitalising its banks—equal to its entire annual defence budget in the midst of a major war.[17] In 1816, Thomas Jefferson had warned that "banking establishments are more dangerous than standing armies."[18] His verdict was proving alarmingly close to the truth, if not in the sense he had intended. The U.K. spent 8.8 per cent of GDP—considerably more than it spends annually on its much-vaunted National Health Service.[19] The Irish sovereign spent over 40 per cent of GDP—more than the typical annual budget of every department of government put together. There could no longer be any doubt. The sovereign had the bankers' backs.

When the dust had settled and the Great Recession set in, the public began to realise what had happened. The banks and their investors had been making a one-way bet. Their business was—just as it always had been—to manage liquidity and credit risk. But if they proved unable to synchronise their payments, the central bank would step in with liquidity support. And if their loans went bad and their equity capital was too thin, the taxpayer would backstop their credit losses. The consequences were, in retrospect, utterly predictable. Around the world, banks had grown in size, reduced their capital buffers, made riskier loans, and decreased the liquid-

"SAME OLD GAME!"

Old Lady of Threadneedle Street. "YOU'VE GOT YOURSELVES INTO A NICE MESS WITH YOUR PRECIOUS
'SPECULATION!' WELL—I'LL HELP YOU OUT OF IT,—FOR THIS ONCE!!"

"Same Old Game" indeed—though today it is not just liquidity,
but also credit, insurance that the sovereign generously doles out.

ity of their assets. More and more had become too big to fail. As
a result, the level of credit insurance that sovereigns had implicitly
been providing had ballooned. Only when the crisis had struck, and
the policy-makers' initial efforts to control moral hazard collapsed,
had the true scale of the subsidy become clear. In November 2009,
a year after the collapse of Lehman Brothers, total sovereign support for the banking sector worldwide was estimated at some $14
trillion—more than 25 per cent of global GDP.[20] This was the scale
of the downside risks, taxpayers realised, that they had been bearing
all along—whilst all the upside went to the shareholders, debt investors, and employees of the banks themselves.

It was a world that Walter Bagehot would not have recognised. The doctrine of the central bank as lender of last resort had become the doctrine of the sovereign as loss-bearer of last resort. This innovation of widespread credit support from national treasuries introduced a dramatic new dimension to the political calculus. When the central bank provides liquidity support, nobody, in principle, loses—and the widely shared benefits of a well-functioning monetary system are preserved. When the government provides credit support, however, taxpayers bear a real cost. The question, of course, is who gains? One answer—the one which garnered most attention in the immediate aftermath of the crisis—is the bankers themselves. When the government bailed out the banks, many bank employees continued, at least for a time, to have their jobs and to earn their bonuses. That was politically contentious, but in reality the bankers themselves enjoyed only one part of the taxpayers' generosity. The banks' bondholders and depositors—those who freely agreed to fund the bankers' lending—were also beneficiaries of the sovereign's unprecedented largesse. When it was refused, as it was to Lehman Brothers, bondholders had to shoulder the losses due to the bad loans that had been made. When it was not, the sovereign relieved them of this unpleasant burden.

Once upon a time, the idea of taxpayers bailing out bank bondholders might not have been politically contentious, because there was little distinction between the two groups. One way or another, via the investments of pension funds and mutual funds, they were by and large one and the same. But in the modern, developed world, two powerful forces have conspired to undermine this convenient correspondence between those who fund the banking system and those who stand to bail it out when things go wrong. The first is increased inequality of wealth and income, which has opened up a divide between the wealthy few who own banks' bonds, and the more modest majority who do not. Spending public money to protect bank bondholders has become an issue of rich versus poor. The second powerful force has been the internationalisation of finance. In countries such as Ireland and Spain, the globalisation of bond markets has meant that domestic taxpayers found themselves footing the bill for bank recapitalisation that benefited foreign bondholders. Firing civil servants to pay for bail-outs meant to save their own pension fund is one thing. Firing them to pay out foreign pensioners is politically quite another. When, on 31 January 2011, Anglo-Irish Bank—which had been recapitalised to the tune of EUR 25.3 billion by Irish taxpayers—repaid in full and on schedule a EUR 750 million bond to its investors, the distribution of risks under the new regime of sovereign credit support for banks was on stark display. The total cuts to welfare spending in that year's Irish budget amounted to a little over the same amount.[21]

The global public's dismay at this state of affairs is therefore not due to an unfortunate misunderstanding of how the financial world does, and indeed has to, work. People are right to smell a rat. The crisis of 2007–8 and sovereigns' response to it revealed a profoundly uncomfortable truth: something has gone terribly wrong with the Great Monetary Settlement. The historic deal struck between the sovereign and the Bank of England in 1694 involved a carefully calibrated exchange of benefits. The private bankers got liquidity for their banknotes. The crown's writ, unlike their own, ran throughout the land, and money that had its blessing could enjoy universal circulation. In return, the bankers provided the financial acumen and the trusted reputation in the City that enhanced the crown's creditworthiness. In modern terms, the crown provided liquidity support to the Bank, while the Bank provided credit support to the sovereign. Yet the policy-makers' response to the crisis revealed a starkly different world. Banks, of course, retained their privilege of issuing sovereign money—and the central bank stood ready to guarantee its liquidity in times of need. But far from receiving support to its credit in return, it was the sovereign that ended up supporting the credit of the banks. The banks—their employees, their bondholders, and their depositors—get both liquidity and credit support. The sovereign—that is, the taxpayer—gets nothing. The crisis revealed that the historic quid pro quo had become a quid pro nihilo: something for nothing.

This was bad enough but there was even worse to come. No

sooner had the crisis exposed with brutal honesty the strange death
of the Great Monetary Settlement that had kept the peace between
sovereigns and banks for three hundred years, than it unveiled the
equally startling revelation that another hoary old veteran of monetary politics was very much alive—and active on a scale never seen
before.

THE COUP D'ÉTAT IN THE CREDIT MARKETS

The great wave of economic deregulation and globalisation that
began in the late 1970s, accelerated in the 1980s and '90s, and reached
its zenith in the pre-crisis years of the early 2000s brought with it
revolutions in the organisation of industries from car manufacturing
to the supply of electricity, and from supermarkets to film-making.
The watchword was decentralisation: the hundreds of activities once
housed in a single corporation could be hived off to smaller and more
specialised companies, and co-ordinated by the market using supply chains and networks of astonishing complexity and length.[22] Of
course, some complained that it went too far—that the costs saved
by moving customer care to a call centre in Bangalore or Manila were
really just offloaded on to the enraged customers on the other end
of the line. But overall, few could deny that in industry after industry
the result for the consumer was a phenomenal reduction in costs and
improvement in choice.

Finance was no stranger to these tectonic shifts in industrial
organisation. Until the late 1960s, lending to companies and individuals remained for the most part a simple and familiar business undertaken almost exclusively by banks. The borrower visited the bank;
the loan officer scrutinised the request and worked it up for approval;
the bank manager signed off on the appraisal; the loan was entered
in the bank's loan book as part of the bank's assets; and a deposit
was credited to the borrower as part of the bank's liabilities. The
whole transaction had only two counterparties—the borrower and
the bank—and the bank's balance sheet was where the management
of credit and liquidity risk took place. But for centuries there had

also existed an alternative way of raising money: by selling financial securities—promises to pay such as shares in the equity of a company or bonds paying a fixed interest over time—directly to investors. The equity capital markets—the stock market, for short—had always been a democratic affair. Even quite small companies could issue shares; they were traded on public exchanges; and there was a vast army of retail investors. The debt capital markets, on the other hand, were more exclusive. Borrowing by issuing bonds was "high finance," the preserve of only the largest corporations, and, above all, of sovereigns themselves. Likewise, the investors in these securities were mostly "institutional investors" such as pension funds, insurance companies, and mutual funds, which aggregated the savings of many thousands of individuals to reach the scale required to play the bond markets. And rather than hawked on stock exchanges like fish in the marketplace, the buying and selling of bonds was done by brokers through their personal networks, like pieces of antique furniture that needed to be found the right home.

Nevertheless, for most borrowers, banks remained the dominant source of debt capital right up until the late 1970s. It was only then that the revolutions in information technology and supply-chain management began to unlock the logic of specialisation and the division of labour in finance as in so many other industries. The debt capital markets, it was realised, represented a vast opportunity to create intermediaries that specialised in individual component activities of banks; and hence the potential for enormous gains in efficiency. Borrowers could continue to come to the bank, and loan officers to scrutinise their requests and knock them into reasonable shape. But the business of actually approving the loans and of monitoring the borrowers could be done just as well—perhaps better—by investors themselves. The bank would merely arrange, rather than implement, the allocation of credit. The loan itself need never appear on the bank's balance sheet. It would become instead a financial security—a bond—owed by the borrower, and owned directly by the individual or institutional investor. The traditional banking model of doing everything in-house began to give way to a new model of "originate and distribute"—of specialising in the identification of borrowers and end-investors, while letting others do the screening, warehousing, and monitoring of the loans. The business of financing companies and individuals was beginning a great migration from the world of banks to the world of markets for financial securities distinguished by their issuers' credit risk—the credit markets, for short.

The shift was most pronounced in the U.S., where securities-based finance had always held a stronger position than in Europe. In the early 1980s, around half of debt capital to U.S. companies was still provided by banks.[23] From the middle of that decade, however, the share of finance arranged instead on the credit markets began to rise. The Savings and Loan crisis of the late 1980s and early 1990s gave this shift a major boost. With a large part of the commercial banking sector in repair mode, the credit markets took up the slack. By the end of 1993, they accounted for more than 60 per cent of U.S. corporate debt finance. A decade later, their share reached 70 per cent. And not only the scale, but the scope, of the credit markets was being transformed. When Michael Milken was almost single-handedly creating the market for bonds issued by small or risky companies from his famous Beverly Hills office in the early 1980s, few would have predicted that two decades later issuance of what were then derisively called "junk" bonds would grow to U.S. $150 billion a year, and displace a substantial part of the banking sector's financing of Main Street U.S.A.[24] An even bigger revolution was taking place in the provision of debt finance to individuals. The development of techniques for pooling and securitising large numbers of mortgage, car, and credit-card loans to individuals generated a near-total shift in the organisation of these types of debt from banks to credit markets. It was a dramatic and fundamental change in one of the most basic functions of the capitalist economy. The days when mainstream finance was the business of banks and the debt capital markets were an obscure specialisation were gone for ever. In 1968, Sidney Homer had been able to lay out in three pages of *The Bond-Buyer's Primer*, his celebrated insider's guide to the debt markets, all the important U.S. corporate bond issuers in existence.[25] There were so few that they all had their own nicknames, speaking quaintly to the simplicity of the corporate landscape of the day: "Rubbers" for the bonds of U.S. Rubber; "Steels" for the bonds of U.S. Steel; and so on. By the late 1990s, such familiarity was unthinkable. There were now tens of thousands of bonds issued by many thousands of issuers—and when the legal structuring was peeled away, most were no longer U.S. household names but just plain U.S. households.

This was just the beginning. In the 2000s, the business of securitisation—the bundling together of many smaller debt securities to make new, larger debt securities—took off. Mortgages, car loans, corporate loans, credit-card debt—any kind of credit could be packaged up, sliced into tranches, assessed by a ratings agency, and then sold on to a new set of investors. The borrowing of money via the credit markets had once been a simple transaction: a bond issued by a company with assistance from a bank was bought by an individual or an institution. Now it could be much more elaborate. A company could still issue a bond. But rather than being bought by the end-investor, it could instead be acquired and "warehoused" by another company specifically established for the purpose. That company could then issue asset-back commercial paper (another type of debt security) to a special-purpose vehicle (another type of company) whose liabilities would in turn be "warehoused" by a fourth company, whose own debt securities could be bought by another special-purpose vehicle which would use it to back collateralised debt obligations (yet another type of debt security) that would be purchased by a hedge fund and finally used as security for a loan from a money market mutual fund. Only then would the end-investor rematerialise, just in time to buy shares in the money market mutual fund and thereby provide the cash which would in the end wend its way back up the chain to the original issuing company—less fees, of course.[26]

This enormous increase in complexity left those weaned on Sidney Homer's *Bond-Buyer's Primer* perplexed. What was the point of it all? They were summarily dismissed as quaint, old fuddy-duddies. Under the powerful spell of the orthodox, modern theories of finance and macroeconomics, the prevailing wisdom was that these

innovations represented the royal road to everything from lower
mortgage rates for homeowners to greater macroeconomic stability.
The International Monetary Fund delivered one particularly memorable verdict in 2006. "There is growing recognition," it said, "that
the dispersion of credit risk by banks to a broader and more diverse
group of investors, rather than warehousing such risk on their balance sheets, has helped to make banking and the overall financial system more resilient."[27] The new arrangements would moreover "help
to mitigate and absorb shocks to the financial system" and amongst
their manifold benefits would be "fewer bank failures and more consistent credit provision."[28] But the real shortcoming of such confident predictions was not their over-optimistic appraisal of what they
thought the new arrangements in the credit markets were doing.
It was the fact that what they thought the new arrangements were
doing was not the main story at all.[29]

The conventional wisdom assumed that the innovations of the
late 1990s and early 2000s were transferring the role of banks in the
creation of credit, but not in the creation of money, to the credit markets. It was an easy enough assumption to make. The global mutual
fund industry had, after all, existed for decades to collect savings and
select creditworthy borrowers for them. The new arrangements had
just increased its size and scope. The business of maintaining synchronisation between payments on long-term assets and short-term
liabilities—the management of liquidity risk, the thing that allows
bank liabilities to be money—that, it was assumed, remained the
unique preserve of banking. After all, only banks have charters from
the sovereign, and only sovereigns can make credit into money. Right?

It was a story that would have seemed horribly naïve to anyone
familiar with the history of the Monetary Maquis. Small-scale curi-
osities like community currencies show that private money can exist
without any help from the sovereign. The episode of the Irish bank
dispute and the precocious success of the sixteenth-century merchant bankers in manufacturing private money demonstrate that
scale is not necessarily an obstacle. History proves that the power
to issue money is an irresistible lure. If sovereigns allow it, whether

by commission or omission, private issuers will take full advantage. The decade before the crisis was no exception to this general rule. To the student of the Monetary Maquis, the only real question would have been how the new arrangements on the credit markets could be pulling it off. The key to issuing money is the ability to make the magic promise of both stability and freedom. The sovereign can do it because it has authority. Community currency clubs are able to do it because they share an ideology. Under the Great Monetary Settlement, banks were able to do it because they combined credit-worthiness with the endorsement of the sovereign. But how could it be done outside the regulated banking system in the wide world of the modern credit markets? How could the ability to create and manage private bilateral credit outside the regulated banking sector be transformed into what had been the Holy Grail of private bankers since at least the time of Nicolas Oresme: the ability to create private transferable credit—private money—without the annoying constraints imposed by the policies of sovereigns and their assorted central banks and regulators?

The answer turned out to be surprisingly simple. It was to make everything surprisingly complicated. With a chain between borrower and end-investor involving seven legal entities in several jurisdictions issuing seven different securities rather than one issuer in one jurisdiction issuing one bond, a sleight of hand could be achieved. Somewhere along the long line of intermediaries, the critical issue of the synchronisation of payments could be conveniently fudged. The traditional credit market transaction, between end-investor and borrower via the medium of a bond, had been stolidly transparent on the matter of liquidity. Buy a three-year bond, and one's money was tied up for three years; buy a ten-year bond, and see it tied up for ten. Of course, if one wanted one's money back sooner, one could try to sell one's bond before it matured—and in normal market conditions, one would be able to. But there was nothing in the prospectus to guarantee this surrogate source of liquidity. There was a clear and simple link between the liquidity terms bought by the end-investor and the liquidity terms promised by the borrower. Like a manual

transmission gearbox in a car, there was a simple, mechanical connection between what you chose and what you got.

The new style of credit market transaction was different. The
end-investor could buy a share in a money market mutual fund that
promised conversion to cash on demand—the credit market equivalent of a bank's demand deposit. The borrower, meanwhile, could
promise a bond that repaid in ten years. The awkward liquidity mismatch between the two could then be systematically obfuscated
somewhere along the long chain of counterparties. Like a car with
automatic transmission, few were equipped to understand exactly
what was going on inside the box, even if the ability to shift gears
without any actual effort from the driver is, when one thinks about it,
rather remarkable. As for consulting the owner's manual, that would
have done no good at all. The theory behind the new arrangements
didn't concern itself with anything so trivial as money. And in any
case: since it all seemed to work, who cared?

As with the demise of the Great Monetary Settlement, it was
only when it was too late that the truth of the matter was discovered. The decades of specialisation and the division of labour had
led in the financial sector to something much more revolutionary—and
less innocent—than they had in other industries. The displacement
of traditional banks by a disaggregated network of specialist firms
linked together by complex supply chains, had not just been about
greater efficiency, more choice, and better value, as it had in the car
or mobile-phone industries. It had been about the reanimation of the
Monetary Maquis: the discovery of a miraculous new means of creating private money outside the control of government. The result,
by 2008, was nothing less than a parallel monetary universe: a vast,
unregulated, "shadow" banking system organised internationally
within the credit markets, alongside the regulated banking systems
of nation states. In the U.S. alone, the balance sheet of the shadow
banking system stood at around U.S.$25 trillion on the eve of the
crash—more than twice the size of the traditional banking system.[30]
In Europe, where securities markets, like automatic gearboxes,
have always been less popular, the new "Army of Shadows" was less
numerous—accounting for a mere EUR 9.5 trillion.[31]

It was only in the teeth of the crisis that these magnitudes began to be grasped and the true size of the challenge facing the world's central banks and sovereigns became clear. Not only was the Great Monetary Settlement in tatters, and the traditional, regulated banking sector rapidly swallowing up billions of dollars in credit support, but there was a gigantic and previously unaccounted for shadow banking sector as well. The failure of this monstrous parasite would kill its host: it could no more be allowed than the collapse of the traditional banks themselves. Liquidity and credit support would have to be extended to it as well.[32] The result was the bizarre sight of the U.S. Treasury providing credit support to an insurance company, and an expansion of central-bank balance sheets on an unimagined scale, as they absorbed the liquidity risk that banks and shadow banks had proved unable to manage alone. In the six weeks between 10 September and 22 October 2008, the balance sheet of the Federal Reserve doubled and the Bank of England's more than tripled.[33] The European Central Bank was initially a more reluctant saviour—but in time it too found itself having to backstop the broken promise of liquidity transformation made by both the traditional and the shadow banking sectors.[34] Analysts expressed horror at this expansion of the money supply, warning of the imminent approach of hyperinflation, the collapse of the U.S. dollar, and the eruption of currency wars. But these lurid fantasies started from a mistaken premise. The news of what had really been happening was only beginning to leak out. The money had been there all along—it had just been hiding in the shadows.

With this coup d'état exposed, attention turned to the sovereigns' response. The U.S.$25 trillion question, it seemed, was whether the regulators have the firepower to bring the system back under control. In the next chapter we will discover the answer.

15

The Boldest Measures
Are the Safest

MONETARY COUNTER-INSURGENCY

The Great Monetary Settlement has become a one-way bet for banks, and the Monetary Maquis has been busy on a scale unparalleled in history. The last four decades, it seems, have seen monetary society burst its political bonds as never before. It is therefore no surprise that counter-insurgency is the order of the day. What might seem a little more improbable is that the global headquarters of the regulatory rapid-reaction force should be a provincial town in north-west Switzerland. The primary international forum for the co-ordination of financial regulation is the Basel Committee on Banking Supervision, based at the Bank for International Settlements—the so-called central bankers' bank. When the crisis struck, Basel was therefore the first port of call for defining a new regulatory response. It was in Basel, after all, that the most important conventional regulatory weapons to mitigate moral hazard had been designed: rules requiring banks to keep a specified quantity of cash or highly liquid securities in their portfolios to reduce the chance of needing to borrow from the central bank, and others requiring banks to maintain a buffer of equity capital sufficiently large that they would not fail in the first place.[1] But over the course of the twentieth century, the size of the protective capital buffers maintained by U.S. and U.K. banks

The picturesque Swiss town of Basel: the unlikely headquarters
of the world's monetary counter-insurgency operations.

had been allowed to fall by a factor of five.[2] The proportion of cash
and highly liquid securities in their portfolios has fallen by the same
amount in only the last fifty years.[3] Basel's diagnosis was that there
was nothing wrong with these tried-and-tested weapons per se, but
that more firepower was needed. In December 2010, a new directive
requiring banks to hold more capital and more liquid assets in their
portfolios was therefore agreed.[4]

Requiring increased holdings of equity capital and liquid assets
acts as a tax on risky activities. Make it more costly for banks to gamble and limit the tables at which they can play, the basic argument
runs, and a healthy equilibrium can be restored. On this view, the
regulatory challenge is a schematic one, familiar from any industry which generates private benefits but also social costs. A chemi-
cal manufacturing plant, for example, might generate profits for its
shareholders and salaries for its employees, but also waste products
detrimental to the local environment. If the factory isn't made to
bear the costs of this pollution, it will enjoy a free ride, and there-

fore produce more than is economically justified. The solution is to impose a tax that ensures the polluter pays the full economic cost of its production.[5]

Many in the regulatory establishment are, however, sceptical that the deep problems revealed by the crisis can really be met success-fully by conventional warfare of this sort. The pollution caused by the banking sector, they warn, is not like the pollution caused by a chemi-cal factory, for two reasons. The first is simply the scale of the prob-lem: the potential social costs of operating the monetary system as currently configured are simply too large to be discouraged through the tax system. Recovering the direct fiscal costs of liquidity and credit support might just about be plausible via a levy on the banks—albeit one that would wipe out most of their profits.[6] But the full bill for the financial instability that came home to roost after 2007 includes the costs of lost GDP, of mass unemployment, and lost capacity. These run into the tens of trillions of dollars: they are, practically speak-ing, uninsurably large.[7] If we stick to conventional warfare, in other words, victory would require an atom bomb so large it would destroy the Earth.

The second reason that taxation will not work, its critics argue, is that the networked nature of the banking system means that the activities of individual banks also generate emergent risks at the level of the system as a whole. So unlike in the case of the polluting chemical factory, an extra tax to discourage activities that generate systemic risks is in theory required. But the system is international—and there exists no multilateral political authority with the legitimacy to levy it.[8] Victory, if we stick to conventional warfare, would require a well-resourced and capable United Nations Army.

The main case against persisting with the Basel strategy of con-ventional warfare rests on nothing more complicated than its exist-ing track record, however. The innovations of the late 1990s and 2000s proved that the financial sector is infinitely inventive at devis-ing ways to circumvent such tax-based regulation. Even worse, the aftermath of the crisis demonstrated that the effects of these conven-tional weapons may even be perverse: requiring banks to raise capital ratios following the crash exacerbated the credit crunch, restricting banks' ability to make loans at precisely the time when companies facing falling demand have a need for credit lines. John Kay, one of the U.K.'s most respected regulatory economists, has put it bluntly: "[t]he belief that more complex versions of the Basel rules would be more effective in future represents the triumph of hope over experience."[9] To continue with the conventional approach would be to risk a regulatory Verdun, with more and more resources committed to the battle, for less and less return.

The regulators have therefore embarked on a fundamental reassessment of strategy; one which recognises that the root problem lies not with the bankers themselves, but with the structure of institutions in which they operate. "Financial stability," warned Daniel Tarullo—the leading authority on bank regulation on the Board of Governors of the Federal Reserve—in June 2012, "is, in important ways, endogenous to the financial system, or at least the kind of financial system that has developed in recent decades."[10] Moral hazard is hard-wired into the system. This is why attempting to mitigate it by tinkering with capital ratios or liquidity requirements would be a Sisyphean task. So long as the nature of banking is to lend long-term by borrowing short-term, and take credit risk whilst promising none, the boulder of moral hazard would forever be tumbling back to the bottom of the hill just as the regulators think they have it fixed. What is needed is reform targeted at the fundamental structure of the banking system, rather than at the behaviour of the bankers within it. The war on financial instability requires not conventional tactics, but a counter-insurgency strategy.

When the excesses of the 1920s ended in the crash of 1929 and the Great Depression that followed, there was a similar depth of soul-searching over the institutional structure of the banking system in the U.S. Then as now, the unwarranted enjoyment of sovereign support by activities inessential to the provision of money to the public was identified as a major cause of the problem. In 1933, the Glass-Steagall Banking Act therefore established a rigid separation of firms permitted to engage in securities dealing, or investment banking, from those permitted to engage in deposit-taking, lending, and payments services to companies and individuals, or commercial banking. And the McFadden Act of 1927 placed effective restrictions on the size of banks by prohibiting National Banks from opening branches outside their home state. Both restrictions lasted right into the 1990s.[11] And it is notable that it was the relaxation of these structural constraints on the activities and size of banks that contributed to the unmanageable size of the problem that was exposed by the 2007–8 crash. It was when the mid-century interlude of strict structural regulation ended that the age of "too big to fail" definitively arrived.[12]

Since the crisis, this historical experience has constituted the default framework for the flurry of legislative activity aimed at changing the structure of the banking sector itself. In early 2009, President Obama appointed an Economic Recovery Advisory Board, chaired by ex-Chairman of the Federal Reserve Paul Volcker, to make proposals on thoroughgoing reform of the financial sector. On the other side of the Atlantic, the newly elected coalition government of the U.K. appointed an Independent Commission on Banking under the leadership of the eminent Oxford economist Sir John Vickers, in June 2010. Both groups recommended a new segregation of banking activities. There were differences of nuance—Volcker chose to distinguish client-oriented and proprietary trading, whilst Vickers drew the line between banks' activities in retail and wholesale markets; and Volcker recommended that segregated activities be done in legally separate companies, whereas Vickers thought "ring-fencing" them within existing conglomerates would be enough—but the underlying philosophy was the same. Let Wall Street and City traders gamble as much as they like on their own tab, was the spirit of both sets of recommendations, so long as sovereign support is henceforth statutorily available only to strictly regulated institutions.

There appears, therefore, to be a rare international consensus on the counter-insurgency tactics of choice. But there remains a problem. "Tactics without strategy," runs the famous maxim of the great Chinese military thinker Sun Tzu, "is the noise before defeat." What exactly is the objective of these structural reforms? At first glance, the answer would seem to be simple: "financial stability." It is financial stability that the new institutions established since the crisis are charged with maintaining.[13] It is financial stability that the newly chastened central banks acknowledge they must aim at, in addition to the overly simplistic objective of low and stable inflation (and perhaps low unemployment) that was their single-minded goal before. Above all, it is financial stability that is the stated goal of all the new legislation.[14] Yet for all the sound and fury, there remains a deafening silence when it comes to the obvious question this raises: what exactly is financial stability?

It is a question to which neither of the dominant intellectual frameworks for contemporary economic policy-making are equipped to provide a sensible answer. As the Governor of the Bank of England has pointed out, modern, orthodox macroeconomics "lacks an account of financial intermediation, so money, credit, and banking play no meaningful role."[15] So as one of the founding members of the Bank of England's Monetary Policy Committee has lamented, it "excludes everything relevant to the pursuit of financial stability."[16] But neither does the modern theory of finance, with its blind spot for money's macroeconomic role, supply any new and specialised theory of financial stability to slake the thirst of the expectant reformers. "For all the attention paid to financial stability analysis in the last few years," Governor Daniel Tarullo of the U.S. Federal Reserve dolefully concluded in October 2012, "it is still—relatively speaking—a fledgling enterprise."[17] The root of the failure in both cases, as we discovered, is the conventional understanding of money. Stuck in its Looking-Glass world, the policy-makers are flying blind. Can the alternative traditions of monetary scepticism help instead?

THE BOLDEST MEASURES ARE THE SAFEST

The global financial crisis has raised the stakes in the debate over regulatory reform. As a result, there is an openness to unorthodox ideas that has not been seen for decades. Fortunately, there is also a rich seam of such ideas to be mined, if we look beyond the last fifty years of economics and finance. Some contemporary thinkers have already begun to float more adventurous proposals. Robert and Edward Skidelsky advocate a hearts and minds campaign—arguing that nothing short of ethical reconstruction is necessary to enable people to answer for themselves the fundamental question of *How Much Is Enough* and thereby free themselves from the militant insatiability intrinsic to monetary society.[18] The philosopher Michael Sandel hints instead at the Soviet strategy. He suggests counter-insurgency by cantonment—reforms to make sure that there remain some things that money can't buy.[19] For others, nothing less than the Spartan solution will do. According to U.S. congressman Ron Paul, for example, the way to solve the intrinsic problems of our current monetary system is simple: *End the Fed.*[20]

The most important thing the unconventional tradition provides, however, is not any one particular proposal. It is the alternative understanding of money not as a thing, but as a social technology. The world, we have to admit, is an uncertain place. King Solomon's biblical warning that "the race is not to the swift, nor the battle to the strong, neither yet bread to the wise, nor yet riches to men of understanding, nor yet favour to men of skill" might sound defeatist—but few would dispute his fundamental point that "time and chance happeneth to them all."[21] It is as true of the field of economic activity, as in every other, that there is a certain amount of inescapable risk in the world. Money is, on the unconventional view, a system for deciding how this risk is shared out. In the jargon of economists, genuine economic risk—uncertainty about whether the harvest will be plentiful or poor, or whether next month's meticulously planned product launch works or it doesn't—is "exogenous": it is essentially beyond our control. Financial risk, by contrast, is "endogenous": we decide, through the design of the monetary system, how those unpredictable economic gains or losses get shared around the community. Money answers the question of who bears which risks under what circumstances. Of course, money is not the only system for organising society that can answer this question. The redistributive engine of the

Western welfare state, in which social rights rather than economic value determine who gets what, is an obvious example of an alternative. But the way that money organises the distribution of economic risk in society—by making a simultaneous promise of stability and freedom—has made it epidemically successful throughout history. It is a brave promise.

For money issued directly by the sovereign, we have seen that the promise works because the sovereign, by definition, has political authority. A sovereign's authority is in turn a function of its legitimacy. That's why, when governments lose their citizens' confidence it becomes much easier for private moneys to circulate, as the example of Argentina's private and provincial currencies showed. In monetary society, how the sovereign can best preserve its legitimacy is therefore a critical question. It becomes all the more pressing because money's promise of stability means that debt crises are bound to arise—and the sceptical tradition has understood since ancient times that a critical prerequisite for the sustainability of monetary society is therefore the safety valve of a variable monetary standard. So long as citizens permit the sovereign a discretionary power to recalibrate the financial distribution of risks by adjusting the monetary standard when it becomes unfair, sovereign money can work. This is why the conventional understanding of money as a physical thing is so dangerous. Whereas with physical concepts it is essential that the standard we use to measure and manipulate them should be an immutable or even a natural constant, with the social concept of value exactly the opposite is true. If money is to generate a just society then it is essential not that the standard of economic value is irrevocably fixed, but that, as Solon showed, it is unflinchingly responsive to the demands of democratic politics.

So much for sovereign money. In the modern world, nearly all the money in circulation is not issued by the sovereign any more: it is issued by banks. So how do banks pull off money's promise to deliver both stability and freedom? The answer—according to the theory, at least—is that banks achieve "liquidity transformation": they "transform" their liquid, short-term deposit liabilities into illiquid, long-term loans. But the notion of "liquidity transformation" is, quite literally, a euphemism.[22] Nothing is actually transformed at all. Banks' liabilities remain short-term and of fixed nominal value, and their assets remain long-term and of uncertain nominal value, and never the twain shall meet. Instead, banks give the impression of achieving a transformation by artfully synchronising the payments in and out of their balance sheets. No matter how artfully this is done, though, there is always the possibility that people will lose confidence in a bank's ability to do it. That is the problem that plagues every private issuer of money—and even did for the great international bankers' money of the sixteenth century in the end. The international shadow banking sector and its horrified regulators relearned the lesson in the early 2000s: private money that sustains itself purely on its own resources works in good times but not in bad. So the only way to make bank money work sustainably is by piggybacking off the sovereign and its authority—that is, by striking a Great Monetary Settlement. For three centuries, this has seemed like a reasonable solution. But the crisis has exposed the fact that the distribution of risks that today's system of bank-based money dispenses has become intolerably unjust.

Such is the alternative understanding of money that our unauthorised biography has described, and the interpretation of what is wrong with the banking system that it implies. Global banking's current structure generates an unjust distribution of risks, where losses are socialised—taxpayers are on the hook for bail-outs—while gains are private—the banks and their investors alone reap any profits. So how can the situation best be fixed? Two extreme options help frame an answer. The first would be to privatise all the risks—to restructure the banking system so that investors bear all potential costs, as well as all the profits. The other would be the opposite: to redesign the system so that the financial system socialises all risks. Taxpayers keep all the downside risk—but now they get the upside too.

The first option is a modern version of the Scotsman's strategy—John Law's revolutionary idea for a structural fix for money. The core principle of Law's plan was the transfer of risk from the sovereign to his subjects, by the creation of what was, in effect, sovereign equity in the form of shares in his conglomerate System. Law's hope had been that these uncertain claims on the revenues of the French economy would come to replace the fixed claims represented by banknotes, *billets*, and other sovereign debt securities. The moribund economic culture of the rentier state would be abolished for ever, and there would be no more debt crises—since there would be no more fixed obligations to get out of kilter with uncertain tax receipts. Two birds would be killed with one stone.

Surprisingly, this fundamental principle is far from alien to the current regulatory response to the crisis. The structural reform proposals of Volcker and Vickers make a nod to Law's fundamental idea of realigning the distribution of risks implicit in the current structure of the banking system. There are more aggressive contemporary reform proposals under debate as well. The prominent U.S. economist and public intellectual Laurence Kotlikoff has put forward one of the more important ones: "Limited Purpose Banking."[23] Under Kotlikoff's radical proposal, banks as we now know them would cease to exist. All economic risk would simply pass unimpeded through an infinitely expandable spectrum of mutual funds from borrowers to savers. The phoney claims of financial intermediaries to practise "liquidity transformation," and the intrinsic mismatches that lie at the root of what is wrong with the current system, would be exorcised once and for all. Only manual gearboxes would be allowed on the roads.

Kotlikoff's vision is a bold one—but even it stops short of taking the Scotsman's strategy all the way to the revolutionary conclusion which John Law himself attempted. Under Limited Purpose Banking, although private banks are henceforth forbidden to issue short-term liabilities of certain nominal value whilst holding long-term assets of uncertain nominal value, the sovereign itself is not. Sovereign money remains just as we know it today at the heart of the system: a safe and liquid promise to pay under all circumstances. Law's idea was to rid money-users of even this last resort of risk aversion. At the heart of his new financial world was to be not sovereign debt, but sovereign equity. Once again, it is an idea that sounds incredible to modern ears—but it is one that has its influential advocates today. The U.S. economist Robert Shiller—a modern Projector, as well as one of the world's most distinguished academic economists—has for many years urged sovereigns to share with investors the risk to the public finances inherent in uncertain economic growth by issuing bonds that pay interest linked to GDP.[24] Shiller's proposals urge a gradual shift towards such innovative financial instruments. In the midst of the greatest economic and fiscal crisis France had ever seen, Law lacked the luxury of time.

Law's strategy of creating a monetary system which privatises all risk represents one extreme option. At the opposite end of the spectrum is a reformed monetary system structured to socialise all risk. This alternative extreme would see the banks replaced not by mutual funds, but by the sovereign. Money's seductive promise would not be abolished. Instead, the one issuer actually capable of making good on it—the sovereign—would be the only issuer permitted to do so. Both capital markets and the banking sector would continue to coexist; and money would remain the special preserve of the latter. But under this extreme option, it would be entirely owned and operated by the state. Once again, it is a reform that sounds dramatic, but is not as far-fetched as it first appears. Indeed it is towards this extreme that the crisis, with governments' nationalisation of banks and central banks' unprecedented interventions in the money markets, has thrust us by default. When the U.S. Federal Reserve has taken over more than U.S.$1 trillion of mortgages, and the balance sheet of the European Central Bank has absorbed everything from car loans to credit card receivables, why not finish the job?[25]

As counter-insurgency strategies designed to disable the Monetary Maquis and secure a new Great Monetary Settlement, these extreme strategies have the merit that they would eliminate once and for all the problematic distribution of risks inherent in the current structure of the banking system. Unfortunately, they would do so only at the cost of destroying monetary society itself. The Scotsman's solution would represent the apotheosis of the vision of modern academic finance: the abolition of banks and money in favour of capital market securities, the value of which would vary in perfect sympathy with the underlying risks present in the real world.[26] The sovereign's ability to redistribute these risks by adjusting the monetary standard would cease, because there would be no sovereign liabilites the value of which was fixed in terms of it. Money would no longer be a tool of government. Instead of a rule for anarchy there would be just anarchy—until some other system for organising society took its place. Rather than reimposing legitimate government, this is defeating the insurrection by permitting a free-for-all.

Meanwhile, the alternative extreme of a return to sovereign money alone—a society in which all money is issued by the state because all banking is operated by it too—presents an equally nightmarish prospect. Money would no longer be a tool of government, it would have become government. All the benefits of decentralised decision-making in finance would be gone, replaced by a monetary system that replaced the injustice of taxpayers' enforced insurance of the bankers by the alternative injustice of their insuring absolutely everybody all the time instead. Like encouraging a descent into anarchy, this is a counsel of despair: defeating the insurgency by becoming a totalitarian state.

If we are to turn the locusts into bees, we do need a radical reform of the banking system. The unconventional view of money suggests three useful principles to begin from: two regarding where we want to go, and one regarding how we get there. First, the solution to the problem of moral hazard at the heart of the modern banking system lies neither in redesigning the system to privatise all financial risk, nor in redesigning it to socialise it. What is required is a closer match—not a perfect one—between the costs and benefits that taxpayers, bankers, and their investors are at risk of bearing. The current regulatory response is on the right track. U.S., U.K., and EU proposals all argue that more risk must be borne privately, and less socialised and borne by the taxpayer. But the reforms they propose do not go far enough.

Second, since money is a tool for organising society, and since the only authority with the political legitimacy to command how society should be arranged is by definition the sovereign, any redesign must maximise the room for monetary policy. Money's fantastic promise to deliver both stability and freedom has become a boondoggle in the hands of the banks: the specious claim of "liquidity transformation" has become camouflage for a one-way bet, and should be forbidden. Yet that same promise is nothing other than the essence of money, one of the most powerful and important tools of democratic government the world has ever known. So long as democratic politics commands the escape valve of a flexible monetary standard, it should therefore be preserved.

A final principle relates to how to get to a system of money and banking reformed in line with these first two. The guiding rule must be that less is more. Conventional warfare will be an infinite regress: attempting to supervise the financial sector is a fool's errand. The current regulatory proposals are correct that structural reform is the key. The trick is to set as few rules as possible and police them rigorously, while setting private initiative and innovation free for the rest. In the field of money—the greatest technology ever invented to liberate mankind's entrepreneurial energies—this canonical rule of regulation is more necessary than ever.

Is there any realistic proposal for banking reform that answers to this daunting job description? Fortunately, there is—and it is not a new one. Eighty years ago, in the depths of the Great Depression, the great American economist Irving Fisher published a famous proposal with the inspiring title *100% Money*.[27] It was remarkably simple. Like the Scotsman's strategy, it sought fundamentally to realign the balance of risks in the banking system. Like today's regulatory response, it advocated doing this by restricting sovereign support to a limited range of activities. But it is simultaneously simpler and more radical. Fisher's proposal was to require that any deposit that could be withdrawn or used to make a payment on demand be backed by sovereign money—and banks which offered such deposits be permitted to do no other business. "The checking deposit department of the bank," Fisher wrote, "would become a mere storage warehouse for bearer money belonging to its depositors and would be given a separate corporate existence as a Check Bank."[28] As for the rest of what banks now do—whether client-facing or not, whether wholesale business or retail—these things would be treated like all other capital market activities, and the institutions that undertake them would neither enjoy special sovereign support, nor suffer special sovereign supervision. The market would decide what products would be offered, and what institutions would offer them. Outside the realm of "Check Banks," even the dodgy promise of liquidity transformation would be permitted. If investors wanted to gamble on an intermediary's ability to synchronise payments in and out of its balance sheet, they would be quite at liberty to do so—because there could no longer be any illusion on any side that such investors would be bailed out if the promise was not met.

Fisher's proposal was taken up in the 1930s by economists at the University of Chicago, after which it became popularly known as "The Chicago Plan." It was revived again in the 1960s by the subsequent Chicago luminary, Milton Friedman.[29] Today, under the banner of "Narrow Banking," it is being advocated once again by some of the world's leading regulatory economists.[30] It has even been the subject of a new study by the International Monetary Fund, which found that testing its consequences using a formal mathematical model strongly corroborates Fisher's argument that it would lead to greater macroeconomic and financial stability.[31]

It is a reform consistent with the principles outlined above. The socialisation of financial risk would not be eliminated, but it would be far more strictly circumscribed. The utility activities of narrow banks would enjoy the support of the sovereign. No other financial institution would: and the clear distinction between narrow banks and everything else would eliminate the ambiguous no-man's-land in which liquidity illusion and moral hazard have allowed the Monetary Maquis to thrive. Sovereign money would remain at the heart of the system, both as cash in the public's pockets and as the only asset held by the narrow banks. Monetary policy, and with it money's integration into the democratic organisation of society, would therefore be preserved. And finally, the necessary structural reforms are simple. The rules for narrow banks would be few but draconian, and anyone wanting a charter for a bank would have to abide by them. For anyone that does not want a bank charter, there would be no rules: just the ceaseless innovation which money itself unleashes, and which the financial sector has shown such a talent for exploiting.

John Maynard Keynes began the final chapter of the most important work of economics of the twentieth century with a realistic diagnosis of the situation seven years into the Great Depression. "The outstanding faults of the economic society in which we live," he wrote, "are its failure to provide for full employment and its arbitrary and inequitable distribution of wealth and incomes."[32] Today, five years into another monumental economic calamity, it is the same outstanding faults of unemployment and an unjust distribution of economic risks that plague us. Money and banking, incorrectly understood, and so incorrectly configured, are what brought us here. Money and banking, correctly restructured, will be what bring us out again.

16 Taking Money Seriously

"So!" interrupted my friend the entrepreneur, "I always knew it!"

"Always knew what?" I answered.

"That you were a closet revolutionary. You don't like capitalism or capitalists like me. And what your story about money boils down to is that you want to soak the rich and hang all the bankers from lamp posts."

"Where did you get that idea?"

"Well, allow me to summarise your argument—or maybe I should call it your murder mystery. You said it would be an unauthorised biography. To me it sounded more like an Agatha Christie novel."

"Oh yes? Who's the victim?"

"Common sense—according to you. But let's see if I've got it straight. You began by explaining that, contrary to first appearances, money is not a thing but a social technology—a set of ideas and practices for organising society. To be precise, you explained that in essence, money comprises three things: a concept of universally applicable economic value; a system of account-keeping whereby that value can be measured and recorded; and the principle of decentralised transfer, whereby that value can be transferred from one person to another. You used that story about Yap to show how absurd it is to think that coins, or any other tokens, are themselves money.

And you used that story about the Irish bank closure to show that although money is usually issued by governments, it doesn't always have to be. I bought all that—but then I asked you what difference it makes to take this view of things. You said a lot—which is why I've been sitting here listening to your so-called unauthorised biography."

"Sounds fair so far."

"Then you began to investigate these ideas that make up money—and especially the most important one: the concept of universal economic value. You explained that a dollar, or a pound, or a euro, or a yen is not a physical thing but a unit of measurement. You explained how some old Polish professor—"

"Witold Kula."

"—that's the one—had looked into the history of physical units of measurement and discovered that both the concepts they measure and the standards they embody have evolved over time. Like a good socialist, you even spoke admiringly of the great strides made by some international bureaucracy."

"That's right—the International Bureau of Weights and Measures."

"But the useful part, if I understood you right, was old Professor Kula's point that both concepts and the standards used to measure them are determined by the uses to which people put them. You made two points. The first was that the concept of universal economic value is just like a physical unit of measurement: the extent of its applicability, and what its standard should be, is properly determined by what it is used for. But the second was that universal economic value is also different from a physical unit of measurement. It is a property of the social rather than the physical world—it's the central component of a technology for organising society, as you put it—so that its standard needs to be political as well."

"Exactly. The right criteria for choosing its standard are not consistency and accuracy—as they are for a physical unit of measurement—but fairness, or political justice, or whatever you want to call the characteristic quality of a well-governed society."

"Right. That was the philosophical part. Then you moved on to history."

"Well: I did argue that there is evidence to support my claims about the nature of money. I claimed that it is because money's central idea is that concept of universal economic value, and because the appropriate standard of value has to be a political one, that money as we know it today was first invented by the collision of the Mesopotamian inventions of literacy, numeracy, and accounting, with the notion of the equal social value of every member of the tribe that the primitive Dark Age Greeks had."

"Ah yes. Well, you could be right about that—but it doesn't seem to be that important if you aren't. After all, money is still with us, so we can test your account of what it really is right here and now. How it was invented doesn't really matter—and since we'll never know, why worry?"

"That's one way of looking at it—ever the philistine. But you're right that the real test of my biography is how well it explains money today—and our problems with it, and how to start solving them. So carry on."

"Well then, the history part. This is where the murder mystery began. You started out by praising the clarity of ancient Chinese monetary thought. You explained that their philosophers and emperors understood perfectly that money is a tool of government, and that the extent to which economic value is used to co-ordinate social activity, and the question of what the standard should be, are therefore to be determined solely by reference to how they contribute to the successful government of the country."

"That's right: to 'peace and order in the sub-celestial realm' as they more poetically put it."

"Revolution, more like, if you ask me. But we'll come to that in a moment. Anyway, then you told the story of Europe's re-monetisation in the Middle Ages. The real story here, you said, was a long-running battle between sovereigns and their subjects over the management of the standard. The Europeans, you seemed to be saying, were less concerned about the applicability of the concept of universal economic value—but they were very much concerned with what its standard was, because both sovereigns and subjects understood only too well that making the pound worth more or less in terms of real goods and services meant the redistribution of wealth and incomes."

"Exactly. And especially, redistribution to the sovereign from his subjects."

"Right. Seigniorage. The story you told was that as the monetary economy grew, so there were more and more subjects interested in the question of the standard—since they didn't want to pay excessive seigniorage to their sovereign. They complained about it a lot. They invented all kinds of clever arguments against it. They hired that French bishop to show why it was wrong. But none of it did much good."

"Because there was no realistic alternative—so they had no way of forcing the sovereign's hand."

"Until, that is, some bright spark rediscovered banking, and with it a viable means of issuing private money on a monster scale."

"Exactly. Turned out to be quite a profitable invention for everybody—but especially for the bankers. The sort of thing I bet you wish you'd thought of."

"Touché. Anyway: once bankers had rediscovered the trick of issuing private money, the boot was on the other foot. Now it was the sovereigns and their seigniorage that were under pressure. This was an unstable situation—monetary insurrection, to use your metaphor. But with the foundation of the Bank of England, a way to secure a permanent peace was found—at least until recently."

"The Great Monetary Settlement. You've got it. But forgive me for interrupting. Only, where's the murder?"

"I can see you don't read many detective stories. It's just about to happen, of course—just when everyone is least expecting it. You see, up until now, everyone might have been arguing over whether the sovereign should manipulate the standard to raise seigniorage, and whether the bankers should be allowed to issue private money, and so on—but at least they all understood what money was. In terms of your 'unconventional' account of money, in other words, common sense still reigned. But just as your Great Monetary Settlement was being struck, somebody murdered monetary common sense. What's worse, having done away with the correct understanding of money, the wicked criminal buried the evidence and put in its place a seductive imposter—a view of money and economic value that looks and sounds awfully persuasive to ignoramuses like me, but one which according to you actually blinds our moral faculties, blunts our economic policies, and—much the most terrible of all—even gave us the banksters currently lording it over Wall Street and the City of London. And in true Hercule Poirot style, you revealed that the culprit was the very last person one would have suspected: none other than the most respected thinker in the land, John Locke."

"Ah, I see."

"And to cap it all, it was what aficionados of the genre call a perfect crime. Nobody noticed that the correct view of money had been swapped for the wrong one—so nobody accused Locke of murder. Quite the opposite, in fact—he seems to have gone down in history as a bit of a hero."

"Absolutely. He did provide the intellectual basis of modern Liberal democracy, after all."

"Right. But it's at this point, I'm afraid to say, that your plot has a hole in it. You see, I'll grant that John Locke might have been able to murder monetary common sense in the course of that particular debate about the recoinage—and even that the imposter he substituted was quite persuasive as a replacement. But given the rule of common sense up to that point—all those thinkers that you mentioned—how on earth did Locke manage to change everyone's mind? I mean, I don't care how influential John Locke was, how can he possibly have managed to fool everyone? Why didn't people notice that his view of money was just wrong? No, I'm afraid your theory just doesn't add up, Mr. Holmes."

"Hang on a minute—you're the detective here. I never said that this was a murder mystery—and I don't think it is.

"John Locke was no murderer—he was the greatest philosopher of his age, one of the greatest of any age, and there can hardly be any doubt that he was motivated by his sincere belief in the rightness of political Liberalism and constitutional government. But in trying to achieve this, he made a mistake. He was a doctor and a don—not a banker or a businessman—he wasn't familiar with the world of finance. He thought the only way to guarantee that the Great Monetary Settlement didn't turn into a giant boondoggle for bankers was to put the standard beyond their—or the sovereign's—control. And that was what his political theory told him must be the case anyway.

"So Locke ended up with the right idea about politics—that it should be Liberal and democratic—but the wrong idea about the monetary standard—that it had to be fixed. John Law was the opposite. He had the right idea about the standard—that it needs to be flexible—but the wrong idea about politics—that absolute monarchy is the right system to determine its adjustment. Now Law really was a murderer—or at least a duellist—but in the world of ideas he was no more a criminal than Locke was. Both of them were trying to solve the political and economic problems presented by the growth of monetary society—and each of them got halfway to the right solution."

"All right. But why was it Locke's view of money that became the conventional one, then? Like I said: if it is so obviously mistaken, why didn't anyone stand up and say, 'all this that Locke's saying isn't true: money isn't silver, it's transferable credit!'? Or rather, why didn't everyone believe Lowndes when he said that?"

"Ah! That is a good question. Part of the answer is because of Locke's prestige, of course. To most people, Locke was a great authority, even if the financial experts didn't think him one on money. Law was a maverick. But the main reason—and this is what explains your 'perfect crime'—is more fundamental. It is that Locke felt that in order to arrive at the conclusion which he felt was necessary to protect the Great Monetary Settlement from itself—that the standard needed to be fixed—one had to understand money as silver and value as a property of the natural world. I explained what the practical consequences of that kind of reasoning have been for economic and financial sector policy, as well as for the ethical disabilities of economics. But naturalistic reasoning of this sort has another effect as well.

"It's well known to sociologists and anthropologists. Once people accept the idea of a particular set of social arrangements as a necessary fact of the natural world, rather than just a social contrivance, it becomes well nigh impossible for them to think critically about it—no matter how progressive they are, and no matter how morally wrong those social arrangements might be. History is full of examples. In the nineteenth century, there was a great fashion for 'positive criminology,' which claimed that felons could be identified by their physical attributes. It sounds bizarre to us today that anyone could believe that you could tell an anarchist by his ears, or a thief by the shape of his nose. But the point is that the people who believed all this had no vested interest in locking up people with unusual faces—they simply believed in the naturalistic explanation of criminality as a product of physiological factors. Likewise, 'scientific racism' was widely accepted as the truth in nineteenth-century America. The inferiority of non-white peoples could be 'proved,' it was believed, by physical differences. And again, it was the hallmark of a liberal outlook—not a reactionary one—to believe this kind of thing. The point is that naturalistic reasoning in the social sciences—claiming to explain social phenomena as objective truths of nature—is self-reinforcing. It spins social and political prejudices into a web of fake facts—and once the web has been spun, it is virtually impossible to escape. Or in terms of our Chinese proverb, naturalistic reasoning like Locke's understanding of money is what fills the fishbowl with water.

"So when it comes to the eclipse of the correct view of money, I don't think it's fair to call it a murder, or John Locke a murderer, Monsieur Poirot—the verdict has to be one of accidental death. And as for the way in which the conventional view of money took over: you are right that if there had been a murder, that would have made it a perfect crime. But I'm afraid to say it's really just a case of mistaken identity—albeit one driven by mass delusion."

"All right," said my friend cautiously, "a case of accidental death and mistaken identity it is, then. But in any case, isn't the whole point of your argument that the rumours of the death of monetary common sense had been greatly exaggerated? There was Law, like you just said—and more to the point, Bagehot, and Keynes, and Kindleberger and those other characters that you went on about. They kept common sense alive—at least on life support. Luckily for you, actually—since you wouldn't have known about it otherwise. You may have moaned that the conventional understanding of money is behind the failings of macroeconomic and financial sector policy that got us into the current mess. But then you brightened up and argued that the way those neglected geniuses thought about money can show us the way out again. And if I understood you right, what you really meant by that was a lot of inflation and debt restructuring to fleece the capitalist rich and bail out the oppressed masses—coupled with a shake-up of the banking sector to make the Big Bang of the 1980s look like child's play. So you don't get off that easily. Even if I buy your argument that there's something wrong with the conventional view of money and that it has led to some big mistakes, I still think your alternatives sound like a load of irresponsible, revolutionary claptrap."

"Ah yes, I'd forgotten—the charge of fomenting revolution. Well, I think you've got me quite wrong there. I've argued that there are three basic policies that are suggested by the alternative view of money.

"The first relates to the management of the monetary standard. You're right that one of the principal differences between the conventional view of money and the alternative view is that the monetary standard can, and indeed should, be deliberately managed. The conventional view implies that economic value is a natural fact. As such, the job of money and finance is to measure it—but not to influence it. The monetary standard is the fulcrum of the scales of political justice, as it were—and just like the fulcrum on a physical pair of scales, it has to be fixed in place in order to be accurate. Any redistribution required in order to even things up between different members of society should be achieved by taxing stuff away from the people on one side of the scales and doling it out to the people on the other—

or perhaps by making the process of accumulating stuff itself more equitable, so that redistribution of this sort isn't needed.

"The alternative view of money sees economic values not as a natural fact, but as a concept invented for the purpose of organising society in the most just and prosperous way. The job of money and finance is therefore not just the measurement of value—but the achievement of this objective as well. There is therefore nothing intrinsically wrong with moving the fulcrum of the scales of justice, since their purpose is not to achieve accuracy—a notion without meaning in the social world—but fairness and prosperity. On the alternative view of money, keeping the fulcrum fixed while shifting weight from one scale to the other via fiscal redistribution is certainly one way of doing things—and quite rightly the usual way in normal times. But the nature of monetary society is such that unsustainable inequalities that cannot feasibly be corrected in this way will inevitably occur from time to time. When that happens, it is time to move the fulcrum to restore balance."

"You and your scales again! I get it. But in practice what you are talking about is higher inflation, right? You think we need to go back to the 1970s."

"Well, you're right that I think many countries are currently at the point where financial inequalities have reached unsustainable dimensions—the point where there's too much debt. And yes, I think that the current strategy of trying to sweat these debt mountains off over time—of trying to amortise the debt gradually—is not politically feasible or economically desirable. If we take a leaf out of Solon's book we will deal with the problem up front instead, either by engineering a few years of significantly higher inflation or by restructuring the debt burden directly. Certainly, the crisis proved that treating low and stable inflation as a sufficient condition for economic stability was a big mistake. The ultimate goal of monetary policy isn't monetary stability, or financial stability, but a just and prosperous society; and no matter how distant that goal might be from the day-to-day business of central banking, it represents the only reliable guide to policy. So yes: I think the time has come to abandon the cult of inflation-targeting and revert to a broader idea of what monetary policy has to achieve—and to allow the central bankers a larger set of tools to attempt these more difficult goals."

"Give a bunch of unaccountable bureaucrats an even larger set of tools? Only a socialist could come up with that!"

"Not so—that brings us to the second policy. Central banks shouldn't be independent. Or at least, not like they are now.

"On the alternative view of money, the question of who decides who should issue money and on what standard is, as we discovered, a vital one. And since money is the ultimate technology for the decentralised organisation of society, there is only one answer that works—the one given by Solon. Only democratic politics provides the sensitivity to current conditions and the legitimacy to deflect criticism that is necessary for money to work sustainably. The fulcrum of the scales will occasionally need to be shifted—and only democratic politics can decide when, and by how much.

"So the alternative view of money doesn't for a moment suggest that we give a wider set of tools to an unaccountable central banker. Quite the opposite. As a result of our current, dire economic circumstances, we are relearning the fact that monetary policy is intensely political; so in monetary policy, as in all policy, the challenge is to govern well—not to pretend there is no need for governing. And if we have any faith whatsoever in our liberal, democratic systems, the only way of doing that is to re-establish the link between the polity and its policy-makers.

"There's another implication too. The alternative view of money shows that the banking sector is really a lot like the civil service. Money is a technology of government—ideally, of self-government—and banks are its bureaucracy. So the bureaucratic virtues of reliability, a public service ethic, and risk aversion are just as important in banking as entrepreneurial energy. And most important of all, the creation and management of money by private banks too should be subject to the ultimate guidance of democratic politics. Of course, I'm not for a moment talking about the sweeping nationalisation of banks— still less a stepping-up of the conventional regulatory arms race we are engaged in at the moment. But the alternative understanding of money most certainly does imply strict regulation of banks' specifically monetary activities in accordance with political priorities."

"Oh yes: how could I forget—your pie-in-the-sky plan for the reform of banking—and money itself!"

"Exactly. The third policy implication of the alternative view of money is that we should go for a more radical reform of money and finance in order that we only have to rely on active political regulation in the smallest possible area."

"And remind me—what's the point of all this?"

"The point is to try to reduce the need for active supervision of money and finance by government—surely not a very socialist objective? The monetary system, as currently configured, is flawed: it is intrinsically unstable. The alternative view of money admits this problem, and implies that the best way to deal with it is to take the frightening step of undertaking radical surgery rather than continuing to prescribe piecemeal treatments. And reforming the banking system is also the only practical way of addressing the even older question of what money's proper place in organising our lives is."

"What? Narrow banking will tell the Skidelskys *How Much Is Enough*, and Professor Sandel *What Money Can't Buy*? That sounds like a bit of a stretch!"

"I don't know whether it will do exactly that. But the biggest difference of all between the conventional and the alternative views of money is that the alternative view acknowledges the genuine dilemma in which people find themselves—today as they did two and a half thousand years ago—over the extent to which money should co-ordinate social life. The sceptical tradition is useful because it warns us what are the wrong answers to the question of what should and should not be weighed in money's scales: the Spartan solution of abolishing money in order to return to traditional society, for example; or the Soviet solution of attempting to impose administrative restrictions on what can and cannot be bought and sold for money. But it is most useful because it also points to the right answer. It is the lesson of the myth of Midas. The root of money's irrepressible imperialising tendency, it warns, is neither morals, man, nor markets: it is money itself. As currently constituted, money's promise looks irresistible—but only because, as Midas discovered, it is actually impossible. Confine that promise to sovereign money alone via the structural fix of narrow banking, and the incentive to mediate everything via money would be radically reduced. Shorn of its specious promise, monetary society would perhaps find natural limits—because Midas would grasp that human relations are just as valuable as financial ones from the outset."

"So: you're going to bin fixed inflation targets and license money-printing in order to escape the debt hangover. You're going to arm the central bankers to the hilt and tell them to keep firing until politicians tell them to stop. You're going to make banking a branch of the civil service, and tell savers that if they want to earn a half-decent return on their nest eggs, they'd better be ready to take some losses as well. And if anyone complains about this marvellous new policy mix, you're going to tell them not to worry because as well as preventing financial crises, it's the only way of avoiding the fate of a deranged despot from story-time. It sounds like a cross between Karl Marx, Ayn Rand, and the Brothers Grimm. I rest my case."

"I'm just getting going: that's only the practical agenda. Given that all these problems originate with the wrong understanding of money, there's not much point fixing the policies if we don't fix the ideas behind them too. So there's an intellectual agenda as well.

"The key, I've argued, is economics. Modern, orthodox economics is a uniquely powerful set of ideas which pervades not only the world's central banks and finance ministries but popular culture and personal ethics as well—and the conventional view of money is ingrained in its core. More important for the long term than any of the practical policies we just discussed is the reform of economics. As with the practical policies, piecemeal reforms won't do. We need finally to bring about the Reformation that never happened. We need to reformulate economics so that it starts from a realistic understanding of money. On the alternative view of money, understanding the economy properly also means understanding politics, history, psychology—and ethics. The practical knowledge of finance and commerce taught in today's business schools and the detailed understanding of institutions and their evolution taught in history departments need to be reintegrated into the teaching of economics, since as Bagehot said, 'no abstract argument, and no mathematical computation' can teach what actually determines trust and confidence in the real world. At the same time, the ability to grapple in a grown-up way with moral and political dilemmas developed in departments of philosophy and politics must also find a place, since as Keynes said, 'economics is a moral and not a natural science,' and an economist must therefore be 'mathematician, historian, statesman and philosopher in some degree.'"

"Right. So once we've inflated away our debts and euthanised the banking sector, all we have to do is rethink economics from the ground up. Forgive me if I sound a bit unimaginative. But to me this all sounds pointlessly radical and utterly unrealistic. I'm sorry: if you're asking me to vote for society, regulation, and government, against individualism, free choice, and the market, you can forget it—they are our only hopes. And if you're asking me to vote to chuck out everything economics teaches at the moment and start again you can count me out of that as well. One thing a career in business has taught me is not to waste time on lost causes—regardless of how worthy they are."

"But I agree with all that. The practical and intellectual agenda I've just described isn't meant to start a socialist revolution—it's meant to stave one off.

"Today, for the first time in a generation or more, many people—and in particular those without a vested interest in business as usual—are losing faith in the ability of the current economic system to deliver peace, prosperity, freedom, and fairness. You know the facts. The median income of American households has hardly risen for more than two decades. Inequalities of wealth are higher now than at any time since the 1930s. The baby boomers own all the houses, and no one under thirty can get on the property ladder. These are not short-term problems—they have built up over decades. The crisis just exposed them and made them worse. I know you'll laugh if I mention the Occupy movement or the *indignados* of Madrid—but these people are asking a question which seems perfectly sensible if you just look at the bare statistics: is capitalism really all it's cracked up to be?

"Now, you and I agree that basically it is—or at least, it's better than anything else. But unless we can explain what's gone wrong, we will lose the argument. You know my answer: the problem is not capitalism, but money and the way we think about it. You may think the policies implied by this answer are too radical and the intellectual revolution impractical. But the alternatives—whether keeping things as they are or kicking capitalism for something else—are worse. I am going to have to rely on a cleverer and more persuasive thinker again to try to convince you. But this time I'll stick to one of the neglected geniuses themselves. You don't like the idea that the monetary standard should be deliberately manipulated and central bankers subject to political control, because you don't believe government should interfere with business. That's quite right as an operational principle in normal times. But as Keynes warned in 1923, those who pursue this principle dogmatically become 'the worst enemies of what they seek to preserve . . . nothing can preserve the integrity of contract between individuals except a discretionary authority in the State to revise what has become intolerable . . . The absolutists of contract . . . are the real parents of revolution.' Likewise, you think the reform of economics is a lost cause—and I agree that it won't be easy. But since, as Keynes wrote in 1936, 'soon or late it is ideas, not vested interests, which are dangerous for good or evil,' it has to be done if money is to be saved from itself.

"So you see: it's not experimenting with the alternative understanding of money that risks a revolution—it's sticking to the conventional one."

"All right, all right," said my exasperated friend, "I give in! Maybe you're right. I'll give you the benefit of the doubt. We definitely are in quite a mess, so I suppose we should be taking some risks with policy. And since I've admitted that we should be thinking about money differently, I suppose we should do the logical thing and try to teach our budding economists differently. Yes, I think I'll write to my old university and tell them they should add a few of those neglected geniuses to the curriculum."

"At last! That's more like it!"

"I'll write to my member of Parliament and tell her to submit a bill to bring in narrow banking."

"Yes! That's the spirit!"

"And what about the head of the International Monetary Fund? Should I email her as well?"

"Absolutely! I think she might even be in favour already!"

"But first of all, I'll write to the new Governor of the Bank of England and tell him he needs to stop fretting about that fixed inflation target and bust us out of this economic hangover with a bout of good, old-fashioned inflation!"

"Bravo! Only . . . there is one other thing I ought to have mentioned."

"What? Don't tell me there's another policy you forgot."

"No, no—it's not that. It's just that there's one other important thing about money—in a sense the most important thing about it—that I realise I forgot to explain."

"After all that? Well, what is it?"

"It's just that, you see, the sovereign doesn't actually control money—so I suppose some of those letters of yours might be wrongly addressed."

"What?"

"No. You see, money is a social phenomenon—like language—so the whole notion that the sovereign or the central bank controls the standard is in fact a myth. It doesn't control the monetary standard any more than the editors of the *Oxford English Dictionary* control the meaning of words."

"You must be joking."

"I'm afraid not.

"You see, because money, like language, is intrinsically social, one certainly can't just invent it on one's own. A famous economist once said that anyone can issue their own money—the problem is getting it accepted. That's exactly right: anyone can write IOUs— and depending on how other people rate the creditworthiness and liquidity of those IOUs, they can circulate as money. But the famous economist was making an assumption that these IOUs are denominated in dollars or euros or pounds or whatever. Because what anyone cannot do is issue their own money—regardless of how creditworthy an issuer they are—denominated in their own, private, monetary unit. The IOUs would be quite literally meaning-less. It would be as absurd for you or I to decide unilaterally on our own monetary standard as it was for Humpty-Dumpty to claim to Alice that his words mean just what he wants them to mean.

"Now the state is not exactly like you and me, of course. It is uniquely large and uniquely influential—and if you have to deal with it regularly, as most of us do, it can, to an extent, dictate terms. So, for example, the state—especially if it is a totalitarian state—can manip-ulate the meaning of words. And when it comes to the monetary standard, the weight of the sovereign's promises to pay does exert a significant effect on its value and on the extent to which the general public use it. That's why hyperinflations are invariably associated with the collapse of sovereign credit, and of the legitimacy of the state itself.

"But the state is not society; so the state's control over the stan-dard is never complete. If the monetary standard, like totalitarian language, becomes so detached from reality as to be useless in the eyes of its users, society can and will improvise an alternative. That's why when inflation gets out of control in emerging markets, peo-ple start to re-denominate prices in dollars or euros even though there may be hardly any dollar or euro notes actually in circulation. Occasionally, like the issuers of the Argentinian *Crédito* or the Italian exchange-bankers of the sixteenth century, they even come up with a new standard all of their own. In either case, they find themselves a monetary standard that will actually serve its stated purpose—the co-ordination of monetary society—to replace the one that the state has rendered quite literally meaningless."

"All right," said my friend suspiciously, "so what? What does all this mean for our revolutionary—sorry, conservative—programme? Are you trying to tell me that there's no point in my writing to the new Governor of the Bank of England after all, because he doesn't actually control inflation, and he's not actually in charge of our money?"

"No—that's not quite the point. It may be indirect but, as I said, the state does exercise a great deal of influence over the monetary standard so I think he should stay on the list. The same goes for all those others you mentioned. National and international monetary and financial policy-makers have a great deal of power over money. Likewise, the academics and finance professionals who are the high priests of economics have enormous influence over the ideas which shape monetary society. So you should definitely lobby them all. It's just that, because money is, like language, in the last analysis, a social phenomenon, none of these people are ultimately in charge of it any more than professors of English are in charge of English or the Académie Française is in charge of French. So if you really agree that money is a social technology, not a thing; that the conventional way of thinking about it is wrong, and makes the technology malfunction, but that the right way of thinking about it is available, and can allow money to fulfil its potential as the greatest tool of self-government ever invented, then it's no good just writing to the experts."

"But who should I write to then? I mean, who is in charge of money?"

"Ah—you of all people will like the answer to that. You are."

"Me and everyone else who uses it, you mean."

"Yes, I suppose that's more accurate!"

"So if we're really going to reform money . . ."

". . . I'm afraid it will ultimately come down to ourselves."

"I knew it," said my friend, with the satisfied look of someone who realises he's been right all along. "If you want anything done properly—you have to do it yourself."

Notes

1 What Is Money?

1. Furness, 1910.
2. *Ibid.*, p. 92.
3. *Ibid.*, p. 93.
4. *Ibid.*, p. 98.
5. *Ibid.*, p. 96.
6. *Ibid.*, p. 97.
7. *Ibid.*, pp. 97–8.
8. Keynes, 1915a.
9. Aristotle, 1932, I.3.13–14. As we shall see in chapter 8, Aristotle also developed a quite different theory, however.
10. Locke, 2009, pp. 299–301.
11. Smith, A., 1981, pp. 37–8.
12. *Ibid.*, p. 38.
13. *Ibid.*, pp. 38–9.
14. The anthropologist David Graeber exasperates himself presenting a catalogue of examples from recent textbooks in Graeber, 2011, p. 23.
15. Dalton, 1982.
16. Humphrey, 1985, p. 48.
17. Kindleberger, 1993, p. 21.
18. Graeber, 2011, p. 28.
19. Smith, T., 1832, p. 11ff.
20. Mitchell Innes, 1913. Like, I expect, most modern readers, I owe the discovery of both this essay and Mitchell Innes, 1914 to Wray, 2004.
21. Statistics from the Federal Reserve Bank of St. Louis and the Bank of England, respectively, for November 2011.
22. Friedman, 1991.
23. See http://www.centralbankmalta.org/site/currency1b.html.
24. Peter Spufford—the leading British historian of money in medieval Europe—discusses the historiographical pitfalls that result from this fact in the introduction to Spufford, 1988.
25. Goetzmann, W. and Williams, L., "From Tallies and Chirographs to Franklin's Printing Press at Passy," in Goetzmann and Rouwenhorst, 2005, pp. 108–9.
26. See Clanchy, 1993, pp. 123–4; and Goetzmann and Williams, "From Tallies and Chirographs to Franklin's Printing Press at Passy," in Goetzmann and Rouwenhorst, 2005.
27. Charles Dickens, 1855, "Speech on Administrative Reform," delivered at the Theatre Royal, Drury Lane, 27 June 1855.

28. *Ibid.*

29. The historian Michael Clanchy has pointed out an exquisite irony in this. At the very moment that Britain's rulers were ordering the deliberate and wholesale destruction of her most important financial records of the past six hundred years in the name of progress and reform, they were instructing the Records Commissioners to begin the first collation of the earliest medieval records in parchment, starting with the Chancery rolls from the time of King John. As Clanchy laments, "The Commissioners would not have dreamed of burning Domesday Book or the Chancery rolls, yet these records of the Exchequer were deliberately destroyed because they were in a medium, wood, which was too uncouth for scholars to appreciate" (Clanchy, 1993, p. 125).

30. Goetzmann and Williams, "From Tallies and Chirographs to Franklin's Printing Press at Passy," in Goetzmann and Rouwenhorst, 2005, describe and analyse one such collection; but they freely admit how difficult it is to know for sure what individual tallies mean.

31. *Irish Independent*, 1 May 1970, pp. 1 and 24.

32. Central Bank of Ireland, 1970, p. 6.

33. *The Times*, 14 July 1970, p. 20.

34. *Irish Independent*, 28 May 1970, p. 30.

35. *Ibid.*, p. 9.

36. *Ibid.*, 13 June 1970, p. 1.

37. Central Bank of Ireland, 1970, p. 47.

38. Murphy, 1978, p. 44.

39. *Ibid.*, p. 45.

40. The characterisation of money as a social technology—a brilliant coinage which has gained even more suggestive power since the advent of internet-based social networks—is due to Ingham, 2004.

41. These three elements form the basis of what is usually called the "credit" theory of money—and set it in opposition to the conventional "commodity" or "metallist" theory: see, for example, Schumpeter, 1954; Goodhart, 1998; Smithin, 2000; Wray, 2004; and, for a concise overview of the differences between the two approaches, Jackson, Werner, Greenham, and Ryan-Collins, 2012. As we shall see throughout the rest of this book, the credit-theoretic approach to understanding money has a rich history.

42. Macleod, 1882, p. 188.

43. *Ibid.*, p. 481.

44. The classic reference is Knapp, 1924. We will hear more about chartalism in chapters 4 and 8.

45. Feynman, R., "How to Enjoy a Trip to the Dentist: The Mystery of Magnetic and Electrical Forces," Episode 3 of *Fun to Imagine*, first broadcast 22 July 1983. Available at http://www.bbc.co.uk/archive/feynman/10702.shtml.

2 Getting Money's Measure

1. The *aristeia* of Diomedes, for example, comprises all of Book V, and the first 236 lines of Book VI of the *Iliad*.

2. The shield is described in *Iliad* XVIII. 478–608.

3. Seabright, 2004, p. 15.

4. *Iliad* II. 272–7.

5. Fragment 23 of the 7th–6th century BC poet and statesman Solon, here in M.L.

West's translation. The identical couplet is also attributed to another aristocratic poet of the seventh century, Theognis of Megara, at lines 1253–6.

6. See Seaford, 1994, pp. 42–53. Seaford summarises: "Collective participation in the ritual as well as in the distribution of meat in a fixed order create community (*koinonia*)." p. 44.

7. See, for example, the first chapter of Macdonald, 2006, p. 14, which provides a useful historical catalogue of the socio-economic institutions of tribal peoples. The classic comparative study of the phenomenon of gift-exchange is Mauss, 1954, the second line of which summarises in a single sentence the results of decades of research on numerous primitive and archaic societies: "In . . . many . . . civilizations contracts are fulfilled and exchanges of goods are made by means of gifts."

8. Parry and Bloch, 1989, pp. 23–4.

9. And, of course, one which has persisted all the way into our own era in the form of the Christian Eucharist.

10. The mysterious standing stones at Göbekli Tepe in modern-day Turkey, carved with elaborate illustrations of people and animals as long ago as 15,000 BC.

11. Nissen, 1988, pp. 70–3. By way of comparison, the urban area of classical Athens was only around 2.5 square kilometres; and Jerusalem, after its expansion around AD 43, attained about 1 square kilometre. Estimates of population sizes for ancient Mesopotamian cities, even very vague ones such as those given here, are necessarily speculative: see Van de Mieroop, 1997, pp. 95–7.

12. The following account of Ur in the early part of the Old Babylonian period (2000–1600 BC) is based on Van de Mieroop, 1992.

13. Van de Mieroop, 1992, pp. 77–8.

14. *Ibid.*, p. 208.

15. The term "command economy" is of course not strictly appropriate, alluding as it does to socialist economies in the twentieth century (AD). There were—especially in the latter part of the Old Babylonian period, as documented in Van de Mieroop, 1992—parts of the Mesopotamian economies which appear to have been under much looser central control. Most probably, the Mesopotamian urban economies incorporated a dominant redistributive, administered temple economy supplemented by a variety of small-scale productive and trading activities outside of the direct control of the bureaucracy.

16. Childe, V. G., 1954, "What Happened in History," p. 93, quoted in Schmandt-Besserat, 1992, p. 6.

17. Schmandt-Besserat traces the earliest version of this theory to William Warburton, who propounded it in his *Divine Legation of Moses* of 1738. See Schmandt-Besserat, 1992, p. 4ff.

18. This last interpretation was not as bizarre as it might sound. Board games were indeed an important feature of Mesopotamian life, as attested by the famous board of the "Game of Ur" that is now in the British Museum. But the sheer number of clay artefacts discovered implied an obsession with games-playing on a rather unlikely scale. The conclusion drawn by the eminent archaeologist Ernest Mackay in his field report from the site of Jemdet Nasr in 1931—"That the games played with these pieces were extremely popular is proved from the great number found"—turned out to be a circular argument.

19. Carleton S. Coon, in his site report on Belt Cave in Iran, cited in Schmandt-Besserat, 1977.

20. See Dantzig, 1930, for more on the history of the concept of number.

21. Schmandt-Besserat, 1979.

22. Schmandt-Besserat, 1992.

23. There were important stages in its development—most notably a stage before about 5500 BC when tokens were mostly undecorated, and the stage afterwards, in which drawing on tokens with a reed pen offered a means of introducing additional flexibility into the system. See Schmandt-Besserat, 1992.

24. UET 5: no. 572, (RS 9), cited in Van de Mieroop, 1992, p. 83.

25. See Hudson and Wunsch, 2000, for more on this fascinating topic.

26. Whilst it is uncontroversial that there was no money in Dark Age Greece, there is some debate over whether or not money existed in the ancient Near East. Seaford, 2004, devotes an appendix (pp. 318–37) to an extensive review of the evidence that it did not; but concedes that there is continuing scholarly disagreement on the question. Any answer will always depend critically on how exactly money is defined. The interpretation followed here is that the systems of financial accounting developed in ancient Mesopotamia did not make the transition to the use of general-purpose money based on a universal concept of economic value deployed throughout society in a decentralised fashion, but instead developed a sophisticated system of limited-purpose units of value for use by the clerical bureaucracy in the course of their economic planning.

27. Kula, 1986, p. 8.

28. *Ibid.*, p. 22.

29. *Ibid.*, pp. 4–5.

30. The set of six basic units themselves had in fact been endorsed as Resolution 6 of the 10th meeting of the General Conference in 1954—but it was Resolution 12 of the 11th General Conference which established it as the *Systeme International*, complete with official abbreviations and a list of supplementary and derived units. At the 14th meeting of the General Conference in 1971, a seventh basic unit, the mole (amount of substance), was added. The story of the creation of the SI—and much else—is told in Robert Crease's fascinating *World in the Balance: The Historic Quest for an Absolute System of Measurement*, 2011.

31. More precisely, "in terms of the wavelength in a vacuum of the radiation corresponding to a transition between specified energy levels of the krypton 86 atom." In 1983, the 17th General Conference on Weights and Measures redefined the metre as the length of the path travelled by light in vacuum during a specific fraction of a second (though it has not yet been possible to operationalise this redefinition).

32. Kula, 1986, p. 42.

33. "Slicing an Apple," *The Economist*, 10 August 2011. The proportions given are of total dollar value.

3 The Aegean Invention of Economic Value

1. Mitchell Innes, 1914, p. 155.

2. B. Applebaum, "A Life's Value May Depend on the Agency, but It's Rising: As U.S. Agencies Put More Value on a Life, Businesses Fret," *New York Times*, 16 February 2011.

3. These verses announce that the cup is the famous drinking vessel belonging to the Homeric hero Nestor—and thereby represent an example of instant sophistication of technique to rival Sterne's *Tristram Shandy*, since this earliest extant specimen of Greek writing is also both the earliest literary allusion—to a passage of the *Iliad*—and the earliest ironic subversion of such an allusion—since the Homeric cup of Nestor was so large and ornate it could barely be lifted, whilst the inscribed

cup is a modest clay bowl. See Murray, O., 1993, pp. 92–101 for further details on the transmission of literacy and its impact.

4. The modern fountainhead of the analysis of the impact of literacy on Greek culture is Jack Goody and Ian Watt's 1963 article "The Consequences of Literacy," reprinted in Goody, J., 1968. Goody and Watt were anthropologists, rather than ancient historians—and their hypotheses were strongly influenced by the anthropological research of the Soviet psychologist Alfred Luria, who made an extraordinary study of the cognitive effects of the transition from oral to literate culture in the unique circumstances to be found in Soviet Central Asia in the 1920s and 1930s (collected in English in his 1976 *Cognitive Development: Its Cultural and Social Development*). The Jesuit Walter Ong's *Orality and Literacy*, 1982, was another foundational contribution. The subject has since come to be seen as fundamental for the understanding of archaic Greek history: see Murray, O., 1993, pp. 98–101 for a concise discussion.

5. Of course, it was not only the flow of new technologies from the ancient Near East that catalysed this intellectual revolution: there were substantive borrowings as well. See West, 1971.

6. Murray, O., 1993, p. 248.

7. Nissen, Damerow, and Englund, 1993, p. 51.

8. The hypothesis that it was the particular ritual of sacrificial distribution that provided the raw material for the idea of universal economic value can hardly be conclusively proved. Nevertheless, the case in its favour is not limited to its unusual role in expressing the equality of the individual within the tribe. There is also important circumstantial evidence: the earliest Greek monetary units were the *obol*—the term for the spits on which celebrants' portions of the sacrificial meat were distributed—and the *drachma*—which originally meant "a handful," presumably of such spits. See Parker, 1996, for details of the ritual itself; Seaford, 1994, and Seaford, 2004, for the exposition of the theory from which the hypothesis here is derived. Evidence in favour of the general hypothesis that abstract monetary units derive originally from social institutions of this broad type has been provided by Grierson, 1977; Grierson's famous lecture made an analogous case for the origins of medieval European monetary units in the similarly egalitarian political ideology of the Germanic tribes of the European Dark Ages, ritualised in that case via the institution of wergild, the conventional compensation for personal injury.

9. See, for example, *Supplementum Epigraphicum Graecum* XII. 391, quoted in von Reden, 2010, p. 36.

10. Plutarch, *Solon*, 23.4, quoted in von Reden, 2010, p. 37.

11. Jeffrey, L. H. and Morpurgo Davies, A. in *Kadmos*, 1970, fig. 1, side A; cited in von Reden, 2010, p. 36.

12. Peter Spufford has demonstrated the intrinsic connection between money and markets in the Middle Ages in his 1988 *Money and Its Use in Medieval Europe*: "One of the striking phenomena of the tenth century in both Germany and England is the great number of new commercial centres deliberately created by imperial or royal fiat . . . The twin grants of the rights to hold a market and to operate a mint added a new dimension to urban life . . . Market and mint went together. The market was not for barter, but for selling and buying with money, and to provide for this a mint was needed" (p. 75). Of one of the very earliest specific examples of such a grant—to the Abbey of St. Gall by the Holy Roman Emperor Otto I in 947, he writes "Mint and market are firmly linked together. Without money there can be no market" (p. 77).

13. Kim, H., "Archaic Coinage as Evidence for the Use of Money," p. 8, in Meadows and Shipton, 2001. The earliest Lydian coinage was minted from electrum, a natural alloy of gold and silver. Most Greek coins were minted from silver—though base metals were sometimes used as well.

14. Von Reden, 2010, p. 40.

15. The first experience of monetisation in Europe, that is. It appears that money may have been invented, independently of the Greeks, in India and China as well—to say nothing of the controversy over whether it was in fact invented in the ancient Near East.

16. Pindar, *Isthmian*, 2.11–12. The sentiment evidently resonated widely, however: Alcaeus too quoted it in one of his poems: see Seaford, 2004, p. 161.

17. Or as Parry and Bloch put it: "By a remarkable conceptual revolution . . . the values of the short-term order have become elaborated into a theory of long-run reproduction. What our culture (like others) had previously made room for in a separate and subordinate domain has, in some quarters at least, been turned into a theory of the encompassing order—a theory in which it is *only* unalloyed private vice that can sustain the public benefit," Parry and Bloch, 1989, p. 29.

18. This and the following examples are taken from M. Sandel, "What isn't for sale?" *The Atlantic*, April 2012. Available at: http://www.theatlantic.com/magazine/archive/2012/04/what-isn-8217-t-for-sale/8902/.

19. The statement ("Remember that you are an Englishman, and have consequently won first prize in the lottery of life") is attributed to Cecil Rhodes by Peter Ustinov in chapter 4 of his 1977 autobiography, *Dear Me*. Elsewhere it is attributed to Rudyard Kipling.

20. Sandel, 2012.

21. Locke, 2009, chapter 11, §106.

4 Financial Sovereignty and Monetary Insurrection

1. De la Torre, Levy Yeyati and Schmukler, 2003.

2. T. Catan, "Argentina Snowed under by Paper IOUs: Pesos or Pacificos? A Dizzying Array of Quasi-currencies Now Fill up the Tills," *Financial Times*, 11 April 2002. The peso was Argentina's currency. The *lecops*, or *Letra de Cancelacion de Obligaciones Provinciales* was a peso-denominated quasi-currency issued by the Argentine National Treasury. The *patacon*, or *Letra de Tesoreria para Cancelacion de Obligaciones* was a peso-denominated quasi-currency issued by the Treasury of the Province of Buenos Aires. Eleven other provinces and cities issued their own quasi-currencies. See De la Torre, et al., 2003, p. 77.

3. Colacelli and Blackburn, 2006, p. 4, fn. 8.

4. *L'Armée des Ombres*—"The Army of Shadows"—is the title of a famous account of the Maquis by Joseph Kessels published in 1943 and filmed by Jean-Pierre Melville in 1969.

5. IMF, "Introductory remarks on the Role of the IMF Mission in Argentina by Anoop Singh, Director for Special Operations, IMF," Press Briefing, Buenos Aires, 10 April 2002. Available at http://www.imf.org/external/np/tr/2002/tr020410.htm.

6. Aukutsionek, 1998.

7. Ryabchenko, P., "Talony vmeste deneg," *Nezavisimaya Gazeta*, 13 October 1998, quoted in Caroline Humphrey's chapter in Seabright, 2000, p. 290.

8. Seabright, 2000.

9. WIR Bank Annual Report 2011, summarised in press release at www.wir.ch.

10. Indeed, one can learn a lot about money from this, one of its simplest incarnations—as the Nobel laureate Paul Krugman often points out. A famous analysis of what one can learn—and the one which initially captured Krugman's attention—is Sweeney and Sweeney, 1977.

11. There are historical examples of just this happening during the early 1930s in Europe, when mutual credit networks gained widespread popularity as a means to escape the economic depression. In Germany for example, the owner of a mine in the Bavarian town of Schwanenkirchen put a scrip currency into circulation, with spectacular economic results: "[N]ews of the town's prosperity in the midst of depression-ridden Germany spread quickly," wrote the American economist Irving Fisher; "[f]rom all over the country reporters came to see and write about the 'Miracle of Schwanenkirchen.'" When the news reached the German government in November 1931, it passed an emergency law banning all private scrip money. See Greco, 2001, p. 64 ff.

12. *Constitution of the United States*, Article 1, Section 8, states that "The Congress shall have power . . . to coin money, [and] regulate the value thereof."

13. Even less popular have been the occasional proposals to endorse officially the co-circulation of existing national currencies. Friedrich von Hayek, for example, proposed this in von Hayek, 1976. When the U.K. Treasury adopted this policy as a serious proposal for how a transition to the euro might work in the early 1990s, it was interpreted by other EU member states as a spoiling tactic.

14. Madison, J., 1788, "Federalist 51: The Structure of the Government Must Furnish the Proper Checks and Balances Between the Different Departments," in Genovese, 2009, p. 120.

15. The protagonist of a more recent constitutional debate also makes just this connection: "If a society were truly moral, a written constitution would hardly be necessary. The moral principles that would guarantee sound money, and our not needing a central bank to maintain it, are honesty, which would reject fraud, and keeping one's word" (Paul, 2009, p. 149). Dr. Paul, however, believes that this Utopia is attainable.

16. Plutarch, *Pericles*, 12; quoted in Trevett, J., "Coinage and Democracy at Athens," in Meadows and Shipton, 2001, p. 24.

17. Trevett, J., "Coinage and Democracy at Athens," in Meadows and Shipton, 2001, p. 24.

18. International Monetary Fund, 2012, Statistical Table 5, p. 65.

19. This is the essence of the chartalist theory of money, the foundation text of which is Knapp, 1924.

20. This is an extreme simplification of the view put forward by the great German philosopher Georg Simmel in his 1907 book, *The Philosophy of Money*, see Simmel, 1978.

21. Plato, *Laws* 5.741e–742b.

22. This estimate of the number of Athenian citizens in the second half of the fourth century BC is from Hansen, 1985, pp. 67–78.

23. Aristotle, 1932, I.3.13–14.

24. *Guanzi* 73, "Guoxu" III: 70, quoted in von Glahn, 1996, p. 29. Von Glahn's superb account of ancient Chinese monetary thought is the primary source for this section.

25. *Guanzi* 74, "Shanguoshi" III: 71, quoted *ibid.*, p. 33.

26. Sima Chen, "Shi Chi 30: Treatise on the Balanced Standard," in Watson, 1961, p. 80.

27. Quoted in von Glahn, 1996, p. 36.

28. *Guanzi* 73, "Guoxu" III: 66, quoted *ibid.*, p. 30.

5 The Birth of the Money Interest

1. "Others, I doubt not, shall with softer mould beat out the breathing bronze, coax from the marble features to life, plead cases with greater eloquence and with a pointer trace heaven's motions and predict the risings of the stars: you, Roman, be sure to rule the world (be these your arts), to crown peace with justice, to spare the vanquished and to crush the proud," Virgil, *Aeneid* VI.847–53 (in H.R. Fairclough's translation).

2. The Roman general Marcus Claudius Marcellus recovered astronomical instruments from Archimedes' academy following the sack of Syracuse—Cicero saw them in his grandson's house—that were probably similar to the Antikythera Mechanism, the extraordinary ancient computer the workings of which were deciphered in 2006 by the international Antikythera Mechanism Research Project. The carvings on the tomb of Marcus Vergilius Eurysaces, a Roman baking tycoon of the Augustan age, proudly depict the mechanised mass production of bread.

3. Cicero, *De Officiis*, 3.59, quoted in Harris, 2008, p. 176.

4. Ovid, *Ars Amatoria*, 1.428, quoted *ibid.*, 2008, p. 178.

5. Horace, *Ars Poetica*, l.421.

6. For example, the jurist Scaevola refers to a certain banker who *paene totam fortunam in nominibus [habebat]* ("had almost his entire fortune in bonds"). The *Digest* of Justinian, 40.7.40.8. See Harris, 2006, p. 6.

7. Andreau, 1999.

8. Cicero, *De Officiis*, 2.87. Quoted in Jones, 2006. Janus was, of course, the two-faced god—though this did not have the same connotations for the Romans as for us.

9. The law was *de modo credendi possidendique intra Italiam* ("Regulating lending and title within Italy").

10. Tacitus, *Annales*, 6.16.

11. Tacitus, *Annales*, 6.17. The history of this and other banking crises is analysed in Andreau, 1999, chapter 9.

12. See Harris, W., "The Nature of Roman Money," in Harris, 2008, p. 205.

13. *Ibid.*

14. Spufford, 1988, p. 9.

15. Spufford, 2002, p. 60 ff. In the most economically advanced and politically coherent parts of Europe it had started even earlier: ". . . in the hinterland of Genoa and Lucca rents in kind gave way to rents in money in the course of the eleventh century, and in the Campania the exploitation of estates began with labour hired for money wages" (Spufford, 1988, p. 97).

16. Spufford, 2002, p. 63.

17. For example, in England, where direct taxation re-emerged at the end of the twelfth century. See Spufford, 2002, p. 65.

18. On the impact of monetisation on social mobility and on the social roles of ambition and avarice, see in particular Murray, A., 1978.

19. Hildebert of Lavardin *Carmina misc.*, 50, quoted in Murray, A., 1978, p. 81. "Money is the man!" was the famous saying attributed to the Argive aristocrat Aristodemus, quoted both by Pindar and by Alcaeus; see chapter 3.

20. Rolnick, Velde, and Weber, 1996, 797.

21. *Ibid.*

22. *Ibid.*

23. Sumption, 2001, p. 195.

24. Johnson, 1956.

25. *Ibid.*, p. 10.

26. *Ibid.*, pp. 19–20.
27. *Ibid.*, p. 38.
28. *Ibid.*, p. 40.
29. *Ibid.*, p. 6.
30. *Ibid.*, p. 17.
31. *Ibid.*, p. 44.
32. *Ibid.*, p. 42.

6 The Natural History of the Vampire Squid

1. Described in Frankel, 1977, p. 15.
2. Élie Brackenhofer was told in 1634 that the Fair of Lyons had been founded in AD 172. See Braudel, 1992.
3. See Spufford, 2002, p. 19 ff.
4. Braudel, 1992, p. 91.
5. The phrase is Braudel's, quoted in Frankel, 1977, p. 15.
6. Amis, 1984, pp. 119–20.
7. De Rubys, 1604, Part IV, chapter 9, p. 499. The pound (*livre*) was the abstract money of account, whilst the *sou* was a coin of the French king.
8. To be more precise, it had not worked as much as they would have liked. By the sixteenth century, the extreme debasements of the Middle Ages were a thing of the past and the Spanish and French sovereign currencies were comparatively speaking fairly stable—in the French case, partly as a result of pressure from taxpayers to limit seigniorage. See chapter 3 of Macdonald, 2006, for details.
9. This is a description of how they achieve the transformation at its most generic, and one which is sufficient as it stands for private banks in the Middle Ages. As we shall see later in this chapter, and in chapter 14, modern banks benefit from a crucial element of external assistance in their business of transforming illiquid claims into liquid ones.
10. Nor is it unique to banking: mutual funds, for example, also manage credit risk in the same three respects.
11. The most important general characteristic of the liquidity risk that is managed by modern banks is the mismatch between the fact that a large part of their liabilities is made up of deposits available for withdrawal on demand, and the fact that their assets generally consist of loans or securities which do not mature and may not be otherwise realisable in the same time frame. Indeed, Walter Bagehot, in his foundational classic of the modern finance literature, identified this characteristic as the one which discriminated banking from other financial activities. "Messrs. Rothschild," he wrote in *Lombard Street*, "are immense capitalists, having, doubt-less, much borrowed money in their hands," and "a foreigner would be apt to think that they are bankers if any one was." But "[t]hey do not take 100*l.* payable on demand, and pay it back in cheques of 5*l.* each, and that is our English bank-ing. The borrowed money they have is in large sums, borrowed for terms more or less long. English bankers deal with an aggregate of small sums, all of which are repayable on short notice, or on demand" (Bagehot, 1873, pp. 212–13). The distinctive business of a bank is in other words "maturity transformation," in the technical jargon—in that they "transform" short-term liabilities to their depositors into long-term loans to their clients. Of course, this jargon is a euphemism. No transformation takes place—alchemy is as impossible in banking as in the natural sciences. Banks really do have a mismatch, which is sustained only so long as their

depositors remain confident in their creditworthiness and the liquidity of their liabilities. We will discover more about banking in chapter 14.

12. Spufford, 2002, p. 38.

13. *Ibid.*, pp. 38–9.

14. *Ibid.*, p. 39.

15. Johnson, 1956, p. 34.

16. Spufford, 2002, p. 40.

17. Huerta de Soto, 2006, p. 75.

18. In essence: its full details were complicated. For a virtuoso overview of the system in all its complexity, see Boyer-Xambeu, Deleplace, and Gillard, 1994.

19. Indeed, Boyer-Xambeu et al. (*ibid.*) argue that under the sovereign monetary policies that were obtained in the mid-sixteenth century, the profits to the exchange-bankers were essentially certain.

20. See *ibid.*, pp. 91–4 for further details on the protocols of the Lyons fair.

21. *Ibid.*, p. xvi.

7 The Great Monetary Settlement

1. R.H. Tawney's Introduction to Wilson, 1925, p. 83. "[A]nd the third person of this inharmonious trinity," Tawney added, "was perpetually at war with the two first."

2. Mayhew, 1999, p. 54.

3. *Hist. MSS. Comm., MSS. of the Marquis of Salisbury*, Pt. I, pp. 162–4, quoted in Tawney's introduction to Wilson, 1925.

4. Montesquieu, *Mes Pensées*, quoted in Hirschman, 1977, p. 74.

5. Montesquieu, *Esprit des lois*, Book XXII, 13, quoted *ibid.*, p. 74 (where it is accidentally attributed to Book XXII, 14).

6. Montesquieu, *Esprit des lois*, Book XXI, 20, quoted *ibid.*, pp. 72–3.

7. *Ibid.*

8. James Carville, quoted in *Wall Street Journal*, 25 February 1993, p. A1.

9. It was published in England in 1767, nine years before Adam Smith's *An Inquiry into the Nature and Causes of the Wealth of Nations*.

10. Steuart, 1966, Vol. 1, p. 278. Quoted in Hirschman, 1977, p. 85.

11. Boyer-Xambeu et al., 1994, p. 30.

12. The extent to which the development of finance in England lagged behind Continental Europe until the late seventeenth century is demonstrated by Thomas Mun's treatment of standard Latin practices such as payments by transfer between bank accounts as unknown in England in his 1621 *Discourse on Foreign Trade*. See also Clapham, 1944, Vol. I, p. 5.

13. The king's adviser Sydney Godolphin, seeking to borrow for the crown from William of Orange in 1680, offered 8 per cent for a loan "secured upon the King's hereditary revenue." This was meant to tempt his target away from lending in the Dutch credit markets, where "at this time no one gives more than 4 per cent for money." See Macdonald, 2006, pp. 170–1.

14. For a detailed discussion of the main Projects, see Horsefield, 1960, pp. 114–24.

15. It was the brainchild of Thomas Neale, the Master of the Mint and a close adviser to the Treasury. Some years later, another larger lottery was held to raise even more money. It was called, imaginatively enough, "The Two Million Adventure."

16. Richards, 1958, pp. 112–13.

17. Curiously enough, the Bank's original charter—itself deliberately tucked away in a corner of a more general public finance bill—did not authorise note issue explicitly. But explicit or not, more than £750,000-worth of notes had been issued by the time the Bank's first public balance sheet had been drawn up in November 1696. See Clapham, 1944, p. 43, for details.

18. Modern scholarship on the nature and significance of this Great Monetary Settlement, starting from the pioneering contribution of Dickson, 1967, is extensive, but it was Ingham, 2004, who first identified its importance as the moment in which the modern, public-private monetary system was born. See especially Ingham, 2004, pp. 128ff.

19. Roseveare, 1991, pp. 14–15.

20. *Clarke* v. *Martin* 1702 *per Holt C. J.*, quoted in Carswell, 1960, p. 18. Holt's efforts to reverse the tide and outlaw the dangerous commercial practice of transferability were defeated by statute within two years. The Promissory Notes Act of 1704 made private credit notes legally transferable.

21. Steuart, 1966, Vol. 2, p. 477.

22. Smith, A., 1981, II.ii.85, p. 320.

23. The 1709 regulation forbade partnerships with more than six members from issuing any kind of note of less than six months' maturity payable on demand—the result of a concerted campaign by the Bank's Directors to muzzle what was then its chief competitor, the Sword Blade Bank. The Bank of England did not receive a monopoly on issuance until the Bank Charter Act of 1844, however—and even then note-issuing banks already in existence were permitted to continue to do so until taken over by banks without the privilege. It was therefore not until the small Somerset partnership of Fox, Fowler & Co., which had received its charter in 1787, was absorbed into Lloyds Bank in 1921, that the last private English banknotes were removed from circulation.

24. H.V. Bowen, "The Bank 1694–1820," in Roberts and Kynaston, 1995, p. 10.

25. Clapham, 1944, Vol. I, p. 102.

26. Speech of 13 June 1781 in the Committee of Ways and Means, as reported by William Cobbett (1806–20) *Parliamentary History of England from 1066 to 1803*, Vol. XXII, cols 517–20, quoted in H.V. Bowen, "The Bank 1694–1820," in Roberts and Kynaston, 1995, p. 3.

27. See above p. 80 and p. 113.

8 The Economic Consequences of Mr. Locke

1. The Mint price of silver—the tariff ordinance which specified the silver content of the sterling monetary units—had been 60d an ounce since 1601, except during the period 1604–26, when seigniorage had been half a penny more, and the Mint price therefore 59½d. Meanwhile, the market price of silver had rarely dropped below this, and in general had been between 62d and 64d an ounce. See Feavearyear, 1931, pp. 109–10.

2. The Mint price was raised by the Act to 62d an ounce, in other words. See *ibid.*, p. 110.

3. By Lowndes, in his 1695 report to Parliament. See Mayhew, 1999, p. 97.

4. Desmedt, L., "Les fondements monétaires de la 'révolution financière' anglaise: le tournant de 1696," in Théret, B., ed., 2007, *La monnaie dévoilée par ses crises*, cited in Ormazabal, 2012, p. 158. The market price of silver reached 77d an ounce in 1695, according to William Lowndes' report of that year.

5. Lowndes, 1695, p. 56.

6. For simplicity's sake, I describe here the mechanics of a recoinage. Lowndes' preferred solution was in fact to execute the official devaluation using the method

more frequently deployed throughout English history of "crying up" the tariffed, nominal value of the existing coinage, rather than going through the practically costly and administratively difficult business of re-minting. The equivalent of a 20 per cent reduction in the silver content would have been a roughly 25 per cent crying up of existing, full-weight coinage. See Lowndes, 1695, p. 123.

7. Feavearyear, 1931, p. 122.

8. Locke, 1695, pp. 1–2.

9. *Ibid.*, p. 9.

10. *Ibid.*, p. 12.

11. See Feavearyear, 1931, p. 124.

12. The full distributional arithmetic was more complex. The counterparty to these gains and losses was in the first place the Exchequer—since it was the Exchequer that was liable to subsidise the re-minting of the collected coins at full weight before the deadline, and the Exchequer that would no longer have to redeem light coins at full nominal value after the deadline. But the Exchequer would need to raise funds for the subsidy (it did so via a window tax), so what it gave with one hand it might take away with another a moment later.

13. Feavearyear, 1931, pp. 129–30.

14. Quoted in Mayhew, 1999, p. 101.

15. Keynes, 1931, p. 394. The book was Hayek's 1931 *Prices and Production.*

16. Barbon, N., 1696, *A Discourse Concerning Coining the New Money Lighter,* quoted in Magnusson, 1995.

17. Liddell and Scott, 1996. Richard Seaford explains the etymology of the word *nomisma* as follows: it "comes from *nomisdein* (to acknowledge), is the object or consequence of *nomisdein*" (Seaford, 2004, p. 142). *Nomisdein* was the verb the Greeks used to denote cognitive commitments, such as belief in the gods, that were the result of convention rather than of active deliberation. To give a flavour of the connotations of *nomisma,* Seaford explains that "[t]he earliest surviving occurrence of *nomisma* is Alcaeus fr. 382 L-P: 'truly she [Athena?] was bringing together a scattered army, inspiring them with *nomisma.*' *Nomisma* here, mysterious enough to be divinely inspired, is the collective confidence, based on custom, that can unite an army . . . Customary collective practice [*nomisma*], *whether coinage or in battle,* depends on and objectifies the collective confidence of the community, for whom it introduces order into potential chaos" (*ibid.*, p. 143).

18. Plato, *Republic,* 2.371b.

19. Aristotle, *Nicomachean Ethics,* 1113a. Similarly at 1133b: "There must therefore be some one standard, and this accepted by custom [*nomos*] (on account of which it is called a convention [*nomisma*]); for such a standard makes all things commensurable, since all things can be measured by money [*nomisma*]."

20. Seaford, 2004, p. 146.

21. Herodotus, *Histories,* 8.26.

22. Aquinas, *Sententia Politica,* lib. 1, l. 7, n. 6.

23. Aquinas, *Sententia Ethica,* lib. 5, l. 9, n. 12.

24. Aquinas, *In Octo Libros Politicorum,* Vol. XXVI of *Omnia Opera,* 1: 7. Likewise at *Sententia Ethica,* lib. 5, l. 9, n. 5.

25. See chapters 1 and 4. The tradition of Aquinas was by no means the only one in medieval monetary thought. In fact, significant parts of the legal tradition rejected monetary nominalism and developed an essentialist theory. For a fascinating, blow-by-blow survey of the medieval debate see Sargent and Velde, 2002, chapter 5.

26. Briscoe, J., 1696, *A Discourse on Money,* p. 18, quoted in Appleby, 1976, p. 65.

27. Feavearyear, 1931, p. 137.
28. Mandeville, 1705.
29. Mandeville, 1988 [1732], Vol. 1, p. 369.
30. Smith, A., 1981, III.iv.4, p. 412.
31. *Ibid.*, III.iv.10, p. 419.
32. *Ibid.*, IV.ii.9, p. 456.
33. *Ibid.*
34. *Ibid.*, III.iv.15, p. 421.

9 Money Through the Looking-Glass

1. Or at least, they certainly did in the headquarters of the international financial institutions in Washington, D.C. Soon after the crisis first broke, in April 2007, I went to the joint IMF–World Bank library to borrow a copy of Kindleberger's standard history of financial crises (Kindleberger, 2000). All the library's copies were out on loan for the first time in many years—as of the previous week.
2. Kindleberger, 1993, p. 264.
3. Reinhart and Rogoff, 2009.
4. Marx and Engels, 1985, Section 1: Bourgeois and Proletarians.
5. Keynes, 1923, pp. 67–8.
6. *Ibid.*
7. *Ibid.*
8. France, 1908, p. 82.
9. "Charity as a Remedy in Case of Famine," *The Economist*, 29 November 1845, p. 192.
10. "Feeding the Irish," *The Economist*, 21 March 1846, p. 370.
11. *Ibid.*
12. *Ibid.* Readers may recognise in the arguments of this editorial precisely the arsenal of rhetorical strategies that the great intellectual historian Albert O. Hirschman identified as characteristic of reactionary argument throughout history in his 1991 study *The Rhetoric of Reaction: Perversity, Futility, Jeopardy*. Yet these arguments were being deployed by one of the leading reform journals of the day, in the cause of radical liberal economic policy. Perhaps they show that it is not just conservatives that have a monopoly on these evidently persuasive strategies.
13. *Ibid.*
14. Quoted in Woodham-Smith, 1962, p. 93.
15. "Faith in Principles," *The Economist*, 2 January 1847, p. 3.
16. Quoted in Woodham-Smith, 1962, pp. 162–3.
17. Quoted *ibid.*, pp. 375–6. Jowett was being a bit disingenuous: he was practically an economist himself, giving a course of lectures on political economy at Balliol every year until he became Master. See "Benjamin Jowett" in Pigou, 1925, pp. 292–4.

10 Strategies of the Sceptics

1. Herodotus, *Histories*, 8.138. Herodotus has the garden located in Macedonia—but Midas was an historical person, and the story has been transposed from Phrygia.
2. Midas' story is told by several classical authors, with numerous variations. The

version given here broadly follows the compound account given by Seaford, 2004, pp. 305–6, with incidental details from Ovid's account in *Metamorphoses*, XI.

3. Ovid, *Metamorphoses*, XI. ll.118–19.

4. *Ibid.*, XI. ll.127–8.

5. Aristophanes, *Frogs*, l.141.

6. Aristophanes, *Wealth*, ll.189–97. A talent was a high-value coin. This was a comic, classical expression of an older idea: Solon, the law-giver of the sixth century, had written: "As for wealth, there is no set limit for mankind; for those who are the richest amongst us hurry on to get twice as much again, and who can satisfy everyone?" (Solon, *fr. 13* ll.71–3). Hirschmann, 1977, follows the trail of this particular aspect of money through the transformation of monetary thought by the Enlightenment philosophers of the eighteenth century. In their hands, he demonstrates, the insatiability of the desire for money, which had long "been considered the most dangerous and reprehensible aspect of that passion," "[b]y a strange twist . . . now became a virtue because it implies constancy." As he points out, this amazing bit of moral gymnastics required something else as well: "to endow the 'obstinate' desire for gain with an additional quality: harmlessness." (pp. 55–6).

7. Sandel, 2012, p. 6.

8. Skidelsky and Skidelsky, 2012.

9. See, for example, Frank, 2011.

10. Aristotle, 1932, 1257b 16.

11. Aeschylus, *Seven Against Thebes*, l.682.

12. *Ibid.*, ll.688–9.

13. *Ibid.*, l.697.

14. This was the boast of Athens' greatest leader, Pericles, in his famous speech extolling her virtues reported by Thucydides in his *History of the Peloponnesian War*, 2.41.

15. As a rite of passage to adulthood, young Spartan men were assigned to secret clubs and sent out to live wild in the countryside, where they lay hidden during the day and emerged at night to murder any members of the peasant caste they could find. See Murray, O., 1993, p. 179.

16. *Ibid.*, p. 160. Murray argues that both Plato and Aristotle admired the Spartan constitution, and believed its failing to be its relentless emphasis on breeding martial valour into its citizens, rather than a broader and more enlightened range of virtues.

17. In the *Republic* 2.371b, Plato admitted that there would have to be money in his ideal state, but at *Republic* 3.416e–17a, he forbade the Guardians—the highest caste—from using it. In the *Laws* 741e–742b, he then proceeded to impose conditions on the use of money by the masses, advocating the issuance of separate moneys for domestic and foreign trade (the former represented by coinage with no intrinsic value, the latter by precious-metal coinage), and explaining that the state should control the allocation to its citizens of the money good for foreign trade.

18. More, 1975, Book II, final page.

19. Bellers, 1696, p. 12.

20. Marx and Engels, 1985, Section 1: Bourgeois and Proletarians.

21. Ilf and Petrov, 1962, p. 29. I owe the example of Ilf and Petrov's novel as an illustration of Soviet monetary policy in the 1920s and 30s to David Woodruff's superlative study, *Money Unmade: Barter and the Fate of Russian Capitalism*, 1999.

22. Ilf and Petrov, 1962, p. 30.

23. *Ibid.*

24. *Ibid.*

25. *Ibid.*, p. 294.

26. In part this had been making a virtue of necessity. The rampant hyperinflation caused by printing money to pay essential workers in the months after the revolution, for example, was quickly hailed as a deliberate effort to accelerate the demise of money by destroying the people's confidence in it. In reality, it was simply a loss of control over the budget and a total collapse of economic and political confidence. See Arnold, 1937, p. 105 ff.

27. Sokolnikov, G.Ya., 1925–28, *Financial Policy of the Revolution*, I, 114, quoted *ibid.*, p. 112.

28. Yurovsky, L.N., 1925, *Currency Problems and Policy of the Soviet Union*, p. 34, quoted *ibid.*, p. 107.

29. Commissariat of Finance, 1921, *Social Revolution and Finance*, p. 42, quoted *ibid.*, p. 107.

30. *Ibid.*

31. Lenin, V.I., 1921, "The Importance of Gold Now and After the Complete Victory of Socialism," in Lenin, 1965, Vol. 33, pp. 109–16.

32. *Ibid.*

33. *Collected Decrees, 1922*, Decree 46, quoted in Arnold, 1937, p. 112.

34. Quoted in Woodruff, 1999, p. 21.

35. The American economist and Soviet expert Gregory Grossman long ago pointed out an irony in all this, that "[f]rom the standpoint of the (Western) monetary theorist, the passive money in the production sector of the Soviet economy is perhaps the closest approximation to that abstract and pure phenomenon, neutral money, neutral because largely powerless as an active determinant of social behaviour." This myth of "neutral money"—the idea that money is not a proactive force in society or the economy—is one of the most important intellectual descendants of Locke's monetary naturalism, and we will meet it in chapter 13. Of course, it was no more true that money was "neutral" in its constrained, Soviet form, than it is in capitalist economies, as Grossman pointed out: "But from the standpoint of the social scientist it is anything but neutral precisely because it is powerless; that is, it has been rendered passive in order not to challenge the regime's political authority." See Grossman, G. (1966) "Gold and the Sword: Money in the Soviet Economy," in Rosovsky, 1966, p. 234.

36. Quoted in Woodruff, 1999, p. 54.

37. An exception to this general statement is the growth of quasi-moneys such as supermarket and airline points systems which have taken advantage of technological change to create viable modern forms of limited-purpose money.

11 Structural Solutions

1. Law had been a protégé of Thomas Neale, the inventor of the Million Adventure whom we encountered in chapter 7.

2. The Bank of Scotland had been established in 1695, but had remained underdeveloped by comparison with the Bank of England, and in 1704 suffered a calamitous run.

3. Law, 1705.

4. *Ibid.*, p. 100.

5. Law, 1720, p. 91.

6. *Ibid.*
7. See chapter 5.
8. Law, 1720, p. 94.
9. *Ibid.*
10. Law, 1705, p. 118.
11. *Ibid.* In his early works—his 1704 *Essay on a Land Bank* and his 1705 *Money and Trade*—Law advocated using land as the standard of monetary value—and it is to land that he is referring here. He believed land to be preferable to precious metals because it was understood by common people to be valuable, of limited supply (thereby imposing a limit on money issuance by the sovereign and quelling fears of overissuance), and under domestic ownership and control. As we shall see, however, once he came to implement his theories a decade later, his thinking had progressed and he had come to believe that the use of land was a halfway house at best.
12. See Velde, 2007, pp. 276–9 for details.
13. Du Tot, N., 1935 [1738], *Réflexions politiques sur les finances et le commerce*, Vol. 1, p. 106; quoted in Murphy, 2009, p. 69.
14. Law, J., *Oeuvres complètes*, Vol. 3, p. 53, quoted in Macdonald, 2006, p. 201.
15. The Duke of Antin, quoted in Murphy, 1997, p. 259.
16. Lee, 1869, p. 189.
17. As James Macdonald points out, however, it was not without precedent, having a close parallel in the corporate structure deployed to organise public finance in the medieval Republic of Genoa (see Macdonald, 2006, pp. 94–100). Moreover, though ahead of its time, the principle of Law's idea is no longer nearly so far-fetched as it once was—as we shall see in chapter 15.
18. Though by no means exclusively in democracies, even if only the circumstantial evidence of the use of coinage is taken as the main indication. See Trevett, J., "Coinage and Democracy at Athens" in Meadows and Shipton, 2001, p. 32.
19. Aristotle, 1932, 1317b, 35–8.
20. Plutarch, *Pericles*, 12, quoted in Trevett, J., "Coinage and Democracy at Athens," in Meadows and Shipton, 2001, p. 24.
21. The hypothesised social and political situation in Athens preceding Solon's reforms presented here is that of Fustel de Coulanges, set out in his 1864 *La Cité antique*, and preferred by Murray, O., 1993, chapter 11.
22. Solon, fr. 13, ll. 5–6.
23. *Ibid.*, ll. 7–8.
24. See Hudson and Van de Mieroop, 2002, pp. 29 ff.
25. *Ibid.*
26. King James Bible, Leviticus 25:8 ff.
27. Murray, O., 1993, p. 187.
28. Solon, *fr.* 37, ll. 9–10.
29. While Chief Magistrate, Solon also introduced new standards of weights and measures for Athens (Aristotle, *The Athenian Constitution*, X). Here is the clearest indication that in money's early days it was easier to understand the difference between a social and a physical standard.
30. *Ibid.*, IX.1.
31. According to Murray, "these objects survived to be discussed by scholars as late as the third century BC; and Plutarch saw fragments of them three hundred years later, preserved in the council office at Athens" (Murray, O., 1993, p. 183). Solon's laws were not in fact the first law-code to have been written down in Athens. A generation earlier, the chief magistrate in 621 BC, Draco, had written down a law-code.

Unfortunately, "the exact scope and nature [of Draco's code] are unknown"—though it was proverbially "extremely harsh (hence the modern word 'Draconian')" (*ibid.*, p. 182).

32. King James Bible, Leviticus 25:10.
33. Law, 1720, pp. 103–4.
34. *Ibid.*, p. 86.
35. It is impossible to say how close and causal the relationship between monetisation and democracy in ancient Greece was. Evidently in the case of Athens, the self-proclaimed "school of Greece" in political matters there was a link, made here, between the social revolution that money brought and the development of her democratic political and legal culture. Some scholars have argued that the link was much broader—at least when it came to the technology of coinage—arguing, for example, that "[t]he anti-democratic ideal was of a world without coinage. Conversely, the democratic *polis*, and Athens in particular, was a world of coins" (Trevett, J., "Coinage and Democracy at Athens," in Meadows and Shipton, 2001, p. 34).

12 *Hamlet* Without the Prince

1. *Focus LSE*, Spring 2009. Available at http://www2.lse.ac.uk/study/meetLSE/pdf/focus/FocusNewsLetter10.pdf.
2. The list of participants in the British Academy conference can be found at http://www.britac.ac.uk/events/archive/forum-economy.cfm.
3. Besley and Hennessy, 2009, p. 3.
4. *Ibid.*, p. 2.
5. *Ibid*.
6. 110th Congress House of Representatives Committee on Oversight and Government Reform (2008), *The Financial Crisis and the Role of Federal Regulators*, hearing of 23 October 2008. Available at https://house.resource.org/110/gov.house.ogr.20081023_hrs15REF2154.raw.txt.
7. The discussion in which Wolf and Summers made these comments is available at: http://ineteconomics.org/net/video/playlist/conference/bretton-woods/V. Summers' response referred to here is his answer to the first question in the interview, starting at 6:04.
8. *Ibid*. Summers also mentioned the 1981 Nobel Laureate James Tobin as an important influence, as well as alluding to the microeconomic literature on bank runs.
9. *Ibid.*, second question starting at 10:58.
10. *Ibid*.
11. It was the short-lived but highly influential economic historian Arnold Toynbee who seems to have coined the name in lectures that he delivered at Oxford in the late 1870s which were published after his death in 1883 as *The Industrial Revolution*.
12. There were fewer than 70,000 Friends even at the height of Quakerism's popularity in the late seventeenth century, and little more than 20,000 by the early nineteenth. See Rowntree, J.S., 1859, "Quakerism Past and Present: Being an Inquiry into the Causes of its Decline in Great Britain and Ireland," cited in Walvin, 2005, pp. 71–4.
13. Anon., 1697, "The Snake in the Grass: or Satan Transformed into an Angel of Light," quoted in Walvin, 2005, p. xvi.
14. Indeed, Barclays was assembled from the merger of three nineteenth-century

Quaker banks, including the Gurney bank of Norwich, and as recently as the turn of the millennium a member of the Gurney family was reputed to be the largest private shareholder in the Barclays register. See Elliott, 2006.

15. The catalyst for this development in the role of the bill brokers seems to have been the financial crisis of 1825, in which the commercial banks were badly burned. The bill brokers stepped in to provide intermediation on their balance sheets where the banks would no longer do so. See Flandreau and Ugolini, 2011, pp. 8–9.

16. Exchange between Bank Directors and members of the 1858 Committee, quoted in Clapham, 1944, Vol. II, p. 237.

17. Capie, 2012, p. 16. The two largest banks at the time were the Midland Bank and the Westminster Bank. As Capie points out, the reason Overend, Gurney could support such an enormous balance sheet was that it ran a much lower ratio of capital to assets: at the time of its failure, Overend, Gurney's ratio was 2 per cent, while most banks had capital–asset ratios of between 9 and 11 per cent.

18. Bagehot, 1999, p. 275.

19. *Ibid.*, pp. 183 and 289.

20. *Ibid.*, p. 164.

21. The famous claim of William Huskisson, the President of the Board of Trade, as quoted *ibid.*, p. 200.

22. The Bank had advanced £9 million to bill brokers, and only £8 million to banks— see *ibid.*, p. 298.

23. Xenos, 1869, p. 64.

24. *Ibid.*, p. 84.

25. Stefanos Xenos, quoted in Elliott, 2006, p. 82. Elliott, however, argues that Edwards, who is held by most earlier scholarship to bear primary responsibility for many of the firm's worst investments, was in fact essentially deployed as a troubleshooter after problems developed, and places most blame on the partners themselves.

26. Another pre-eminent securities-dealing partnership—Goldman Sachs—pulled off a similarly well-timed public offering in 1999. Despite the partners' good fortune in selling out months before the bursting of the dotcom bubble in March 2000, there was however no suggestion on that occasion that the conversion to a public company had been done to escape bankruptcy.

27. *The Economist*, no. 1142, Saturday, 15 July 1865, p. 845.

28. King, W., 1936, p. 240.

29. *Bankers' Magazine*, 1866, p. 639, quoted *ibid.*, p. 243.

30. *The Times*, Saturday, 12 May 1866, p. 243, quoted *ibid.*, p. 243.

31. *The Times*, Friday, 11 May 1866, p. 11.

32. Sir Launcelot Holland, in testimony to the 13 September 1866 meeting of the Court of Proprietors of the Bank of England, quoted in Bagehot, 1999, p. 165.

33. Clapham, 1944, p. 265.

34. *Ibid.*, p. 270.

35. Quoted in Elliott, 2006, p. 188.

36. Bagehot, 1999, p. 273.

37. Quoted in Keynes, 1915b, p. 375. Bagehot believed this to be to his advantage—since he viewed Mill's powerful influence on economic thought to have been essentially unproductive. "[T]here is little which is absolutely original in his great work," he wrote (and in his obituary of Mill in *The Economist*, no less), "and much of that little is not, we think, of the highest value," quoted in Keynes, 1915b, p. 374.

38. Keynes, 1915b, p. 269.

39. *Ibid.*, p. 371.

40. Bagehot, 1999, p. 1.
41. *Ibid.*, p. 189.
42. *Ibid.*, pp. 158–9.
43. *Ibid.*, p. 22.
44. *Ibid.*, p. 323.
45. *Ibid.*, pp. 68–9.
46. *Ibid.*, p. 35.
47. *Ibid.*, p. 20.
48. *Ibid.*, p. 35.
49. *Ibid.*, p. 42.
50. *Ibid.*, p. 196.
51. *Ibid.*, pp. 197–8.
52. *Ibid.*, p. 197.
53. *Ibid.*

13 . . . and Why It Is a Problem

1. Say, 2001, I.XXI.32.
2. Mill, 1848, III.7.9.
3. Bagehot, 1999, pp. 66 and 190.
4. Say, 2001, I.XV.3.
5. Joplin, 1832, p. 219. Say himself also observed the results of the British crisis of 1825 and revised substantially his earlier teachings, as pointed out by DeLong, 2012, pp. 7–9. The argument of this section is heavily indebted to DeLong's brilliant ongoing research into the lessons of the macroeconomic debates of the nineteenth century for today's theoretical and policy morass.
6. Smith, A., 1981, II.4.4., p. 351.
7. Say, 2001, I.XV.7.
8. Mill, 1848, Preliminary Remarks 9.
9. *Ibid.*, III.7.8.
10. Keynes, J.M., Letter to Lydia Lopokova, 18 January 1924, cited in Skidelsky, 1992, p. 175. Evidently, Keynes had forgotten the maxim attributed to Gladstone that "not even love has made so many fools of men as pondering the nature of money."
11. Keynes, 1936. He also wrote his *A Treatise on Money*, 1930, along the way.
12. See chapter 12, n. 9.
13. In today's monetary regimes, the two are linked. Whereas in Bagehot's day, the Bank of England was only able to issue sovereign money against either gold (in the normal course of things) or private debt (in a crisis), modern central banks have typically been licensed to issue money only against government debt—at least until the crisis of 2008–9 forced many of them to start issuing money against various types of private debt (notably mortgage-backed securities in the case of the U.S. Federal Reserve; corporate bonds in the case of the Bank of England; and a very wide range of private debt in the case of the European Central Bank).
14. Walras, 1874.
15. Hicks, 1937.
16. Arrow and Debreu, 1954.
17. Hahn, F., "On Some Problems of Proving the Existence of a General Equilibrium in a Monetary Economy," in Hahn and Brechling, 1965, pp. 126–35. In fact, Arrow and Debreu's pioneering 1954 paper had been quite explicit in proving the existence

of general equilibrium in an economy without any money—some might say a strange thing to do, but what they did nonetheless. The target of Hahn's critique was really a second generation of "monetary general equilibrium" models (specifically, in Hahn and Brechling, 1965, the model set out in Patinkin, 1956), which aimed to prove the Arrow–Debreu result for an economy that did include money. The basic challenge these models had to overcome was to show why one commodity would be chosen and valued as a medium of exchange in a general equilibrium. Hahn's famous critique demonstrated that these models had not succeeded in this. The class of general equilibrium models pioneered by Arrow and Debreu, 1954, are intrinsically models of a non-monetary economy: solutions that include money always encompassed by simpler solutions that do not.

18. McCallum, 2012, p. 2.

19. The way was to allow the assumption that some nominal prices are "sticky"—that is, they take time to adjust. This generates both a rationale for proactive monetary policy—since sticky prices will cause inefficient relative price changes in the presence of inflation—and the means for it to be effective—since by changing the nominal interest rate, the central bank can manipulate the real interest rate. Since money itself does not exist in the model, credit and liquidity risk—and other factors emphasised by the unconventional view of money—do not appear, and hence are not considered either as factors of instability or objects of policy.

20. King, M., 2012, p. 5. Outside of the orthodoxy, there remained independent-minded scholars who nevertheless persevered with the project of understanding the economy as a system in which money and banks play an irreducible role, as, for example, Smithin, 2000; Wray, 2004; Werner, 2005; and Werner, 2011, demonstrate. There were also attempts within the mainstream to establish a more realistic theory of the microeconomic foundations of money: Kiyotaki and Moore, 2001; Kiyotaki and Moore, 2002a; and Kiyotaki and Moore, 2002b, jointly constitute an important example. It took the crisis of 2008, however, to alert orthodox macroeconomics to the urgency of what such scholars had been doing.

21. The classic references for these innovations are Markowitz, 1952, Sharpe, 1964, and Black and Scholes, 1973.

22. Mehrling, 2011, p. 85.

23. Tobin, 1969.

24. Black, F., 1995, "Hedging, Speculation, and Systemic Risk," *Journal of Derivatives*, 2(4), pp. 6–8, quoted in Mehrling, 2005, p. 10. Mehrling cites this as an example of how diametrically opposed the worldviews of academic macroeconomics and academic finance had become by the mid-1990s, calling it "[f]or a macroeconomist . . . a shocking statement."

25. High and volatile inflation is a macroeconomic ill in New Keynesian models essentially because in the presence of sticky prices, it generates inefficient relative price changes which reduce output to below its potential.

26. The idea of central-bank independence, unlike inflation targeting, is not associated specifically with New Keynesian theory—its origins lie in an earlier literature, notably Rogoff, 1985—though it was only once the New Keynesian approach had become the most widely used framework for policy-making that it achieved a concrete institutional impact.

27. Turner, 2012.

28. Minsky, H., "The Financial Instability Hypothesis: Capitalist Processes and the Behaviour of the Economy," in Kindleberger and Laffargue, 1982.

29. King, M., 2002, pp. 162 and 173.

30. *Ibid.*

14 How to Turn the Locusts into Bees

1. See http://en.wikipedia.org/wiki/Locust_(finance). The term became widely used in political debate in the run-up to the September 2005 federal elections in Germany.
2. See chapter 8.
3. The title of Novi, E., 2012, *La dittatura dei banchieri: l'economia usuraia, l'eclissi della democrazia, la ribellione populista.*
4. "Banksters: How Britain's Rate-fixing Scandal Might Spread—and What to Do About It," *The Economist*, 7 July 2012.
5. "How to Tame Global Finance," interview with Adair Turner in *Prospect* magazine, 27 August 2009.
6. "The Only Useful Thing Banks Have Invented in 20 Years Is the ATM," *New York Post*, 13 December 2009.
7. In the U.S. there are the 849 pages of the Dodd-Frank Wall Street Reform and Consumer Protection Act, incorporating the Volcker Rule and establishing the Financial Stability Oversight Committee. In the U.K. there was the 2009 Turner Review of what went wrong with the supervision of the banking sector, which has led to the wholesale rearrangement of the U.K.'s regulatory institutions, and the 2011 report of the Independent Commission on Banking, on which the Draft Financial Services (Banking Reform) Bill is based. Even in the Eurozone—where even more existential challenges have dominated policy-makers' attention—serious structural reforms were proposed in October 2012 by the High-level Expert Group on Reforming the Structure of the EU Banking Sector.
8. In November, 2008. The remark was reported and subjected to sceptical ridicule in the *Wall Street Journal* on 28 January 2009: http://online.wsj.com/article/SB123310466514522309.html.
9. U.K. Financial Services Authority, 2007.
10. This was the title of the U.K. House of Commons Treasury Committee's 2008 report on the episode and the authorities' response to it: U.K. House of Commons Treasury Committee, 2008.
11. See chapter 6.
12. U.K. Financial Services Authority, 2007.
13. The nationalisation of Northern Rock was done under special legislation, and no consideration was paid for the existing shareholders' equity. On 1 January 2010, the Treasury—by then the sole shareholder—injected £1.4 billion of capital into the bank. See UKFI, 2012, p. 26.
14. U.K. House of Commons Treasury Committee, 2008, Vol. I, p. 74.
15. In a debate in the U.K. House of Commons on 10 December 2008, the then prime minister Gordon Brown made what became an infamous slip of the tongue. He claimed that the policies of his government in the heat of the crisis had "saved the world" before correcting this claim to the more modest one that they had only "saved the banks."
16. Laeven and Valencia, 2012, Table 1, p. 6, and *passim* for details. In addition to liquidity and capital support, all but three of these countries ramped up the guarantees provided by the sovereign on bank deposits and other liabilities—a further form of sovereign support.
17. In fiscal year 2011, federal outlays on defence were 4.7 per cent of GDP. See Congressional Budget Office, 2012, Table F.4, p. 139.
18. Thomas Jefferson to John Taylor, Monticello, 28 May 1816, in Ford, 1892–99, Vol. 2, p. 533.

19. The total spending of the U.K. Department of Health was 7.6 per cent of GDP in 2011–12. See HM Treasury, 2012, Table 5.1, p. 73, and Table F.2, p. 206.
20. Alessandri and Haldane, 2009, p. 2 and Table 1.
21. EUR 870 million. See Whelan, K., 2011, "Anglo's January 31st Bond," available at http://www.irisheconomy.ie/index.php/2011/01/. A lively and expertly informed debate on the merits of the particularly extreme strategy of liquidity and capital support undertaken by the Irish sovereign is available on the excellent joint blog *The Irish Economy* (www.irisheconomy.ie) in which this post appears.
22. The multinational origins of the Apple iPhone mentioned in chapter 2 are a contemporary example of the kind of industrial organisation that resulted in the consumer electronics industry.
23. The share of corporate bonds in total corporate debt financing (excluding mortgages) averaged 51 per cent between 1980 and 1984. These and the related data in this paragraph are calculated from Table B.102 of Board of Governors of the Federal Reserve System, 2012.
24. Martin, 2011, 1. Data from Citibank Credit Investment Research.
25. Homer, 1968, pp. 27–29.
26. What is described here is the illustrative, generic, credit intermediation process of the international shadow banking sector as set out in Pozsar, Adrian, Ashcraft, and Boesky, 2010, pp. 10–12 and Exhibits 2 and 3.
27. International Monetary Fund, 2006, p. 51.
28. *Ibid.*
29. In the IMF's defence, it did warn on the same page as the infamous quotation above that "while these markets increasingly facilitate the 'primary' transfer of credit risk, secondary market liquidity is still lacking within some segments, creating the potential for market disruptions"—a statement which at least intimated that the new system of credit market intermediation was being expected to manage liquidity as well as credit risk, but that its ability to do so remained untested.
30. Poszar and Singh, 2011, p. 5. This estimate is for the end of 2007.
31. Bouveret, 2011, p. 18. Note that this estimate is as of the end of 2010, and so not strictly comparable with Poszar and Singh's estimate for the U.S. above (but instead with their end-2010 estimate of the size of the U.S. shadow banking system at U.S. $18 trillion).
32. The details of how central-bank assistance found its way to the shadow banking sector—as well as a superlative history of the evolution of the U.S. financial sector and its relationship to the evolution of economic and financial theory—can be found in Mehrling, 2011, a brilliant and profound book to which I am much indebted in this chapter.
33. Total assets of the U.S. Federal Reserve rose from U.S.$927 billion to U.S.$1.8 trillion. See Board of Governors of the Federal Reserve System, Credit and Liquidity Programs and the Balance Sheet website: http://www.federalreserve.gov/monetarypolicy/bst_recenttrends.htm. Total assets of the Bank of England rose from £93 billion to £292 billion. See Bank of England Bank Return, available at www.bankofengland.co.uk.
34. It took until the beginning of 2012 for the total assets of the European Central Bank to double from their level of approximately EUR 1.5 trillion in October 2008.

15 The Boldest Measures Are the Safest

1. In Basel Committee on Banking Supervision, 2006, commonly called the Basel II Framework. The Basel Committee is simply an international forum, and until the

crisis its main focus was on harmonising the measurement of bank capital (rather than liquidity) and standards of its adequacy. Most of the definition and all of the implementation of prudential regulatory standards remains in the hands of national regulators, however—and after the crisis, many national regulators too proposed more stringent capital or liquidity requirements in addition to those agreed on in the Basel III accords (see n. 4 below).

2. Alessandri and Haldane, 2009, p. 3 and Chart 2.

3. *Ibid.*, p. 3 and Chart 3.

4. Basel Committee on Banking Supervision, 2010, commonly called the Basel III Framework. As its name suggests, the Basel III Framework incorporated a more explicit focus on internationally co-ordinated measurement and standards of bank liquidity as well as capital.

5. This analogy is drawn from Haldane, 2010.

6. *Ibid.*

7. Haldane, 2010, presented illustrative estimates of the present value of the total economic cost of the global financial crisis, depending on how much of the output loss proved permanent. They ranged between 90 per cent and 350 per cent of the world's output in 2009.

8. Alistair Milne, Perry Mehrling, and others have proposed models for systemic risk insurance and premiums to support it that could be levied from banks. See Kotlikoff, 2010, p. 172 ff. for a discussion and references.

9. Kay, J., "Should We Have Narrow Banking?" in Turner et al., 2010, p. 219.

10. Tarullo, 2012a, p. 9.

11. The restriction on banking activities was in practice eroded over time, but it was in 1999 that the Gramm–Leach–Bliley Financial Services Modernization Act revoked the central provisions of the Glass–Steagall Act. The McFadden Act restriction was repealed by the 1994 Riegle–Neal Interstate Banking and Branching Efficiency Act.

12. Having been roughly stable for more than sixty years from the 1930s to the 1990s, the average size of U.S. banks relative to national income tripled in the space of twenty years (see Haldane, 2010, p. 8 and Chart 1). And the biggest beasts of all were the ones that grew the fastest. In 1990, the three largest U.S. banks accounted for only 10 per cent of all banking sector assets. By 2007, they made up 40 per cent (*ibid.*, p. 9 and Chart 2).

13. The Financial Stability Oversight Committee in the U.S., the Financial Policy Committee of the Bank of England in the U.K., and the international Financial Stability Board founded by the G20 in London in April 2009. (The Financial Stability Board was in fact re-founded as a successor institution to the G7's Financial Stability Forum—see http://www.financialstabilityboard.org/about/history.htm for details.)

14. As Daniel Tarullo, the leading regulatory expert on the Board of Governors of the U.S. Federal Reserve, has put it, "the primary aim" of the Dodd–Frank Act is "a reorientation of financial regulation towards safeguarding 'financial stability' through the containment of 'systemic risk,' phrases that both recur dozens of times throughout the statute." Tarullo, 2012b, p. 1.

15. King, M., 2012, p. 5.

16. Buiter, W., "The Unfortunate Uselessness of Most 'State of the Art' Academic Monetary Economics," Willem Buiter's maverecon, *Financial Times* website, 3 March 2009. Available at http://blogs.ft.com/maverecon/2009/03/the-unfortunate-uselessness-of-most-state-of-the-art-academic-monetary-economics/#axzz2AgdwP9Yz.

17. Tarullo, 2012b, p. 22.

18. Skidelsky and Skidelsky, 2012.

19. Sandel, 2012.

20. Paul, 2009.

21. King James Bible, Ecclesiastes 9:11.

22. The *Oxford English Dictionary* defines a euphemism as "[t]hat figure of speech which consists in the substitution of a word or expression of comparatively favourable implication or less unpleasant associations, instead of the harsher or more offensive one that would more precisely designate what is intended."

23. Full details of Professor Kotlikoff's proposals can be found in Kotlikoff, 2010.

24. This is only the least adventurous of Shiller's ideas (GDP-linked bonds have already been issued by several emerging market sovereigns); he has plenty of others. For an overview see Shiller, 2003.

25. The ongoing European sovereign debt crisis has forced the ECB to broaden the spectrum of assets that it accepts as collateral for its liquidity support to its banking sector significantly more than either the U.S. Federal Reserve or the Bank of England have done. A particular stir was caused in 2011, when it was revealed that the ECB had even been lending against securitised Australian automobile loans. It should be noted that in the ECB's case, acceptance of such assets is as collateral under repo agreements, so that the credit risk that the central bank bears is not strictly speaking that of the financial security in question but of the bank that is taking liquidity support. Likewise, the U.S. Federal Reserve is in principle indemnified against credit losses on its holdings of mortgage debt by the U.S. Treasury. In both cases, in other words, there is in theory no credit support being granted.

26. It would be the world that James Tobin realised that the models of academic finance implied at their logical limit, in which "[t]here would be no room for discrepancies between market and natural rates of return on capital, between market valuation and reproduction cost. There would be no room for monetary policy to affect aggregate demand. The real economy would call the tune for the financial sector, with no feedback in the other direction" (Tobin, 1969, p. 26).

27. Fisher, 1936. The ultimate origins of Fisher's plan were to be found in a book published in 1926 by the British monetary thinker Frederick Soddy: Soddy, 1926. Soddy's book would have been dismissed as an instant classic of monetary crankery had it not been for the credibility he had as a winner of the Nobel Prize in Chemistry. Even then, it made little impression on either the public or the official imagination, in part because it was overshadowed by another more popular, but ultimately disappointing, proposal for monetary reform, the Social Credit Movement of Major C.H. Douglas: Douglas, 1924. Soddy's ideas were taken up by Frank Knight at Chicago, from whom Fisher learned of them.

28. Fisher, 1936, p. 10.

29. Friedman, 1960, and Friedman, 1967.

30. See for example Kay, 2009 and Kay, J., "Should We Have Narrow Banking?" in Turner et al., 2010. Laurence Kotlikoff's proposal for *Limited Purpose Banking* likewise effectively includes narrow banking as one of its component parts—see Kotlikoff, 2010, p. 132 ff.

31. Benes and Kumhof, 2012. In order to explore in detail the consequences of the Chicago Plan in the context of a formal model of the U.S. economy, Benes and Kumhof are obliged to go beyond Fisher's narrow prescription for the reform of banks' monetary activities and specify a novel structure for the provision of credit services. This is an extremely useful exercise; though it is not necessary—and perhaps, as Kay, J., "Should We Have Narrow Banking?" in Turner et al., 2010, pp. 4–5 argues, not desirable—to prescribe a structure for this non-utility tier of the financial system in advance.

32. Keynes, 1936, p. 372.

Bibliography

In addition to the works cited in the endnotes, there are a number of others which deserve special acknowledgement because their influence pervades the whole of this book.

My own interest in the topic began with reading Charles Goodhart's article "The Two Concepts of Money: Implications for Optimal Currency Areas" (Goodhart, 1998)—a brilliantly concise and eloquent overview of the two main traditions in Western monetary thought, combined with a prescient warning concerning their implications for the then novel project of the euro.

I read that article in 2002 when I was just beginning a doctorate in monetary economics. My timing turned out to be fortunate because in 2004 three extraordinary books on money, by scholars from three different disciplines, were published. All three were profound influences on the present book.

The first was *The Nature of Money* by the sociologist Geoffery Ingham (Ingham, 2004) a masterful investigation of the history of money and monetary thought. *The Nature of Money* opened my eyes—and I am sure those of many other classically trained economists—to many fundamental questions about money that were abandoned by our own discipline over the course of the twentieth century, and still better, supplies historically compelling answers to them.

The second was *Money and the Early Greek Mind*, by the classicist Richard Seaford (Seaford, 2004), a profound and dazzlingly imaginative book on the origins of money in ancient Greece and the impact of monetisation on philosophy and art, the extensive influence of which on the present book will be obvious to all who know it.

Thankfully, the economists were not completely left behind in this bumper year for monetary thought. The year 2004 also saw the publication *Credit and State Theories of Money: the Contributions of Alfred Mitchell Innes*, edited by L. Randall Wray—an economist who has long been at the forefront of promoting and popularising more realistic approaches to money in economic analysis (Wray, 2004). This book did a particular service by recovering for contemporary readers two of the most extraordinary articles on the nature of money written in the twentieth century: Alfred Mitchell Innes' "What is Money?" and "The Credit Theory of Money" (Mitchell Innes, 1913 and 1914).

All three of these books are required reading for anyone who wishes to learn more about the topic of the present book.

And 2004 turned out not to be the only great vintage for books on money. In 1977, three further books which were major influences on the present work were published. The first of these was Philip Grierson's *The Origins of Money* (Grierson, 1977), where I found for the first time a serious attempt to answer the critical question of what monetary units of account actually are and where, historically speaking, they might have come from.

The second was Herbert Frankel's *Two Philosophies of Money: The Conflict of Trust*

and Authority (Frankel, 1977)—an inexplicably little-known work which probes the political and social underpinnings of monetary society.

The third, and most famous, was Albert Hirshman's scintillating essay in the history
of economic thought, *The Passions and the Interests: Political Arguments for Capitalism
Before Its Triumph* (Hirshman, 1977).

Two other more recent books that were general influences were the extremely
valuable collection of essays edited by John Smithin, *What is Money?* (Smithin, 2000),
and James Buchan's marvellously evocative literary-historical treatment, *Frozen Desire*
(Buchan, 1997).

Several of these works investigate not only the nature of money today, but the
history of money and of monetary thought. There is a vast literature in this area,
of course, and many essential and standard works are cited in the notes. Here too,
however, I owe special acknowledgement to a number of books: Joseph Schumpeter's great, unfinished *History of Economic Analysis* (Schumpeter, 1954); Charles
Kindleberger's *Manias, Panics, and Crashes* (Kindleberger, 1978) and his *Financial His-
tory of Western Europe* (Kindleberger, 1993); Thomas Sargent and François Velde's
The Big Problem of Small Change (Sargent and Velde, 2002); James Macdonald's *A Free
Nation Deep in Debt: The Financial Roots of Democracy* (Macdonald, 2006); and Antoin
Murphy's books *John Law: Economic Theorist and Policy-Maker* (Murphy, 1997) and
The Genesis of Macroeconomics: New Ideas from Sir William Petty to Henry Thornton
(Murphy, 2009).

From the literature on comparative monetary systems, two modern books in par-
ticular were crucial in my education. The first of these is the political scientist David
Woodruff's brilliantly imaginative study *Money Unmade: Barter and the Fate of Russian
Capitalism* (Woodruff, 1999). The second is the essay collection *The Vanishing Rouble:
Barter Networks and Non-Monetary Transactions in Post-Soviet Societies,* (Seabright, 2000).
Both these books may at first seem to be simply studies of the disintegration of mon-
etary order during the collapse of the Soviet Union, but both in fact have profound
lessons for the understanding of money more generally.

A final thing I have tried to do in the present book is to show why a clear and
realistic understanding of money is not just of academic interest, but an important
tool for confronting contemporary economic and social challenges. As I was writing,
Andrew Jackson, Richard Werner, Tony Greenham, and Josh Ryan-Collins produced
a supremely accomplished example of how this could be done in their book *Where
Does Money Come From? A Guide to the UK Monetary and Banking System* (Jackson, Werner, Greenham, and Ryan-Collins, 2012)—essential reading for anyone who wants to
understand how modern banking systems work and what could be done to improve
them.

That book focuses on the U.K. banking system (though its relevance is much
broader). For American readers, and anyone interested in particular in how "high
finance"—the global, wholesale capital markets—works, then Perry Mehrling's *The
New Lombard Street: How the Fed Became the Dealer of Last Resort* (Mehrling, 2011) is an
exceptional treatment by a distinguished economist who truly understands not only
the workings of today's financial markets, but also the developments both in financial
practice and theory that made them. It was a fundamental influence on the present
book.

Finally, two significant books on money were published in the U.K. when I was
already in the midst of writing, with the unfortunate result that I was not able to absorb
and make reference to them as I would in retrospect have liked. These are Philip Coggan's *Paper Promises: Money, Debt, and the New World Order* (Coggan, 2011) and David
Graeber's *Debt: The First 5,000 Years* (Graeber, 2011).

BOOKS AND ARTICLES

Alessandri, P., and Haldane, A. (2009), *Banking on the State*. London: Bank of England.

Amis, M. (1984), *Money: A Suicide Note*. London: Vintage.

Andreau, J. (1999), *Banking and Business in the Roman World* (tr. Lloyd, J.). Cambridge: Cambridge University Press.

Appleby, J. (1976), "Locke, Liberalism, and the Natural Law of Money." *Past and Present* 71, 43–69.

Aristotle (1932), *Politics*. London: William Heinemann Ltd.

Arnold, A.Z. (1937), *Banks, Credit and Money in Soviet Russia*. New York: Columbia University Press.

Arrow, K., and Debreu, G. (1954), "Existence of an equilibrium for a competitive economy." *Econometrica* 22(3), 265–90.

Aukutsionek, S. (1998), "Industrial Barter in Russia." *Communist Economies and Economic Transformation* 10(2), 179–88.

Bagehot, W. (1999) [1873], *Lombard Street*. New York: John Wiley & Sons Inc.

Basel Committee on Banking Supervision (2006), *International Convergence of Capital Measurement and Capital Standards: A Revised Framework*. Basel: Bank for International Settlements.

Basel Committee on Banking Supervision (2010), *International framework for liquidity risk measurement, standards and monitoring*. Basel: Bank for International Settlements.

Bellers, J. (1696), *Proposals for Raising a Colledge of Industry of all Useful Trades and Husbandry, with Profits for the Rich, a Plentiful Living for the Poor, and a Good Education for the Youth*: available at http://archive.org/stream/proposalsforraisoobellrich#page/n7/mode/2up.

Benes, J., and Kumhof, M. (2012), "The Chicago Plan Revisited." *International Monetary Fund Working Paper* 12/202.

Besley, T., and Hennessy, P. (2009), *Letter to Her Majesty the Queen*, 22 July, 2009: available at http://www.britac.ac.uk/news/newsrelease-economy.cfm.

Black, F., and Scholes, M. (1973), "The Pricing of Options and Corporate Liabilities." *The Journal of Political Economy* 81(3), 637–654.

Board of Governors of the Federal Reserve System (2012), *Flow of Funds Accounts of the United States*. Washington, D.C.: Board of Governors of the Federal Reserve System.

Boswell, J. (1986), *The Life of Samuel Johnson*. New York: Penguin Classics.

Bouveret, A. (2011), "An Assessment of the Shadow Banking Sector in Europe." *Observatoire Français des Conjonctures Economiques Working Paper*: available at http://papers.ssrn.com/sol3/papers.cfm?abstract_id=2027007.

Boyer-Xambeu, M.-T., Deleplace, G., and Gillard, L. (1994), *Private Money and Public Currencies*. London: M. E. Sharpe.

Braudel, F. (1992), *The Wheels of Commerce: Civilization and Capitalism 15–18th Century*, Vol. 2. Berkeley, CA: University of California Press.

Buchan, J. (1997), *Frozen Desire*. London: Picador.

Capie, F. (2012), "200 years of financial crises: lessons learned and forgotten." Mimeo: available at http://www2.uah.es/financial_crisis_spain/congreso2012/papers/Forrest%20Capie.pdf.

Carswell, J. (1960), *The South Sea Bubble*. London: Cresset Press.

Central Bank of Ireland (1970), *Report on Economic Effects of Bank Dispute 1970*. Dublin: Central Bank of Ireland.

Clanchy, M. (1993), *From Memory to Written Record: England 1066–1307*. Oxford: Blackwell.

Clapham, J. (1944), *The Bank of England: A History*, 2 volumes. Cambridge: Cambridge University Press.

Coggan, P. (2011), *Paper Promises: Money, Debt, and the New World Order.* London: Allen Lane.

Colacelli, M., and Blackburn, D.J.H. (2006), "Secondary Currency: An Empirical Analysis." Mimeo: available at http://la-macro.vassar.edu/SecondaryCurrency.pdf.

Congressional Budget Office (2012), *The Budget and Economic Outlook: Fiscal Years 2012–2022.* Washington, D.C.: Congressional Budget Office.

Crease, R. (2011), *World in the Balance: the Historic Quest for an Absolute System of Measurement.* New York & London: W.W. Norton.

Dalton, G. (1982), "Barter," *Journal of Economic Issues* 16(1), 181–90.

Dantzig, T. (1930), *Number: The Language of Science.* London: Allen and Unwin.

De la Torre, A., Levy Yeyati, E., and Schmuckler, S.L. (2003), "Living and Dying With Hard Pegs: the Rise and Fall of Argentina's Currency Board." *Economia* 5(2), 43–107.

DeLong, B. (2012), "This Time, It Is Not Different: The Persistent Concerns of Financial Macroeconomics." Mimeo: available at http://delong.typepad.com/20120411-russell-sage-delong-paper.pdf.

De Rubys, C. (1604), *Histoire Veritable de la Ville de Lyon.* Lyon.

Dickson, P. (1967), *The Financial Revolution in England: A Study in the Development of Public Credit, 1688–1756.* London: Macmillan.

Douglas, C.H. (1924), *Social Credit.* London: C. Palmer.

Eatwell, J., Milgate, M., and Newman, P., eds (1989), *The New Palgrave: The Invisible Hand.* London: Macmillan.

Elliot, G. (2006), *The Mystery of Overend and Gurney.* York: Methuen Publishing Ltd.

Feavearyear, A.E. (1931), *The Pound Sterling.* Oxford: Clarendon Press.

Fisher, I. (1936) [1935], *100% Money.* New York: Adelphi Company.

Flandreau, M. and Uglioni, S. (2011), "Where It All Began: Lending of Last Resort and the Bank of England During the Overend, Gurney Panic of 1866." *Norges Bank Working Paper* 2011/3: available at http://papers.ssrn.com/sol3/papers.cfm?abstract_id=1847593.

Ford, P.L., ed. (1892–99), *The Writings of Thomas Jefferson.* New York: G.P. Putnam's Sons.

France, A. (1908), *The Red Lily* (tr. Whale, W.S.). London: John Lane, The Bodley Head.

Frank, R. (2011), *The Darwin Economy.* Princeton, NJ; Oxford: Princeton University Press.

Frankel, S.H. (1977), *Money: Two Philosophies—The Conflict of Trust and Authority.* Oxford: Blackwell.

Friedman, M. (1960), *A Program for Monetary Stability.* New York: Fordham University Press.

—(1967), "The Monetary Theory and Policy of Henry Simons." *Journal of Law and Economics* 10, 1–13.

—(1991), "The Island of Stone Money." *Hoover Institution Working Papers in Economics* E91-3.

Furness, W. (1910), *The Island of Stone Money: Uap of the Carolines.* Philadelphia, PA: Washington Square Press.

Genovese, M., ed. (2009), *The Federalist Papers.* New York, NY: Palgrave Macmillan.

Goetzmann, W.N., and Rouwenhorst, K.G., eds (2005), *The Origins of Value: The Financial Innovations that Created Modern Capital Markets.* Oxford: Oxford University Press.

Goodhart, C. (1998), "The two concepts of money: implications for the study of optimal currency areas." *European Journal of Political Economy* 14, 407–432.

Goody, J., ed. (1968), *Literacy in Traditional Society.* Cambridge: Cambridge University Press.

Graeber, D. (2011), *Debt: The First 5,000 years.* Brooklyn, NY: Melville House Publishing.

Greco, T. (2001), *Money: Understanding and Creating Alternatives to Legal Tender.* White River Junction, VT: Chelsea Green.

Grierson, P. (1977), *The Origins of Money*. London: Athlone Press.

Hahn, F. and Brechling, F., eds (1965), *The Theory of Interest Rates: Proceedings of a Conference by the International Economic Association*. London: Macmillan.

Haldane, A. (2010), *The $100 bn Question*. London: Bank of England.

Hansen, M. (1985), *Demography and Democracy: The Number of Athenian Citizens in the Fourth Century B.C.* Herning: Forlaget Systime.

Harris, W.V. (2006), "A Revisionist View of Roman Money." *The Journal of Roman Studies* 96, 1–24.

—(2008), *The Monetary Systems of the Greeks and Romans*. Oxford: Oxford University Press.

Hicks, J. (1937), "Mr. Keynes and the 'Classics': A Suggested Interpretation." *Econometrica* 5(2), 147–59.

Hirschman, A. (1977), *The Passion and the Interests: Political Arguments for Capitalism Before Its Triumph*. Princeton: Princeton University Press.

—(1991), *The Rhetoric of Reaction: Perversity, Futility, Jeopardy*. Cambridge, MA & London: Belknap Press of Harvard University.

HM Treasury (2012), *Public Expenditure Statistical Analysis 2012*. London: The Stationary Office Limited.

Homer, S. (1968), *The Bond Buyer's Primer*. New York: Salomon Bros. & Hutzler.

Horsefield, J.K. (1960), *British Monetary Experiments*. Cambridge, MA & Harvard University Press.

Hudson, M., and Van de Mieroop, M., eds (2002), *Debt and Economic Renewal in the Ancient Near East*. Bethesda, MD: CDL Press.

Hudson, M., and Wunsch, C., eds (2000), *Creating Economic Order: Record-keeping, standardization, and the development of accounting in the ancient Near East—a colloquium held at the British Museum, November 2000*.

Huerta de Soto, J. (2006), *Money, Bank Credit, and Economic Cycles*. Auburn: Ludwig Von Mises Institute.

Humphrey, C. (1985), "Barter and Economic Disintegration," *Man* 20(1), pp. 48–72.

Ilf, I. and Petrov, E. (1962) [1931], *The Golden Calf* (tr. Richardson, J.). London: F. Muller.

Ingham, G. (2004), *The Nature of Money*. Cambridge: Polity.

International Monetary Fund (2006). *Global Financial Stability Report 2006*. Washington, D.C.: International Monetary Fund.

—(2012), *Fiscal Monitor April 2012*. Washington, D.C.: International Monetary Fund.

Jackson, A., Werner, R., Greenham, T., and Ryan-Collins, J. (2012), *Where Does Money Come From? A Guide to the UK Monetary and Banking System*. London: New Economics Foundation.

Johnson, C., ed. (1956), *The De Moneta of Nicholas Oresme and English Mint Documents*. London: Nelson.

Jones, D. (2006), *The Bankers of Puteoli*. Stroud: Tempus.

Joplin, T. (1832), *An Analysis and History of the Currency Question*. London: James Ridgway.

Kay, J. (2009), *Narrow Banking: The Reform of Banking Regulation*. Mimeo: available at http://www.johnkay.com/wp-content/uploads/2009/12/JK-Narrow-Banking.pdf.

Keynes, J.M. (1915a), "The Island of Stone Money." *Economic Journal* 25(98), 281–283.

—(1915b), "The Works of Walter Bagehot—Review Article." *Economic Journal* 25(99), 369–375.

—(1923), *A Tract on Monetary Reform*. London: Macmillan.

—(1930), *A Treatise on Money*. London: Macmillan.

—(1931), "The Pure Theory of Money. A Reply to Dr. Hayek." *Economica* 13(34), 387–97.

—(1936), *The General Theory of Employment, Interest, and Money*. London: Macmillan.

Kindleberger, C. (1993), *A Financial History of Western Europe*. New York and Oxford: Oxford University Press.

—(2000) [1978], *Manias, Panics, and Crashes: a History of Financial Crises*. New York, NY & Chichester: Wiley.

Kindleberger, C., and Laffargue, J-P., eds (1982), *Financial Crises: Theory, History, and Policy*. Cambridge: Cambridge University Press.

King, M. (2002), "No money, no inflation—the role of money in the economy." *Bank of England Quarterly Bulletin*, Summer 2002.

—(2012), "Twenty Years of Inflation Targeting." Speech at the London School of Economics, October 9, 2012.

King, W. (1936), *History of the London Discount Market*. London: Routledge.

Kiyotaki, N. and Moore, J. H. (2001), "Evil is the Root of All Money." Clarendon Lectures in Economics, University of Oxford.

—(2002a), "Evil is the Root of All Money." *American Economic Review* 92 (2), 62–66.

—(2002b), "Inside Money and Liquidity." Mimeo: London School of Economics.

Knapp, G. (1924), *The State Theory of Money*. London: The Royal Economic Society.

Kotlikoff, L. (2010), *Jimmy Stewart Is Dead: Ending the World's Ongoing Financial Plague with Limited Purpose Banking*. Hoboken, NJ: Wiley.

Kula, W. (1986), *Measures and Men*. Princeton, NJ & Guildford: Princeton University Press.

Laeven, L., and Valencia, F. (2012), "Systemic Banking Crises Database: An Update." *IMF Working Paper* 12/163.

Law, J. (1705), *Money and Trade Considered, with a Proposal for Supplying the Nation with Money*.

—(1720), *The Present State of the French Revenues and Trade, and of the Controversy betwixt the Parliament of Paris and Mr. Law*. London: J. Roberts.

Lee, W., ed. (1869), *Daniel Defoe: His Life, and Recently Discovered Writings: Extending from 1716 to 1729*, Vol II. London: John Camden Hotten.

Lenin, V.I. (1965), *Collected Works*: available at http://www.marxists.org/archive.

Liddell, H.G., and Scott, R. (1996), *Greek–English Lexicon*. Oxford: Clarendon Press.

Locke, J. (1695), *Further Considerations Concerning Raising the Value of Money, Wherein Mr. Lowndes's Arguments for it in his late Report concerning An Essay for the Amendment of the Silver Coins, are particularly Examined*. London: A. and J. Churchill.

—(2009) [1698], *Two Treatises of Government* (ed. Laslett, P.). Cambridge: Cambridge University Press.

Lowndes, W. (1695), *A Report Containing an Essay for the Amendment of the Silver Coins*: available at http://openlibrary.org/books/OL23329564M/A_report_containing_an_essay_for_the_amendment_of_the_silver_coins.

Luria, A. (1976), *Cognitive Development: Its Cultural and Social Foundations*. Cambridge, MA & London: Harvard University Press.

Macdonald, J. (2006), *A Free Nation Deep in Debt: the Financial Roots of Democracy*. Princeton, NJ & Oxford: Princeton University Press.

Macleod, H. (1882), *The Principles of Political Economy*. London: Longmans, Green, Read, and Dyer.

Magnusson, L., ed. (1995), *Mercantilism*. London: Routledge.

Mandeville, B. (1705), *The Grumbling Hive, or, Knaves Turn'd Honest*. London.

—(1988) [1732], *The Fable of the Bees, or, Private Vices, Publick Benefits*, 2 Volumes. Indianapolis: Liberty Classics.

Markowitz, H. (1952), "Portfolio selection." *Journal of Finance* 7(1), 77–91.

Martin, F. (2011), "Global High Yield: The Big Winner from the Banking Crisis." *Thames River Capital Monthly Newsletter*. London: Thames River Capital.

Marx, K. and Engels, F. (1985) [1848], *The Communist Manifesto*. London: Penguin.

Mauss, M. (1954), *The Gift: Forms and Functions of Exchange in Archaic Societies* (tr. Cunnison, I.). London: Cohen & West.

Mayhew, N. (1999), *Sterling: The Rise and Fall of a Currency*. London: Allen Lane.

McCallum, B. (2012), "The Role of Money in New Keynesian Models." *Banco Central de Reserva de Perú Working Paper* 2012–2019.

Meadows, A., and Shipton, K., eds (2001), *Money and Its Uses in the Ancient Greek World*. Oxford: Oxford University Press.

Mehrling, P. (2005), "The Development of Macroeconomics and the Revolution in Finance." Mimeo: available at http://economics.barnard.edu/profiles/perry-mehrling/perry-mehrling-recent-papers.

—(2011), *The New Lombard Street: How the Fed Became the Dealer of Last Resort*. Princeton, NJ: Princeton University Press.

Mill, J.S. (1848), *Principles of Political Economy: With Some of Their Applications to Social Philosophy*. London: J.W. Parker.

Mitchell Innes, A. (1913), "What Is Money?" *Banking Law Journal* 30(5), 377–408.

—(1914), "The Credit Theory of Money." *Banking Law Journal* 31(2), 151–68.

More, T. (1975) [1516], *Utopia*. New York: Norton.

Murphy, A.E. (1978), "Money in an Economy without Banks: The case of Ireland." *The Manchester School of Economic and Social Studies* 46(1), 41–50.

—(1997), *John Law: Economic Theorist and Policy-Maker*. Oxford: Clarendon Press.

—(2009), *The Genesis of Macroeconomics: New Ideas from Sir William Petty to Henry Thornton*. Oxford: Oxford University Press.

Murray, A. (1978), *Reason and Society in the Middle Ages*. Oxford: Clarendon Press.

Murray, O. (1993), *Early Greece*. London: Fontana Press.

Nissen, H.J. (1988), *The Early History of the Ancient Near East: 9000–2000 BC*. Chicago & London: University of Chicago Press.

Nissen, H.J., Damerow, P., and Englund, R.K., eds (1993), *Archaic Bookkeeping: Early Writing and Techniques of Economic Administration in the Ancient Near East*. Chicago & London: University of Chicago Press.

Ong, W. (1982), *Orality and Literacy: The Technologizing of the Word*. London: Methuen.

Ormazabal, K. (2012), "Lowndes and Locke on the Value of Money." *History of Political Economy* 44(1), pp. 157–80.

Parker, R. (1996), *Athenian Religion: A History*. Oxford: Clarendon Press.

Parry, J., and Bloch, M. (1989), *Money and the Morality of Exchange*. Cambridge: Cambridge University Press.

Patinkin, D. (1956), *Money, Interest, and Prices: An Integration of Monetary and Value Theory*. Evanston, IL: Row, Peterson.

Paul, R. (2009), *End the Fed*. New York, NY: Grand Central Pub.

Pigou, A., ed. (1925), *Memorials of Alfred Marshall*. London: Macmillan.

Pozsar, Z., Adrian, T., Ashcraft, A., and Boesky, H. (2010), "Shadow Banking." *Federal Reserve Bank of New York Staff Report* 458.

Pozsar, Z., and Singh, M. (2011), "The Nonbank-Bank Nexus and the Shadow Banking System." *International Monetary Fund Working Paper* 11/289.

Reinhart, C., and Rogoff, K. (2009), *This Time Is Different: Eight Centuries of Financial Folly*. Princeton, NJ & Oxford: Princeton University Press.

Richards, R.D. (1958), *The Early History of Banking in England*. London: Cass.

Roberts, R., and Kynaston, D., eds (1995), *The Bank of England: Money, Power and Influence 1694–1994*. Oxford: Oxford University Press.

Rogoff, K. (1985), "The Optimal Degree of Commitment to an Intermediate Monetary Target." *The Quarterly Journal of Economics* 100(4), 1169–89.

Rolnick, A., Velde, F., and Weber, W. (1996), "The Debasement Puzzle: An Essay on Medieval Monetary History." *Journal of Economic History* 56(4), 789–808.

Roseveare, H. (1991), *The Financial Revolution, 1660–1760*. London: Longman.

Rosovsky, H., ed. (1966), *Industrialization in Two Systems: Essays in Honour of Alexander Gerschenkron*. New York, NY: John Wiley.

Sandel, M. (2012), *What Money Can't Buy: The Moral Limits of Markets*. London: Allen Lane.

Sargent, T., and Velde, F. (2002), *The Big Problem of Small Change*. Princeton, NJ & Oxford: Princeton University Press.

Say, J.-B. (2001) [1803], *A Treatise on Political Economy*. New Brunswick, NJ & London: Transaction Publishers.

Schmandt-Besserat, D. (1977), "The Earliest Precursor of Writing." *Scientific American* 238(6), 50–58.

—(1979), "Reckoning before Writing." *Archaeology* 32(3), 22–31.

—ed. (1992), *Before Writing*, Vol. 1. Austin: University of Texas Press.

Schumpeter, J. (1954), *History of Economic Analysis*. London: Allen & Unwin.

Senner, W., ed. (1991), *The Origins of Writing*. Lincoln, NE & London: University of Nebraska Press.

Seabright, P., ed. (2000), *The Vanishing Rouble: Barter Networks and Non-monetary Transactions in Post-Soviet Societies*. Cambridge: Cambridge University Press.

—(2004), *The Company of Strangers: A Natural History of Economic Life*. Princeton, NJ & Oxford: Princeton University Press.

Seaford, R. (1994), *Reciprocity and Ritual in Tragedy: Homer and Tragedy in the Developing City-State*. Oxford: Clarendon Press.

—(2004), *Money and the Early Greek Mind*. Cambridge: Cambridge University Press.

Sharpe, W. (1964), "Capital Asset Prices: A Theory of Market Equilibrium Under Conditions of Risk." *Journal of Finance* 19(3), 425–42.

Shiller, R. (2003), *The New Financial Order: Risk in the 21st Century*. Princeton, NJ & Woodstock: Princeton University Press.

Simmel, G. (1978) [1907], *The Philosophy of Money* (tr. Bottomore, T.). London: Routledge & Kegan Paul.

Skidelsky, R. (1992), *John Maynard Keynes: The Economist as Saviour, 1920–37*. London: Macmillan.

Skidelsky, R., and Skidelsky, E. (2012), *How Much Is Enough?* London: Allen Lane.

Smith, A. (1981) [1776], *An Inquiry into the Nature and Causes of the Wealth of Nations*. Indianapolis: Liberty Press.

Smith, T. (1832), *An Essay on Currency and Banking*. Philadelphia, PA: Jesper Harding.

Smithin, J. (2000), *What Is Money?* London: Routledge.

Soddy, F. (1926), *Wealth, Virtual Wealth, and Debt: The Solution of the Economic Paradox*. London: Allen & Unwin.

Spufford, P. (1988), *Money and Its Use in Medieval Europe*. Cambridge: Cambridge University Press.

—(2002), *Power and Profit: the Merchant in Medieval Europe*. London: Thames & Hudson.

Steuart, J. (1966) [1767], *Inquiry into the Principles of Political Oeconomy*, Vol 1. Edinburgh & London: published for the Scottish Economic Society by Oliver & Boyd.

Sumption, J. (2001), *The Hundred Years War: Part II—Trial by Fire*. London: Faber & Faber.

Sweeney, J., and Sweeney, R. (1977), "Monetary Theory and the Great Capitol Hill Baby Sitting Co-op Crisis." *Journal of Money, Credit, and Banking* 9(1), 86–89.

Tarullo, D. (2012a), "Shadow Banking After the Crisis." Washington, D.C.: Board of Governors of the Federal Reserve.

—(2012b), "Financial Stability Regulation." University of Pennsylvania Distinguished Jurist Lecture 2012. Washington, D.C.: Board of Governors of the Federal Reserve.

Tobin, J. (1969), "A General Equilibrium Approach to Monetary Theory." *Journal of Money, Credit, and Banking* 1(1), 15–29.

Turner, A. (2012), "Macro-prudential policy for deflationary times." Speech during the Financial Policy Committee regional visit to Manchester, July 20, 2012: available at http://www.fsa.gov.uk/library/communication/speeches/2012/0720-at.shtml.

Turner, A., et al. (2010), *The Future of Finance Report*. London: London School of Economics.

UKFI Ltd. (2012), *Annual Report and Accounts 2010–11*. London: The Stationary Office Limited.

U.K. Financial Services Authority (2007), Statement: "Liquidity support for Northern Rock plc," September 14, 2007: available at http://www.fsa.gov.uk/library/communication/statements/2007/northern.shtml.

U.K. House of Commons Treasury Committee (2008), *The Run on the Rock, Fifth Report of Session 2007–08*. London: The Stationary Office Limited.

Ustinov, P. (1977), *Dear Me*. London: Heinemann.

Van de Mieroop, M. (1992), *Society and Enterprise in Old Babylonian Ur*. Berlin: D. Reimer.

—(1997), *The Ancient Mesopotamian City*. Oxford: Clarendon Press.

Velde, F. (2007), "John Law's System." *The American Economic Review* 97(2), 276–279.

von Glahn, R. (1996), *Fountain of Fortune: Money and Monetary Policy in China, 1000–1700*. Berkeley, CA & London: University of California Press.

von Hayek, F. (1931), *Prices and Production*. London: G. Routledge.

—(1976), *Denationalisation of Money: An Analysis of the Theory and Practice of Concurrent Currencies*. London: Institute of Economic Affairs.

von Reden, S. (2010), *Money in Classical Antiquity*. Cambridge: Cambridge University Press.

Walras, L. (1874), *Éléments d'économie politique pure; ou Theorie de la richesse sociale*. Lausanne.

Walvin, J. (2005), "Quakers, business, and morality." Gresham College lecture, April 25, 2005: available at http://www.gresham.ac.uk/lectures-and-events/quakers-business-and-morality.

Watson, B. (1961), *Records of the Grand Historian of China*. New York, NY & London: Columbia University Press.

Werner, R. (2005), *New Paradigm in Macroeconomics: Solving the Riddle of Japanese Macroeconomic Performance*. Basingstoke: Palgrave Macmillan.

—(2011), "Economics as if Banks Mattered: A Contribution Based on the Inductive Methodology." *The Manchester School* 79 Issue Supplement s2, 25–35.

West, M. (1971), *Early Greek Philosophy and the Orient*. Oxford: Clarendon Press.

Wilson, T. (1925) [1572], *A Discourse Upon Usury, by Way of Dialogue and Orations, for the Better Variety and More Delight of All Those That Shall Read This Treatise*. London: G. Bell.

Woodham-Smith, C. (1962), *The Great Hunger: Ireland 1845–9*. London: Hamish Hamilton.

Woodruff, D. (1999), *Money Unmade: Barter and the Fate of Russian Capitalism*. Ithaca, NY & London: Cornell University Press.

Wray, L. R., ed. (2004), *Credit and State Theories of Money: The Contributions of Alfred Mitchell Innes*. Cheltenham: Edward Elgar.

Xenos, S. (1869), *Depredations, or Overend, Gurney & Co. and the Greek & Oriental Steam Navigation Company*. London.

Acknowledgements

There are so many teachers, friends, and colleagues from whom I have learnt over the years, and to whom I owe my sincere thanks, that it is almost invidious to pick out individuals. But since the opportunity to acknowledge publicly people who have done so much not just for me but for many other students comes round so rarely, I would like to thank here Tom Earnshaw, Steve Spowart, John Birkin, Peter Noll, and Lorne Denny; Jasper Griffin, Oswyn Murray, and the late Oliver Lyne; Mike Veseth and the late Pat McCarthy; and Chris Adam, Anthony Courakis, Colin Mayer, the late John Flemming, and my incomparable doctoral supervisor Antoni Chawluk.

This book is a work of synthesis, obviously—and as such, I owe an enormous debt of gratitude to the many brilliant scholars and practioners on whose research and ideas it draws. In addition, I would like to thank especially several of them who were exceptionally generous with their time and knowledge in commenting on or discussing with me chapter drafts. My very sincere thanks in this regard to Richard Seaford, Antoin Murphy, James Macdonald, Hannah Dawson, Edward Skidelsky, Arthur Edwards, Wendy Carlin, Simon Wren-Lewis, Colin Mayer, Andy Haldane, Richard Harrison, Gregory Thwaites, John Kay, Perry Mehrling, Robert Skidelsky, and Mark Bearn. Ben Tobias provided invaluable help with research. Needless to say, any errors or infelicities that remain are mine.

The practical business of writing the book was greatly helped by the Centre for Global Studies in London, which hosted me as a research associate in the first half of 2012. My sincere thanks to Olga Bogomazova and to the Centre for so generously providing the ideal environment in which to work.

I owe special thanks to two people—Ha-Joon Chang and Robert Skidelsky—who encouraged me actually to write this book rather than just to talk about writing it. Likewise, Will Goodlad, Joy de Menil, Philip Delves Broughton, Nicole Aragi, Tim Moore, Barnaby Martin, Joanna Kavenna, Anna Webber, Rory Stewart, and Aleksandar Hemon all provided masterful and greatly appreciated practical advice and encouragement. As for my agent, Natasha Fairweather, she is simply in a class of her own. I cannot thank her and the rest of the team at A. P. Watt—Linda Shaughnessy, Lucy Smith, and Donald Winchester—enough.

I have been incredibly fortunate to have had two exemplary editors in Stuart Williams at The Bodley Head and Andrew Miller at Knopf. Of course, this book would never have seen the light of day without their support and meticulous attention. But even if it had, it would have been much worse—and also much longer. I am enormously grateful to both of them, and to the rest of The Bodley Head team in London and the Alfred A. Knopf team in New York.

Finally and most importantly, I must thank my daughters for putting up with my absence; and above all my wife, Kristina—without whom neither this book, nor many other much more important things, would exist. Thank you, my darling, for everything.

Index

Illustration Credits

A NOTE ABOUT THE AUTHOR

Felix Martin was educated in Britain, Italy and the United States and holds degrees in classics, international relations and economics, including a doctorate in economics from Oxford University. He worked for the World Bank and for the European Stability Initiative think tank and is currently a partner in the fixed-income division at Liontrust Asset Management PLC. He lives in London.

A NOTE ON THE TYPE

This book was set in Monotype Dante, a typeface designed by Giovanni Mardersteig (1892–1977). Conceived as a private type for the Officina Bodoni in Verona, Italy, Dante was originally cut only for hand composition by Charles Malin, the famous Parisian punch cutter, between 1946 and 1952. Its first use was in an edition of Boccaccio's *Trattatello in laude di Dante* that appeared in 1954. The Monotype Corporation's version of Dante followed in 1957. Although modeled on the Aldine type used for Pietro Cardinal Bembo's treatise *De Aetna* in 1495, Dante is a thoroughly modern interpretation of the venerable face.

Composed by North Market Street Graphics,
Lancaster, Pennsylvania

Printed and bound by Berryville Graphics,
Berryville, Virginia